THE TREE OF LIFE AND PROSPERITY

21st Century Business Principles from the Book of Genesis

MICHAEL A. EISENBERG

A WICKED SON BOOK
An Imprint of Post Hill Press
ISBN: 978-1-63758-070-7
ISBN (eBook): 978-1-63758-071-4

The Tree of Life and Prosperity:
21st Century Business Principles from the Book of Genesis

Cover Design by Tiffani Shea

Post Hill Press
New York • Nashville
posthillpress.com

Published in the United States of America
1 2 3 4 5 6 7 8 9 10

Table of Contents

For Yaffa: my wife, partner, and a paragon of ethics, morals, and self-improvement

Preface

My wife thinks that I look at everything through an economic lens, and I am guilty as charged. The world is inherently, naturally economic. In the words of the wisest of all men, "Money is the answer to everything" (Ecclesiastes 10:19). Or as Liza Minnelli sang in *Cabaret*, "Money makes the world go round."

Moral and ethical principles are, in my view, part of an economy's foundations and drivers, so I view my wife's words as a compliment, even a blessing.

The co-head of the yeshiva where I studied when I was nineteen years old, Rabbi Yehuda Amital, once challenged me to "move to Israel and open a plant that would employ 10,000 people earning a dignified living." He told me that this would be the best way to fulfill the great mitzvah (commandment) to settle Eretz Yisrael (the land of Israel), for a good living is the basis for sustaining a family and a society. I do not (yet) own such a plant, and I do not know whether the companies I have invested in employ as many as 10,000 people in Israel. So I do not consider myself at liberty to desist from Rabbi Amital's challenge. His words encourage me to reread the equation in both directions: the Torah and commandments are influenced by economics and also influence it.

This book—the first volume of a five-volume series, one for each book of the Bible—seeks to lay bare the fundamentals of modern economics and to show that systemic understanding and daily encounters with the reality of contemporary economies gives a completely different perspective on the Torah. That same Torah informs economics as well.

Throughout this volume, and in subsequent volumes, we will encounter contemporary economic issues, such as the "universal basic income" promoted by Facebook founder Mark Zuckerberg, Tesla founder Elon Musk, and one-time presidential and current New York City mayoral candidate Andrew Yang, among others, which Adam in the Garden of Eden already faced. The initiatives and inventions of both Noah and Alfred Nobel will come into focus; Abraham and Andrew Carnegie will develop divergent approaches to wealth; and Jacob and Laban will behave in accordance with the principles of game theory. After we see dramatic economic changes relating to agriculture, urbanization and the undesirable results of too much market intervention, we will conclude with entrepreneurs and managers and their impact on national economies and values. Along the way, we will meet Esau, whose lifestyle was incompatible with the economic changes taking place around him and who was unable—or unwilling—to adapt.

The world of the twenty-first century, which is undergoing a radical change from an industrial to a technological economy, raises the same questions: Will everyone adapt? Is the world compatible with everyone's lifestyles and skills? What about societies that are not yet industrial? The Book of Genesis is a foundational document for a real-world economy, and contemplating it is vital.

The global economy is shifting from an industrial paradigm to one driven by knowledge and data. Nations and states are torn by social and economic rifts and political upheaval. Under changing conditions, we must always seek out first principles. These are what anchor our lives and constitute our moral conscience. Family, social, and moral values are part of the laws of economics. A model that examines the values expressed by the economy and chooses to work toward realizing the best ones is a recipe for economic, financial, and political success.

WHAT I HAVE LEARNED AS AN INVESTOR

My years of venture capital investment have taught me that one of the strongest signals of a good investment is when everyone who hears about it thinks it is impossible, impractical, or even foolish.

My first professional investment was in a company called PictureVision. It was 1995, and the internet was still in its infancy. I was sitting on a plane to Tel Aviv next to Gur Shomron, a veteran high-tech entrepreneur, and we got to talking. I was young and curious but completely inexperienced. I had heard Gur's name before, but did not meet him until that moment, when we were sitting next to each other in uncomfortable economy seats. Gur was well over six feet tall, and I am a bit above six feet. He had a heavy Israeli accent, and I was a young, recent American immigrant to Israel. At some point he said to me: "I have a friend, really an acquaintance, near Jerusalem. He is having a hard time raising funds. He has an idea related to the internet. Have you heard anything about that?"

Several days later, I received a call at our small office in Jerusalem from someone identifying himself as Yaacov Ben

Yaacov. To tell the truth, I thought it was my cousin prank-calling from the United States.

It took me a few minutes to realize that Yaacov Ben Yaacov was actually a real person, an entrepreneur with a start-up company that had developed an early method for transferring images over the internet. Today it seems simple, but back then, people were still using cameras with film and negatives, and the internet was running on dial-up modems. We could barely keep our email running smoothly in Jerusalem, so I did not believe he would manage to transfer images. But my curiosity got the better of me.

I traveled to Givat Ze'ev, a suburb of Jerusalem. There, in the home of Yaacov Ben Yaacov, with the children gallivanting around the house, we sat in his attic with a plate of supermarket cookies and a bottle of Coca-Cola, and he proudly presented his development. I would end up spending many more long hours in that attic, in unbearable heat or with the din of rain on the roof, but that first visit was barely over two hours.

Yaacov scanned a negative, uploaded the file to a local computer, and over the course of more than an hour, he transferred it over the internet to another computer via a landline. Just displaying the picture on the second computer took two minutes and several clicks of the "refresh" button. Yaakov's venture was penniless, and he was living off the fumes of an idea that was not yet a business. Other investors, including those suggested by Gur Shomron, had rejected it. Yet something about it enchanted me.

I had immigrated to Israel with my wife in 1993, two years before. Our families still lived abroad, and we now had a baby girl. The idea that we could send pictures to our parents and grandparents overseas excited me more and more every time I saw it done. Today we call this "photo sharing," but we did not know what to call it then because PictureVision was the first to do it.

As noted, I was a novice investor. I knew nothing, so I called a lot of experienced investors. Some asked, "What's an internet?" Some thought it would be impossible to send a picture over a line with such narrow bandwidth. Like our daughter, the internet was still in diapers, and the Israeli venture capital industry was likewise in its infancy. "Sophisticated" investors asked where they would find all the scanners for the negatives and where and how we would install them. In a word: impossible.

Nevertheless, despite the skepticism, the doubters, and the risk, my partner Shlomo Kalish and I pledged to invest about $50,000 in the company, although we did not have the money. In addition, we would help the company raise money in exchange for a cash fee and some warrants to buy stock. PictureVision was clearly somewhat desperate to use novices like us, and we were somewhere on the spectrum between over-optimistic and reckless. Our naïve assumption was that if we succeeded, we would receive a fee in the amount of $50,000, and that would be the investment that we committed to Yaacov and his partners.

We contacted private investors and asked if they wanted to send pictures to their nearest and dearest through something called "the internet." In essence, we were working with the crowdfunding concept that is so popular today, in which people preorder a product that is under development. We did not have a "crowd," but we did find a handful of believers. These were not typical "angels," as they are now known, a concept that would have been foreign to most of the investors we contacted.

Fast-forward a bit more than two years and the dying company from Givat Ze'ev was sold to then-communications giant AOL and photography giant Kodak. Those initial investors, who were following their hearts and a vision of what could be over what was solid and established, multiplied their investment more than tenfold. While this was not a venture capital home run, it was a very meaningful outcome for the earliest investors.

In retrospect, this story reflects the strategy for both investing and living that I have tried to apply for the past quarter-century. Strategy often starts as passion or instincts driven by your unique way of looking at the world of investments. It is comprised of the knowledge and insights you developed or fused from your education, experiences, and beliefs.

Every product has an underlying theme and advances an agenda. Behind every transaction and innovation there are people. Human spirit has been invested in every technological development. Every negotiation of value is influenced by the principles of the parties involved. There are some people whose transactions reflect the principles they champion, and those principles influence how they determine economic value. The investors in PictureVision were people for whom the importance of keeping in touch with distant family members resonated strongly.

Daniel Kahneman (after collaboration with Amos Tversky) won a Nobel Prize for suggesting that humans were not strictly rational economic beings. Venture capital, where I have spent the last twenty-five years of my professional life, is a service business. We service entrepreneurs, who are the heroes of innovation and the ones who propel the world forward by leaps and bounds, (mostly) improving our lives along the way. However, entrepreneurs generally—and technology entrepreneurs—specifically, are not rational economic beings. There are easier ways for bright and ambitious people to make money. What they truly want to do is make change. They are impelled by a need to change something, to fix or improve it. In my world, their canvas is technology.

Broadly, there are three investment strategies for a venture capitalist. You can invest in a technology change, in a market evolution or revolution, or in people. As venture capitalist Keith Rabois says, you can make money at all three, but you better be among the best at one of them. I do not know much about technology and markets, so I focus on people.

I started off investing with no strategy that I could explain. I was curious, driven, and, in many ways, desperate to prove myself. I had a degree in political science—whatever that means—and edited the college newspaper, and even created some troubles for my university's administration, but mostly, I had spent my time studying Torah. In retrospect, it is fair to say that my investment strategy reflected more of my Torah values than science, technology, and markets. Perhaps this is passion re-narrated as strategy.

One of the key attributes of Torah study is *chavruta* or "learning in pairs." If you have ever been to a house of Torah study, you will hear pairs of students yelling at each other, arguing over ancient and modern texts that cover almost every realm of life from holidays and blessings to economics and torts. The leading yeshivas actually spend most of their time on the tractates that cover economics and torts.

Many approaches to Torah view within it hidden, even mystical meanings. Others provide metaphysical interpretations, many of which are necessary and important. Still, others use the text as a diving board into homiletics. For me, it is real life. After this first volume of my series on the Torah came out in Hebrew, Rabbi Benny Lau remarked, "I learned from your book that people are people. Economics is economics, and families are families. Things have not changed fundamentally in thousands of years since the Torah was written." I think he is right.

Our biblical patriarchs and matriarchs were great people, and the Torah provides eternal truths, but we can only learn them if we are willing to say they are applicable. That people are people. That Abraham had family issues and dealt with wealth and economic hardship. That Isaac had family strife and had to reinvent his business and shift his livelihood from livestock to farming. That Jacob had tension with his wives and children and hence in his family business, and that Joseph's rags-to-riches story shows that you can create policy responses to economic crises, but you cannot predict their outcomes. At the same time that we strive for Torah-inspired moral clarity and greatness, we must apply its relevant lessons and examples to everyday challenges. Woven into the stories it tells is timeless wisdom about ethics and values. These lessons permeate the text and are an integral part of the narrative.

When people seek my advice, I often tell them that I would not ask someone like me for guidance. After all, who would ask someone for advice who is wrong as often as he is right? The venture capital business can be brutal. Half the time, you lose your money. You invest in the unknown, live with uncertainty, and often snatch defeat from the jaws of victory. In sum, it is a business steeped in faith. Faith that the future will be better. Faith in people, entrepreneurs, and changemakers. And in my case, a faith in God and the eternal wisdom of the Torah.

Like film and gaming, venture capital is commonly referred to as a home-run business. More accurately, it is a Grand Slam Home-Run Business. Similar to Hollywood or gaming where most products fail, most technology startups fail as well. A small number succeed, and they can succeed big. One venture investment in eBay, Facebook, Cisco, or Google can make up for a lot of losing ones. Still, according to Correlation Ventures, out of 21,000 venture financings from 2004 to 2014, 65 percent lost money. Two and a half percent of investments made 10–20x their money. One percent made more than a 20x return, and half of 1 percent—only about 100 companies—earned 50x or more.[1]

Sometime in 2005, I decided to reflect on my failures. I came to three conclusions: First, I know little about technology, and the more complex technology involved in the investment, the worse I do. At a minimum, I need to be able to explain it to other people so that they know I am not completely making it up. Second, even in my failures, if I stood up for what was right, I was proud of the investment, even if it was less financially successful. Moreover, that ethical stance was reputation building.

Lastly, I had not spent enough time with certain founders and co-investors to see if we had common values. I concluded that shared values and a culture of ethics, excellence, and innovation mattered a lot. This was not an investment in the stock market or an Exchange Traded Fund. It was an investment in people you had to believe in. It was almost a marriage.

One particularly nettlesome investment involved the digital imaging space. I understood the company, and we even had good people. When the tech bubble burst in 2001, its board decided not to pay severance to employees in the United States and instead focused on an Asian market. This was too much for me to accept. Together with the CEO, I objected, was outvoted, and resigned from the board immediately. As the Torah says, "Do not keep with you the wages of your laborers until the morning" (Leviticus 19:13).

Here I failed twice: I lost our investors' money and failed to persuade the board that we needed to pay US employees. More deeply, however, I failed in my investment philosophy. The trend the company bet on and the product it created became successful. They were the inventor of the now popular photobook, which many households have today to show off their digital pictures in paper form. We picked a lousy business strategy, trying to build everything ourselves instead of partnering with printing houses. However, more troubling was that when the chips were down, there was an ethical failing. Reflecting on that caused me to double down and search for greater guidance from the Torah.

When Daniel Schreiber pitched me his idea for a new type of insurance company in an area he initially called "P2P Insurance," I responded immediately. Daniel and I had been friends for thirty years. We had studied in yeshiva together. I had backed his first company, Alchemedia, which was, shall we say, not exactly a roaring success. However, Daniel was a leader, a fearless entrepreneur, and a mensch. Over coffee and a croissant at Café Michael in Jerusalem, he laid out a plan for building a new kind of insurance company from the ground up. A company that would align its interests with its customers instead of making money when it made its customers miserable by rejecting their claims. Daniel was not a technologist but talked about the power of data, AI, and behavioral economics with only a PowerPoint. He did not yet have product or technology, but I knew I wanted to invest. This was an idea rooted in values and giving back to the community of policyholders, and it was a fundamental values-driven change. It probably helped that even a technological idiot like me could explain it.

I introduced Daniel to Shai Wininger, a product and technology whiz I had known for a decade. Shai was also a visionary who saw and promoted the good technology could create. He was a unique entrepreneur and person of deep values and boundless creativity, and he had a deep desire to make the world a better place. Shai did not go to yeshiva with me nor was he raised on learning Torah, but he reflected those values in his own way.

Lemonade—so named because when life gives you lemons, insurance should give you lemonade—did not yet have an insurance license. It was a coin flip as to whether they would be granted one by the regulators in NYC. The fledgling company needed a lot of money up-front. Moreover, these inspired entrepreneurs were seeking a 10x change in a stodgy, conservative industry as well as a fundamental values-based realignment. But we were in. As the Torah says, "When you see the ass of your enemy lying under its burden and would refrain from raising it, you must nevertheless raise it with him" (Exodus 23:5).

Before the Beginning

We do not often speak about principles in a world of balance sheets, contracts, and markets. The dry letter of the law obliges us to focus on the bottom line—the profits of a company and its stakeholders. This is the fiduciary duty of the board of directors and rightly so. In the course of our daily lives, it is not always convenient to clarify and sharpen our moral principles as we consume, transact, and forge personal and economic relationships. But it is likely the difference between success and failure.

This does not mean that scoundrels do not make money. It means that their bad practices eventually catch up with them. It means that in a world that is becoming ever more transparent, ethics in business and the values of brands and products will be scrutinized more and will differentiate winners from losers.

In 1989, when I was a first-year student at Yeshivat Har Etzion in a small town called Alon Shvut in the Judean Hills, thirty minutes south of Jerusalem, I approached Rabbi Dr. Aharon Lichtenstein with a youthful question. Like many American Orthodox Jewish kids, I spent a year studying Torah at an Israeli yeshiva. I had just finished my freshman year at Yeshiva University in New York. At YU, you studied Torah in the morning and liberal arts in the afternoon. I was eighteen and impressionable but even thirstier for knowledge. Rabbi Lichtenstein was the reason I had chosen this yeshiva. He had emigrated to Israel in the early 1970s, giving up a clear path to success at YU, where he was likely to become the head of the institution.

To us, "Rebbe," as we called Rabbi Lichtenstein, cast a tall, imposing figure and possessed a towering intellect. More importantly, he was a beacon of ethics. As my friend Rabbi Amnon Bazak has said, everybody's heart skipped a beat when they approached him with a question. Over my time in yeshiva, Rabbi Lichtenstein's work ethic, clear moral compass, and personal example of leadership were key sources of inspiration for me and thousands of other students.

Those were the days of cassette tapes, which could be inserted into a radio cassette player to record and listen to music. I had a "double cassette" player, which allowed me to copy music from one tape to another. I asked Rabbi Lichtenstein whether halakha (Jewish law) allows you to copy music that you had purchased to another cassette.

His answer made a strong impression: "If you bought it, then it is permitted. They cannot tell you what to do with the tape once you have purchased it. However, you will not win any medals for fulfilling, 'You shall be holy.'"

Rabbi Lichtenstein clearly meant that one must distinguish between what is permitted and what is appropriate and proper. His reference to the commandment "be holy" alluded to the comments of Ramban (Nachmanides): "One should not be a scoundrel with the license of the Torah." In other words, don't be a jerk and then justify yourself by pointing to the letter of the law.

I tell this story to my children every year on the Sabbath when we read the Torah portion where this verse appears. The importance of this message opens a window to an issue that is far from simple: the reciprocal relationship between law and morality.[2] Law is a structured framework, and as such, it is unable to capture the full complexity of the human condition. Laws are crafted and administered by the state, religions, or other bodies in an attempt to order societies. Ethics and morals fill in many gray areas. It is these normative, universal, and religious dictates that requires adherence. However, these dictates can often come into conflict in practical ways, even if they derive from the same sources. They also prepare us for life, in which we often encounter scoundrels (even scoundrels clothed in religious rhetoric or cloaking behind religious laws) and are frequently tempted to cut ethical corners ourselves.

Today, almost thirty years since I left yeshiva, I have concluded that Rabbi Lichtenstein was righter than he knew. Principles, ethics, and morals are not merely questions of lifestyle that parallel the laws of economics; they must also be part of its foundations. My claim is that principles affect worth—values improve value—especially in the modern, digital age. Capitalism is a fundamental engine of change and growth. It is, perhaps, the greatest driver of human potential, innovation, and improvement in human history. Innovation and freedom are the fuel that drives it. However, without timeless ethics and morals, both the system and individual businesses can become runaway trains than can run over others—or, as we will see with Noah, subvert humanity itself.

Today, people are moving more and more toward ethical investments. While each person defines his ethics slightly differently, ethical investing is unquestionably gaining momentum. Environment, social, and governance-based funds, often called "sustainable funds," grew four times from 2018 to 2019, reaching over 20 billions of capital inflows. Consumers are checking the ethical practices of brands and choosing not to support those that use sweatshops or fossil fuels.

Most of this attention has been focused on environmental issues. Lemonade, for example, announced that it would not invest in fossil fuel companies. We can debate each company's ethical stance, but we cannot deny that consumers and investors increasingly look for investment decisions that reflect their personal values and ethics.

Principles are part of all successful business considerations. They built the economy, the free market, reputations, and long-term wealth, not short-term economic strategies that were greedy and impatient. Principles are part of every product, service, and economic decision, not just an external balance or brake. As my friend Marc Benioff, founder and CEO of Salesforce.com says, building a successful business is the best way to promote your principles. This works in the opposite direction as well. Principles, as a component of business, are a competitive advantage, as they are a core component of identity.

An Anchor and Seven Satellites

To implement the idea of investing in initiatives that will make the world better and drive better financial returns, I employ a loose framework that I call "an anchor and seven satellites." Again, this might be passion and instincts narrated again as strategy. The anchor, as we will see, is a fear of God and the timeless wisdom of His Torah merged with sensible humanism. For God wants us to fear as well as love Him: "You shall fear your God; I am the Lord" (Leviticus 19:14 and 19:32).

A satellite is launched into the sky and traverses space, but it is guided in orbit around planet Earth. Satellites increase in value as more communications pass through them. It has all but evaded our detection that satellites have become an integral part, foundational infrastructure, of our daily functioning. These are the kinds of investments I am talking about: technological products or services that become part of our functional infrastructure and that serve to advance human development.

The seven satellites—the tools I use to examine principled initiatives—are as follows:

1. **The customer is willing to pay a premium for a product or service out of principle.** Intuitively, we all know that we pay more for quality products. I can simply pay more for the product. I can choose to purchase from someone I admire or feel close to. Or I can share my purchasing power with others. The Torah's injunction not to desire the property or wives of others necessarily incurs a premium, as does the injunction against collecting interest on loans to members of the Tribe. That premium should be reflected in the product itself and not just in price gouging or brand premiums.

2. **The more I use a service or product, the more helpful it is for others, not just for me.** Clearly, if I use a product that erodes value to others, I am harming them. So-called network effects—wherein the more people use a product, the better it gets—are the holy grail of

investing. WhatsApp and fax machines generate network effects because the more widely they are used, the better communication gets for everyone. The same framework can be used to think about economics.

3. **The service's, product's, or company's competitive advantage does not stem from a special government concession or from preventing competition.** The Torah, quite broadly, built market rules, not market regulation. Three traders in the market can rule on cheating or price gouging in real time, without waiting for a court ruling. When the prophet Samuel is asked to appoint a king, he warns the people that the king can exercise eminent domain on their possessions and family members. This shows the Bible's emphasis on restraining the powers of government and the connected class.
4. **The service or product is sufficiently trustworthy that people will share their confidential information.** Fundamentally, trust is the lubricant of every economy and is a value that drives increased monetary and economic value for all.
5. **The feedback on and reviews of the service or product denote both "value" and "values" and a high index of customer loyalty.** Monotheism frees the mind and the person by acknowledging that it is not just their doing that has created wealth. It is the values behind the products and not the products themselves that drive their beauty and value.
6. **The success of the initiative does not undercut other elements vital to the long-term health of the economy.** In my opinion, the Torah's approach to "investment

products" clearly mandates that we should not create or market products that impoverish others.

7. **The innovation generally benefits humanity and does not exploit one segment of the population.** When we meet Noah and Alfred Nobel, we will begin to understand destructive innovation. This is not be confused with Clay Christensen's disruptive innovation or Josef Schumpeter's creative destruction, which are both positive. Innovation employed or deployed to exploit others is both corrosive and ultimately turned on its creators.

Products, services, technologies, and innovations are expressions of our values. The same is true of investments. Even benign investments require an "anchor" so they don't become unethical. Others are transformative and therefore unpredictable. They are necessary to move the world forward and should not be artificially restrained. However, when creating or investing in these critical technologies, we need anchors. For me, that anchor is biblical ethics and the timeless laws and lessons of the Torah. I am not Pollyanna. I make mistakes and get things wrong, both when it comes to people and investments. But Torah values are a North Star, a beacon that beckons.

When I began my career, they told me about *The Wall Street Journal* test. The test is very simple. If something you did makes the front page of the most important business paper in the world, how would you feel about it? Would you be proud? Ashamed? The anchor of conscience enshrined in this test provides us with who we are, what we believe in, and who we want to be. Unfortunately, I have since learned that not everything written in the papers is true, and their values have increasingly become relativist, if not some newfangled groupthink.

Competition is healthy, and in all competitions, there are losers. This is important for the advancement of humanity and the improvement of our general standard of living. The profit motive is one of the greatest human motivators, and it should by no means be contemned or invalidated. It is a healthy and even heavenly motivation, as well as an integral part of creation. However, as I will discuss below, technological advancement can produce total ruin if it is not accompanied by principled support for its customers and communities.

Satellites soar skyward because the sky is the limit, both when it comes to business opportunity and when it comes to the ability to sustain an array whose individual units do not conflict with one another. Like many models, however, this abstraction does not perfectly correspond with reality. These are signals, signs, and pathways that indicate whether a product, investment, or business is aligned with ethical principles. The satellites must be anchored in their orbits by eternal values that can and should be capitalized upon. The question is how to differentiate passing fads from solid values.

Looking Backward from the Future

In venture capital and entrepreneurship, we should think about the kind of world we want our children to live in and invest in the kind of ventures that can advance that vision. This mental habit is called "back casting." In forecasting, we try to predict the future based on variables that are currently known. In back casting, we know what future we want to see and try to create the tools that will realize it.

In my view, the better future is not a future with more candy, free money, or mindless entertainment and frivolity. Instead it is one in which the moral values of freedom, equality, knowledge, kindness, hard work, and service to others are realized. It is a world in which technology can drive down the cost of essential services and spread benefits to a broad swath of the world's population. It uses digital technology to improve health and welfare and to increase societal and economic resilience. It is an economic system that is less subject to the accumulation of catastrophic risks and expresses spiritual objectives through which people become part of something bigger than themselves.

This is the world in which most people want to live, so I look for enterprises that can be the building blocks for such a world. In the fullness of time, there should be robust consumer and enterprise demand for these kinds of products. Hence, these values guide me toward investing in projects that will form the infrastructure and resources of a world in which everyone wants to live and whose products and services they will want to buy.

I do not mean this in the narrow sense of "attain ownership" or "purchase for use"; they will want to be a part of it and buy *into* it. This is said of God: "Lord most high, buyer (*koneh*) of heaven and earth" (Genesis 14:22), and Eve said, when she first gave birth: "I have bought (*kaniti*) a person with God" (4:1). When the Lord or Eve "buys" something, it means that they have invested in them and built something that is lasting. God is invested in the future of heaven and earth, and Eve is investing in her family.

Back casting should be a model for policymakers who are responsible for the sustainability of society and state several generations hence, and for laying down the necessary infrastructure. Instead, most politicians focus on present needs. In general, they react. They contend over today's voters, not over what kind of society their children and grandchildren will live in.

I prefer the approach of entrepreneurs who see the world in terms of what could be and tackle a problem that they want to solve. These entrepreneurs think of their product in terms of how much it will help and how many people will buy, use, adopt, and gain benefit from it.

Investors are the necessary link between these worldviews. By raising capital and making investments, fund managers and investors, consciously or not, decide what kind of future to develop. Unlike entrepreneurs, investors are not swallowed up in the daily grind of launching and running a business, and this means they can look toward more distant horizons. The investor is not the change agent or hero; that is the entrepreneur. However, an investor can choose entrepreneurs who have the fuel to make a difference and maintain necessary guardrails on the road to success. To paraphrase the words of Matthew Arnold (a beloved saying of Rabbi Lichtenstein): the investor's job is to see the venture steady and see it whole while riding the roller-coaster of capitalist growth and disruptive technology.

The strategy of the "principled model" is to determine which principles the product advances and whether the world will want or subscribe to it. The model considers whether the product will lay the foundation of a new and improved social reality. Before any investment is actually made, the investor and entrepreneur must see eye-to-eye regarding the product, its development, and the short and long-term objectives that will guide it. They must also make sure that moral principles are always represented at the table and not drowned out by the voices of expediency and egotism.

The Principles of Principals

I invested in Riseup, founded by Yuval Samet, Tamara Cohen, and Iftach Bar, largely due to their view that everyone in Israel deserves a "family office"—that is, high-level, customized financial services, which today, only the wealthy can afford. It is rare to find a successful entrepreneur who wants to help the social periphery, where customers have less to spend. They also said that if their first idea did not succeed in the Israeli market, they would develop something else for it.

In twenty-five years, I had never encountered an entrepreneur who focused exclusively on the Israeli market. Israel is a country of nine million people and is not a large market for most products. Yuval explained: "I grew up poor in Israel. My goal is to create a company to solve problems that affect the society in which I grew up and to help people like me overcome challenges like the ones I faced."

Much of Western society has been characterized by overconsumption and driven by profit motives, lower marginal costs, and an advertising culture that encourages massive consumption of unneeded wares. I do not share the view that we ought to regulate businesses to stop these practices. But I do think companies need values that anchor their marketing approaches. Values that see the moral hazards of overconsumption, which often leads to obesity and credit debt. Values that see the monetary and societal costs of putting people in penury and risking their health. Jumbo potato chips and jumbo loans are the same: short-term thrills with long-term costs.

For most of my life, mortgaging the future to consume in the present has been considered a good business model. Yuval, Tamara, and Iftach wanted to turn this on its head. They believed in a model that would prevent overspending—and they thought people would pay for it.

Yuval is a businessman, not a philanthropist. His goal is to make money. That is my goal too. This is not impact investing or a social experiment with a basic business model.

Importantly, though, his moneymaking enterprise is changing people's lives. When I released the Hebrew version of this book in 2019, Riseup had just launched. Already, tens of thousands of Israelis have gotten out of debt and begun saving money—and they are paying Riseup a premium for the privilege. It turns out that Israel is a sufficient market to build a venture capital outcome in financial services but that by succeeding in Israel, we can launch Riseup to other parts of the world and create better futures for many other people. "From Zion shall go forth the Torah." (Isaiah 2:3)

Riseup disrupts a fundamental principle of many financial services: consumers pay to borrow money, and banks make money by raising their credit limits. Riseup only wants you to use financial products you can actually afford. It looks not only at the risk to the bank but the risk to its consumers. According to what Eldar Shafir of Princeton calls the "scarcity mindset," people make worse decisions when they are in financial stress. Riseup is like a blinking yellow light that helps drivers avoid a speed trap. Neither paternalistic nor patronizing, it engages your rational brain and helps you assess your personal risk. Of course, the collective risk of those who borrow money becomes society's risk. That is a price we all paid during the mortgage lending bubble of 2008.

As an investor, the horizon I look at is much broader. It is the values-based product of a good company that people use not just to save money, but to bring about change that's good for everyone. They use it not only for personal reasons but to become part of a newer, better zeitgeist.

As is well-known, the Torah forbids lending with interest (at least to other members of the Tribe—a point I will discuss in detail in the forthcoming book on Leviticus): "If you lend money to My people, to the poor among you, do not act toward them as a creditor; exact no interest from them. If you take your neighbor's garment in pledge, you must return it to him before the sun sets; it is his only clothing, the sole covering for his skin. In what else shall he sleep? Therefore, if he cries out to Me, I will pay heed, for I am compassionate" (Exodus 22:24-26).

The words "My people" and "the poor among you" indicate that the prohibition against lending with interest reflects the value of social solidarity. The point of this prohibition is to prevent a lender swallowing up a borrower's wealth, as described by *Sefer HaChinuch* (§68): "Among the roots of this commandment is that the benevolent God desired the settlement of His people which He chose. He therefore commanded to remove the obstacle from their path, that one should not swallow up the wealth of his friend without his feeling it, until he finds his house empty of all good...."

It is a mitzvah to lend and support a friend in need. But it is forbidden to exploit their situation and distress for personal profit. It is useful for everyone to have a tool that helps consumers bring their expenditures into proportion with their income or gives consumers credit that they can manage. Many products sold today are marketed with messages such as, "You must get what everyone else is getting! Everyone must have this!" Or, "A new smartphone for just ninety dollars.*" (The fine print tells you it's ninety dollars a month for thirty-six months, subject to the terms of the company.) The implication is this: Borrow now so you can buy and pay with your future earnings at 18 percent interest.

If everyone consumed within their means, including credit they can afford, the erosion of future earnings would shrink, if not cease entirely. A world in which people spend within their means—rather than follow dreams promoted by advertisers and dictated by the latest fashion—is a world that I want my children to live in. When everyone understands how much better it is to avoid ruinous credit card debt, Riseup's tool will become the Waze of personal economic management.

Lemons to Lemonade

As mentioned above, some six years ago, I invested in a new digital insurance company called Lemonade. I introduced the founders to each other in 2015. Both of them envisioned making financial services friendlier and more principled.

Insurance companies do not pop up overnight. In the Western world, the average age of insurance companies is 125 years. Lemonade dared to establish a new insurance company that was based on technology, artificial intelligence, and a simple and intuitive user experience.

Not only did Lemonade lower prices through its direct approach to customers, making the need to pay insurance agents unnecessary; it also changed the business model from an adversarial model to one of alignment, based on shared interests. Instead of profiting like other insurance companies by minimizing payouts on claims to the degree possible—thus giving them a built-in incentive to reject its customers' claims—Lemonade's income is determined as a fixed percentage of the price of the premium. After covering the claims of its customers, whatever funds remain are given to charities chosen by the premium payers.

On some level, insurance is a case of tragedy of the commons. We all band together and form a pool of capital that allows us to help each other in times of need. It should be the world's greatest social good business. However, people cheat. Duke University professor Dan Ariely has often said that if you want to design a business that would *not* build trust and would instead bring out the worst in people, it would look like a traditional insurance company.

For a biblical perspective on this question, consider the following passage from Bereishit: "Jacob resumed his journey and came to the land of the Easterners. There before his eyes was a well in the open. Three flocks of sheep were lying there beside it, for the flocks were watered from that well. The stone on the mouth of the well was large. When all the flocks were gathered there, the stone would be rolled from the mouth of the well and the sheep watered; then the stone would be put back in its place on the mouth of the well" (Genesis 29).

In biblical times, access to water was a social good, one that needed to be available to all. The rock on the well, which required all shepherds to be present to remove it, was the visual representation of an ethical code. This code served to prevent a tragedy of the commons, wherein a few bad actors might take an unfair share, thus raising the risk (and cost) for everyone else. (We will discuss why Jacob removed the rock singlehandedly in Chapter 8.)

Insurance companies are the industry most hated by customers, but they are also an industry that everyone needs. Only a team that took a principled approach, changing the supplier-customer relationship from an adversarial to a cooperative one, could find a "rock" large enough that prevented people from cheating. The brilliant minds and principled souls of Lemonade's team in Tel Aviv and New York answered this challenge and developed an approach that neutralizes the conflict of interest between the company and its customers, thereby creating a true sense of partnership. Beyond the administrative fees, which are fixed as a percentage of the premium—thus synchronizing interests—the balance is transferred to charitable organizations chosen by the customers. Thus, the company and its customers strive together toward a worthy horizon.

Because Lemonade created an insurance model with common moral values, it is adding customers—who come from several continents—at a dizzying pace. When I published the Hebrew version of this book in 2019, Lemonade was the fastest growing insurance company in the world and the highest rated for customer satisfaction. Using the AI technology it developed, it lowered costs for clients, as well as the percentage of fraudulent claims. I knew we were on to something when we attracted veteran employees from the insurance industry. John Peters, Lemonade's Chief Insurance Officer held very senior positions at one of the largest US insurance companies. He joined Lemonade early on and saw his new role as head of Lemonade's insurance department as attractive and challenging, even though he was only overseeing a small number of policies and an even smaller number of employees.

In its short few years in existence, Lemonade has managed to donate over two million dollars to charity on behalf of its members each year. In the early summer of 2020, Lemonade held an Initial Public Offering on the New York Stock Exchange at the height of the COVID-19 pandemic. The ticker symbol, LMND, serves as living proof that a business approach based on moral principles has significant, venture scale investment value.

In the internet age, digital services are creating customer bases ten times larger than anything that could have been imagined a decade ago. Lemonade is now the first transnational property and casual insurance carrier, servicing customers in the United States, the Netherlands, France, and Germany. It is therefore vital to our economic future that ethics and principled identification be among the factors influencing the customer's decision to adopt a service or place trust in a product.

Moreover, services and products that are not principled will ultimately be seen as harmful and will consequently disappear. Thus, a short-term strategy of maximizing profit, with nary a thought about values and principles, not only impoverishes future generations; it also hurts the suppliers themselves. It also stands to reason that in a more transparent world, in which reputations are judged on social media each day, customers and investors will not be as forgiving toward people who violate their principles.

Much has been made of Silicon Valley losing its way, working on social networks instead of cures for cancer. I find this criticism a bit overwrought. It has become a useful tool in the hands of politicians who are threatened by technology and the growing power of tech CEOs. Social networks added much-needed transparency and connectivity to the world. However, like Noah who did not add an ethical framework to his invention, the entrepreneurs behind social networks did not install time-honed and time-honored ethical frameworks around theirs. This has come back to bite them and harm our society. Like the flood in Noah's times, social networks have the potential to be destructive.

In recent years, I have increasingly found a common language with entrepreneurs who speak of a better world that their products will advance. This approach is gaining momentum in Israel. Broadly speaking, the entrepreneurs of Tel Aviv are more deeply focused on efforts that are driven by values than their brethren in Silicon Valley. The Torah of values-driven entrepreneurship is going forth from Zion, even though modern technological Zion is in Tel Aviv and not Jerusalem.

"When you build a new house, you shall make a parapet for your roof, so that you do not bring bloodguilt on your house if anyone should fall from it" (Deuteronomy 22).

The Bible as a Source of Economic Wisdom

The Book of Books is a treasure trove of responses to economic and commercial challenges that do not belong only to the past. People are people, and from our tradition, we can learn how to handle the challenges posed by the economy, family, negotiation, invention, technological advances, and new-old ideas such as universal basic income and the welfare state. According to the straightforward meaning of Scripture, as well as a straightforward understanding of human beings then and now, the Torah deals comprehensively with these challenges.

Of course, the world has changed and advanced, but people and their challenges do not fundamentally change. On the contrary, a significant part of the wisdom inherent in Scripture can be investigated and understood only in our time. Historical perspective and modern discoveries allow us to examine models that in the distant past were theoretical and only implemented later. Indeed, the more generations advance, the more the study of Scripture is reinvigorated. For time is cyclical, much like the Jewish people's return to the land of Israel.

Some might say this is too religious for a philosophy of investment. Others might find it blasphemous to read the Torah through an economic lens. Some might say that once the discussion turns to moral principles and values, it becomes preachy. Others will shake their heads and argue that my strategy cannot be implemented. But anyone who seeks stability and longevity, something that rests on solid ground and basic principles, must connect with the foundations of human existence.

Scripture is the most studied book in history. Believers and unbelievers alike quote and relate to its contents, and new interpretations and structures are built on it to this day. Ultimately, Scripture has the largest number of "users" on earth. If you are looking for something that speaks to everyone, Scripture is it. People are not always aware of this fact, but many of our basic presuppositions, worldviews, and aspirations are taken from Scripture.

Moreover, even now, new religions are emerging in Silicon Valley. Historian Yuval Noah Harari's belief that the world is basically biology and made-up human storytelling soothes relativists' souls. Sam Altman, the CEO of Y Combinator, the Silicon Valley-based accelerator that birthed Airbnb and Stripe, has said, "Politics is the new religion." I don't think he actually believes that but perhaps, it may be so for those who have replaced timeless texts and principles with temporal tweets and rhetoric. It is also quite odd given the distrust of the US government held by many in Silicon Valley. Perhaps he meant that certain post-modern political views have taken on a cult-like significance.[3]

I do not suspect that Google or Facebook were established for unworthy purposes. On the contrary, Google opened access to knowledge and produced massive economic and moral value. Facebook was founded to connect people. However, the bigger they grew, the more their power skyrocketed, and their self-deification increased. Their power and the strength of their hand spurred them to possess more capabilities. They became kingmakers and have literally determined presidential elections. Eternal principles were beneath them.

Sure, they praised values and principles as they wielded their double-edged swords. And yet Facebook and Twitter are effectively restraining freedom of thought and creating societal rifts in a manner that can best be termed Orwellian. In fact, Facebook's profits grow based on uniformity and narrowness. The company collects data on its subjects and fills their newsfeeds with things that already interest them, instead of challenging them with things that are different. The order of results in a Google search, which the company tightly controls, transforms it into a modern idol that dictates the world order and determines what is important. Other platforms have deleted mobile applications, further constraining freedom of thought. A modern tower of Babel, where there is a central unifying principle and difference is disdained.

In sum, these companies are a digital Tower of Babel, seeking to glorify themselves while suppressing human difference and promoting uniformity, as in the Biblical description: "Everyone on earth had the same language and the same words" (Genesis 11:1). As we will see in the second volume of this series, it is hard to be a contrarian in the politically correct and corrosive discourse of social networks. Unfortunately, since publishing this book in Hebrew, that same conformity has been imposed by well-known newspapers and "cancel culture." The agenda driven news media has become an echo chamber of like-mindedness. Enforced uniformity of acceptable language and thought constrains freedom. But God did not punish the builders of the Tower of Babel. He scattered them and gave them different languages and new platforms. In so doing, he unshackled them.

A social network is not inherently devoid of values. A search engine can develop in different directions; the question is what is permitted and what is forbidden. Which values influence its evolution. Therefore, from my perspective, how these platforms are managed through their life cycle is no less important than the setup and initial phases. After the product or service is launched, does its governance draw on eternal values or on relativistic ones? Is it in effect a new religion whose ethical code dwells in the mind of one person or publisher, or is it open to public criticism? We must also ask whether those criticizing these technology driven platforms are drawing on eternal values or reflecting political expediencies.

I take inspiration from the revelation at Mount Sinai, where God appeared in public. It was not a secret revelation of commandments to one individual, but a public spectacle, where "all the people saw the thunder" (Exodus 20:14). As Isaiah said, "From the first, I have not spoken in secret" (Isaiah 48:16). Sunlight is indeed, as Justice Louis Brandeis said, the best disinfectant. It ensures the longevity of principles.

Innovation and Interpretation Are One

Yeshiva University professor Aaron Koller interpreted the Scroll of Esther as a celebration and triumph of the Diaspora Jews and their broad influence in Persia. My book *The Vanishing Jew* laments the mass assimilation of the Jews of Persia and reads Esther as a wake-up call, not just for them but for Jews in the contemporary United States—urging them to move to Israel so that they may preserve and develop their Jewish identities. We both think that we correctly interpreted the straightforward meaning of Scripture and the intent of the verses. We both think we viewed the scroll in its proper historical context. Yet we arrived at diametrically different conclusions.

Koller once asked me if I think there is one objective interpretation or whether each exegete brings their own personal baggage to the interpretation of Scripture. My answer was that Scripture was written in a particular context, and it stands to reason that the author of Esther had his or her own interpretation of its meaning. Nevertheless, for the most part, exegetes cannot fully comprehend the context of an ancient work; hence, there can be no expectation of attaining any final, "authentic" interpretation.

Texts are unvarying, especially foundational texts like the Torah and Tanakh. This is an iron anchor. But the context from which we look at them changes.

The generation in which we are fortunate to live, with the return of the Jewish people to Eretz Yisrael, the mature synthesis of economic comprehension, and the emergence of globalization, encounters Tanakh, the biblical canon, at new junctions. The lived reality of the Jewish people in its homeland challenges us anew to build a model society—but it must be realistic, not utopian. Economics and moral principles are a central part, if not the actual center, of that reality.

In analyzing the sources, I have hewed closely to the straightforward meaning of the verses. I used relatively few midrashim, and then only to illuminate that meaning. I see the placement of stories and verses themselves as being important: Why does the narrative sometimes deviate from chronological order, and what does this tell us about the story that appears early or late? What does context teach us? What can we derive from comparisons between verses and words?

One of the novel aspects of this book is its attention to word choice. One of the Hebrew words for a word is *teivah,* which also means "box," indicating that a word is a container that holds meaning. Even in English, the word "content" can refer to the meaning of a text or the matter held by a receptacle. Readers often see words as building blocks from which sentences are constructed. They do not pay attention to words that are part of ordinary conversation. They look at the map, but do not focus on the treasure before them. Consider words like "property" (*rekhush*), "city" (*ir*), "vapor" (*eid*) instead of precipitation (*geshem*), and "a spring" (*ma'ayan*) instead of "a well" (*be'er*). What is the *kesitah* with which Jacob purchases a field? Why was he cooking, of all things, lentils when his brother came in starving from the hunt? Such questions are the doors to worlds of content and illuminate various aspects of commerce, economics, and society.

Ideally, the order of the chapters would have been thematic. Essays on the same general topic (free market economics, entrepreneurship, leadership, management) might have been placed in the same section, and the contents of one chapter would support or complement the preceding or succeeding one. In the end, I chose to organize the chapters according to the order of the Torah itself, or more precisely, the traditional division of the Torah into portions (each known as a *parashah*) that are read in synagogue each week. These weekly portions express our way of listening to the Torah and resonate with the requirement that we pay attention to the contents, which still speak to us today.

Moreover, the reading of a different parashah each week reflects the Torah's constant presence, all year long, reminding us that moral principles themselves demand consistency. An investor whom I hold in high regard revealed to me that in his twenty-nine year career, he only made money in nine years. Nonetheless, all twenty-years were vital, and had he not remained active during the bad years, he would not have profited during the good ones. The world of investments is built on ups and downs, but we must hold to our principles at all times and in all circumstances.

Organizing this book by parashah gives expression to my belief that the moral universe envelops every step we take. Economics are dynamic; people are always making changes, and tomorrow always has surprises in store. So I did not want to present readers with final, closed interpretations. Rather, my goal is to challenge everyone to examine their moral worlds and to ask how these worlds find expression in life's weekly junctures. This strategy leaves room for those who come after me to build further and to edify themselves.

Naturally, venture capitalists are optimists who believe in technology's ability to create a better future. So it is only natural that I connect with the utopian visions of the prophets.

The Torah strives to shape a people whose daily life would powerfully project moral and just principles—and economics is the core of daily life. Throughout history, we Jews have believed that if we are good, we will merit the fulfillment of God's benevolent promises. This worldview guided the development of halakhah toward the increase of safeguards, hedges, and stringencies, to prevent us from stumbling. It was an eminently moral approach, and many Jews gave their lives to its observance.

Technological advancement and the implementation of the principled model can initiate an entirely new process. The principles that will be manifested when people choose worthy, benevolent products and services will bring about the realization of all the good prophecies. Of their own will, "nation will not lift up sword against nation" (Isaiah 2:4) not even to wage currency wars, and "the wolf will lie with the lamb" (Isaiah 11:6). Competition will be disruptive but not predatory.

When moral principles manifest in every step, perhaps we will be able to remove the prohibitions and safeguards that were added out of concern lest.... Perhaps we will even bring about, with our own hands, a reality in which "commandments will be annulled in the future" (BT *Niddah* 61b) and these *mitzvot* will be fulfilled naturally, without any commandment. Indeed, "You will eat your bread to satiety, and you will dwell securely in your land" (Leviticus 26:5).

1
Parashat Bereishit

MISSION (IM)POSSIBLE

Universal Basic Income

There is no work, however vile or sordid,
that does not glisten before God.

—John Calvin

The brute's existence is an undignified one because it is a helpless one.... Only the man who builds hospitals, discovers therapeutic techniques and saves lives is blessed with dignity.

—Rabbi Joseph B. Soloveitchik[1]

THE DIGNITY OF LABOR

Technology does not stand still. Actually, it is accelerating—and automation is accelerating even faster.

Meanwhile, the world is getting smaller. The latter part of the twentieth century and the first part of the twenty-first saw an explosion in globalization. Globalization encompasses not only our ability to travel almost anywhere but more importantly, the interconnectedness of supply chains and the global supply of labor.

As a percentage of the US GDP, manufacturing has dropped by almost 50 percent in the last forty years. Why? Because it is cheaper to manufacture in the East. Initially, this was because the labor was cheaper. However, over time and in increasing volumes, the Southeast Asian manufacturing partners simply automated their lines, driving costs down further and speeding up production time. With the standardization of shipping containers and more frequent cargo flights and ship routes, the global supply chain was born.

These two forces, automation and labor arbitrage, have created a general sense that in the near future, many traditional jobs will be eliminated. Marc Andreessen, the entrepreneur behind the first commercial web browser, famously said that "software is eating the world." It is unquestionably eating many jobs. Perhaps more accurately, digitization is making many jobs unnecessary. We can see this clearly in a few examples. As newspaper production goes down because people consume news on digital devices, we have lost the jobs of people who work the presses, drive the trucks, and throw the papers at your door. Robots are replacing many manufacturing floor jobs. We even invested in a company that provides a robotic supermarket, reducing the need for human labor by over 80 percent.

As I write these lines, 20 percent of the US labor force has gone on unemployment due to COVID-19. This was partially driven by an economy coming to a halt. It was also due to a belated recognition that automation has made many jobs obsolete, and they are not coming back.

We have been thrust into quickly dealing with the impacts of a more automated world. There are two parts to these job losses: the economic costs of unemployment and the human costs. We therefore need to consider our responsibility as a society to the individuals who have lost their jobs. What is our financial obligation to them, and what is our humane obligation?

Whether you believe these losses will ultimately be made up with new areas of productivity (as I do) or that they are permanent (like Mark Zuckerberg), we need to address the value of "work qua work" versus work as a means to put food on the table. Put differently, is the only role of work to earn an income or is there value to work in itself? Have we thought through the societal and individual consequences of this dilemma?

These questions can be illuminated by the Torah. In fact, it is among the first topics that the Torah deals with. Adam's life in the Garden of Eden and his ultimate expulsion from that cocoon of workless income is a good starting point for the urgent debate we are having at the beginning of the twenty-first century, thirty years into the digital economic revolution.

Universal Basic Income (UBI)[2] is hardly a new idea. Also called citizen's income, citizen's basic income, basic income guarantee, basic living stipend, guaranteed annual income, or universal demo grant, it is a theoretical public program providing a periodic payment to all citizens without a means test or work requirement. The advent of technology, however—specifically innovations like artificial intelligence—and the economic changes these developments bring, have pushed the idea to the forefront.

In recent years, CEOs of technology companies like Mark Zuckerberg and Elon Musk and politicians across the spectrum have advocated UBI for every citizen. Ongoing trials in Finland

and Scotland were scheduled to finish in 2020. In Barcelona, an experiment is underway that assesses the behavioral differences between people who receive a basic income and those who do not.[3]

Supporters of the idea believe that UBI will give people the opportunity to take risks, innovate, and try new things that will lead to greater success, wealth, and happiness, as Zuckberg said:

> And yes, giving everyone the freedom to pursue purpose isn't free. People like me should pay for it. Many of you will do well and you should too.[4]

Others see it as a potential solution to the problem of disappearing jobs and professions, while still others see it as a way to establish equality in a time of widening social gaps.[5]

The proposal is so charged and controversial that some policy thinkers insist the very future of humanity depends on it, while others maintain it would herald the end of the world. These latter thinkers raise the concern that man would not fill his time with positive behaviors and principled, goal-oriented initiatives. Rather, his freedom would degenerate into behavior that would prove not only personally problematic, but a burden to society at large.[6]

Neither group of thinkers sees value in work per se. Work in itself is not vital; it is only necessary as a means to ensure man's continued existence. Man is charged to provide for himself and his household, and this burden fills his day and obligates him to follow the rules.

The Torah takes a different view. Man's labor is part of his essence. It is literally his life's work for work gives life. Without it, his vitality suffers, and his procreation is inhibited. In a sense, the Torah believes that a lack of labor is corrosive to the human being. The absence of a labor of love will lead to a vacuum of love for the next generation. Man cannot live, in all senses, without work.

This is not only true for individuals. Man's labor is necessary for the earth itself to flourish and hence necessary for providing for humanity. It is necessary for the earth to evolve and bring forth its fruits. It is necessary to build future generation and to build the future.

THE FIRST EXPERIMENT IN HISTORY

Parashat Bereishit, the first portion of the book of Genesis, touches on all of the questions that relate to man's existence in God's world. In its description of creation—light and darkness; the heavens and the earth; water and land; the sun, the moon, and an infinite number of stars—the Torah addresses man and the roles and responsibilities he has been assigned: "God blessed them and God said to them, 'Be fertile and increase, fill the earth and master it; and rule the fish of the sea, the birds of the sky, and all the living things that creep on earth'" (Genesis 1:28). The discussion of creation in Chapter 2 then goes further: "This is the story of heaven and earth when they were created. When the Lord God made earth and heaven, when no shrub of the field was yet on earth and no grasses of the field had yet sprouted, because the Lord God had not sent rain upon the earth and there was no man to till the soil" (2:4–5).

The Torah indicates two reasons that the trees and shrubs have not yet grown: God has not yet brought rainfall, and man is not there to work the land. The world was designed and created for man to actualize the hidden potential in nature and to uncover the world's natural resources by cultivating the land, thus paralleling God's active intervention from above in the form of rain.[7]

Indeed, the verse that immediately follows presents the solution to these two missing elements: "But a mist[8] would well up from the ground and water the whole surface of the earth. The Lord God formed man from the dust of the earth. He blew into his nostrils the breath of life, and man became a living being." (2:6–7).

The mist quenches the earth and is effectively a substitute for rain. Man is also fashioned from the earth, thereby demonstrating that man is specifically connected to the earth and "understands it." His work is critical to growth and prosperity. We fully expect man to fulfill his potential and function in accordance with the role designed for him, causing grass and shrubs, fully ripened and ready, to grow. But the Torah surprises the reader with the story's continuation:

> The Lord God planted a garden in Eden, in the east, and placed there the man whom He had formed. And from the ground the Lord God caused to grow every tree that was pleasing to the sight and good for food, with the tree of life in the middle of the garden, and the tree of knowledge of good and bad. (2:8–9)

The Torah diverges from what should have occurred. After the mist welled up from the ground and man was created from the earth, God intervenes and creates something entirely different: a garden of trees as opposed to the bushes and grasses that man was meant to cultivate. In fact, the mist that rose from the ground foreshadowed the change of direction that man finds upon entering the Garden. The mist derives from the land and quenches the earth in order to fulfill the provision "because the Lord God had not sent rain upon the earth."

The difference is striking. Rather than God sending rain from the heavens, the mist arises on its own. Rain is dynamic, while mist is static—it is continuously present and fills the expanse. A mist is simply vapor that is always present in the air. It cultivates plant life consistently, though in limited amounts. A mist is not like scattered rain showers. The difference between mist and rainfall corresponds to the difference between man who tills the soil, as originally planned, and man who, like a child, enjoys the passive existence of living in an orchard. God's planting of a garden in Eden rendered man's labor unnecessary. God is the one who created the growth of trees that were "pleasing to the sight and good for food."

This was the first experiment in the history of humanity—an experiment in which man received the equivalent of a universal basic income. In the Garden of Eden, man was granted everything he could possibly need, ready for use. He could exist without exerting any effort at all.

As noted in the introduction, UBI is predicated on the assumption that it makes time and space for creativity and initiative, specifically in light of God's blessing to man in Chapter 1, charging man to be fruitful and multiply and conquer the world. Accordingly, the story continues: "A river issues from Eden to water the garden, and it then divides and becomes four branches" (2:10).

By definition, a river is active. As Heraclitus said, "No man ever steps in the same river twice." It flows and separates into different streams and tributaries, crossing continents and functioning as a thoroughfare between different regions and countries. A river transports man and that which develops on his account, and it replaces the mist in sustaining the Garden of Eden. Replacing the mist with a flowing river symbolizes the expectation of man to get up and travel the length of the river, search and discover, and improve his quality of life.[9] He is no longer meant to remain planted in a static garden, since the garden is only intended to be his supportive framework. Instead, man is supposed to collect, pick, gather, and harness the strength of the flowing river to his own benefit. The river represents the power of activity, and from it, man needs to learn that it is proper to strive, act, and advance from within the supportive environment of the Garden.

Perhaps the very act of planting the Garden communicates a similar message, a message that man was unable to understand at that time. The chapter begins with the anticipation of God sending rain and man working the land. However, God "surprises us" when He plants the Garden instead and places man there. This change, similar to the reference of the rushing river that has the ability to move and travel great distances, was intended to stimulate man to try to be like God: to think "out of the box" or out of the Garden and create new things.

Indeed, following the instantiation of the river, man does become curious. He follows the rushing rivers and makes great discoveries:

> The name of the first is Pishon, the one that winds through the whole land of Havilah, where the gold is. The gold of that land is good; bdellium is there, and lapis lazuli. The name of the second river is Gihon, the one that winds through the whole land of Cush. The name of the third river is Tigris, the one that flows east of Asshur. And the fourth river is the Euphrates. (2:11–14)

Man travels great distances. He finds gold. Good gold. Alongside the river, he discovers precious gems that captivate the heart. With gold in hand, man continues to travel the length of the second river and discovers the lands of Cush and Asshur. Slowly, though, the discoveries subside. Does the Euphrates lack gold reserves, or was man simply satiated from the gold discovered by the Pishon? It seems that this is unimportant. It does not even matter where the Euphrates River flows. Man understands the principle: This is yet another river. His investigations ended with wealth and boredom. Research stimulates and ignites the imagination, but the end of the process necessarily demands a practical dimension, one of action. Or in the words of the Torah: "The Lord God took the man and placed him in the garden of Eden, to cultivate it and safeguard it" (2:15).

From where has God taken man? From his travels alongside the rivers and his futile search to find things. As he wanders along the river, he is busy investigating and researching, but he does not create. He documents everything; he picks and gathers food to eat. But at the end of the day, he is overwhelmed by boredom. It is just a river in his eyes. It has become just a river in his eyes and he no longer is even curious even if it is "Just the Euphrates."

The answer is to bring man back from his nomadic travels and assign him an explicit task: "to cultivate it and to safeguard it." This is the first divine command. The basic level of "and from the ground the Lord God caused to grow every tree that was pleasing to the sight and good for food" was established by God. From this point onward, man would need to continue the work.

Indeed, Rabbi David Zvi Hoffmann explains the phrase "to cultivate it and safeguard it": "Man was not placed in the Garden of Eden for his pleasure and enjoyment. He was rather placed there to fulfill his destiny, namely—'to cultivate it.'" My esteemed teacher, Rabbi Lichtenstein, also expanded on these two levels of "cultivating" and "safeguarding" as part of the world's genetic code: The first answer is that, indeed, the world was created perfect—but part of that perfection, and one of the components within that order, is human activity. Part of "And

He found it very good" is man, not existing simply as a biological being enjoying the world, but rather as a functional being who contributes, creates, and works. The need for man to work is not part of the curse subsequent to the sin; man was originally placed in the Garden in order to cultivate it. The curse was that man would have to battle with an unwilling earth: "Thorns and thistles shall it sprout for you.... By the sweat of your brow shall you get bread to eat" (Genesis 3:18–19). But the fact that one needs to work at all is part of the primeval, primordial order, irrespective of any element of sin. This had been intended from the beginning. Simply put, this is indeed a perfect order, provided that man does his part. If man does not, then one of the pieces of the picture has fallen out, and the world is no longer perfect.

According to this approach, both *leovdah* ("to cultivate it") and *leshomrah*" ("to safeguard it") are designed to maintain the world at its present level, and this entails two components: passively guarding against damage and actively working in order to replenish. We need to work so that natural processes repeat themselves; if you do not contribute your share, the seasons come and go, but nature will not replenish itself.

The second approach assumes the *leovdah* is a mandate to go beyond the original state of creation. *Leovdah* is not meant simply to maintain the original standard; rather, we have been given the right and the duty to try to transcend it. While the former approach asserts that man was asked to maintain the world as God had created it, this answer claims that man was empowered and enjoined to create something better, as it were.[10]

In the absence of a real need to work, in an environment where his basic needs are guaranteed, the command "to cultivate it and safeguard it" does not endure for long. Man becomes bored again, and this time, he is brought to sin.

MAN'S TOOLBOX

The impact of UBI on human loneliness is widely disputed. Professor James Ferguson of Stanford University and Oxford University fellow Max Harris contend that in the absence of a supportive social network, UBI will increase people's isolation. If all their needs are provided for, man will not look to build a community and develop social relationships. Others, such as Kate McFarland, instructor at Ohio State University and fellow at the US Basic Income Guarantee Network, maintain that even if a person gives up professional social interactions, they will not become isolated. Rather, it will ensure that people will have more free time and will neither compromise the strength of the community nor inhibit social interaction. Moreover, developing and enriching these areas of socialization can be legislated in conjunction with UBI.[11]

In the Garden of Eden, man's boredom and lack of peace of mind (precisely when he has nothing to do) are expressed in the next verse: "The Lord God said: 'It is not good for man to be alone; I will make a fitting helper for him'" (2:8). It was not good for man to be alone, without goals, and with too much free time. His food grew on its own. The solution had to be sought on the social plane:

> And the Lord God formed out of the earth all the wild beasts and all the birds of the sky and brought them to the man to see what he would call them. And whatever the man called each living creature, that would be its name. And the man gave names to all the cattle and to the birds of the sky and to all the wild beasts; but for Adam no fitting helper was found. (2:19–20)

Why does God bring all of the animals to man? Apparently, they were candidates to serve as man's "helper" and to potentially engage together in agricultural work with him. Animals are strong creatures that are endowed with brawn and might that can be harnessed for different tasks. Encountering the animals should have ignited man's imagination about what they might accomplish, work, and cultivate together. Yet the garden produced enough fruits on its own, and man was not motivated to struggle and strain with an ox or donkey to sow a field, plant seeds, gather produce, thresh, and grind. Man did not find a helper or assistant, and he remained idle.

God did not despair:

> So the Lord God cast a deep sleep upon the man; and, while he slept, He took one of his ribs and closed up the flesh at that spot. And the Lord God fashioned the rib that He had taken from the man into a woman; and He brought her to the man. Then the man said, "This one at last is bone of my bones and flesh of my flesh. This one shall be called woman, for from man was she taken." Hence a man leaves his father and mother and clings to his wife, so that they become one flesh. (2:21–24)

The narrative suggests that the first man and woman did not set out to accomplish much of anything together. They did not roll up their sleeves and set out to cooperatively cultivate and safeguard the Garden of Eden. In the absence of a joint endeavor, it seems that they did not even have anything to talk about. Are we shocked, then, when this "fitting helper" engaged in conversation with the serpent rather than with man?

THE SHATTERED DREAM

As everyone knows, Eve succumbed to the serpent's temptation and then persuaded Adam to taste the forbidden fruit. The Torah's discussion of their punishment teaches that they sinned because they were bored and had nothing to do with themselves:

> To Adam He said, "Because you did as your wife said and ate of the tree about which I commanded you, 'You shall not eat of it,' Cursed be the ground because of you; by toil shall you eat of it all the days of your life. Thorns and thistles shall it sprout for you. But your food shall be the grasses of the field. By the sweat of your brow shall you get bread to eat, until you return to the ground—For from it you were taken. For dust you are, and to dust you shall return" (3:17–19).

The punishment seems confusing. Why was man sentenced to eat bread by the sweat of his brow? Why was the ground cursed on his account? And how do these punishments relate to the fact that man listened to his wife and his wife to the serpent?

"Cursed be the ground because of you": The experimental establishment of an array of fruit trees that would function as man's safety net did not succeed. Unstructured, unproductive time does not inspire man to work and create. It instead leads to boredom and results in sin.

"But your food shall be the grasses of the field": This is a reference to the very same grasses that did not grow earlier in the story, in the absence of human cultivation. Meaning—the original plan that lacked a safety net and demanded hard work—would be reinstated. We thus conclude that when man's basic needs are met, there is nothing that compels him to act. In contrast, beyond the supportive environment of the Garden of Eden, man needs to work hard to tame the thorns and thistles. He must break a sweat to ensure his very existence because hard work is an integral part of his life.

Consider the following verse: "So the Lord God banished him from the garden of Eden, to till the soil from which he was taken" (3:23). The phrase "the soil from which he was taken" indicates and symbolizes a return to God's original plan. God sent man from the Garden of Eden because of the divine imperatives "to cultivate it and safeguard it" and so that he not eat from the Tree of Life. These imperatives would not be fulfilled in an environment where everything grows on its own, and man's connection to life does not take hold existentially. Divine commands evaporate in an atmosphere devoid of activity and creative energy, and with them, so does the meaning of life and the purpose of creation.

The story of the Garden of Eden illustrates that UBI, an idea with a pedigree of half a millennium, can exist only on an intellectual, theoretical plane. It cannot be implemented. Biblical Man and modern people need to work to earn a living simply because they need to work. People must exert effort and break a sweat. This is the only way to develop a decent and moral society.[12] The ability to grant UBI to every individual does not make this "new-old" concept useful and positive. The Torah does not believe in leisure culture nor in man's ability to create and initiate from a place of complacency.[13] Complacency causes people to disengage from the turbulent tide of life, and their lack of involvement will bring them to a state of emotional boredom. On the contrary, a person who feels that their continued existence is contingent upon their active involvement will connect to both the world that surrounds them and the society in which they live, thereby infusing their life with meaning. This, in turn, creates a better world.

An expression of Judaism's approach to the inherent importance of work and its significance in human life appears in a midrash (homiletical exposition) that discusses the desire of Abraham to live in the land of Israel:

> When Abraham walked through Aram Naharayim and Aram Nahor, he saw the people eating, drinking, and acting loosely. Abraham said to himself: I hope that I do not have a portion in this land. When he arrived at the Ladder of Tyre [northern border of the land of Israel], he saw people busying themselves with weeding during the weeding season and hoeing during the hoeing season. He said I hope that I will have a portion in this land. (*Bereishit Rabbah* 38:9)

The land of Israel and its inhabitants seek livelihood that derives from a strong work ethic rather than a free ride. This is the way to establish a healthy society, a creative society that takes an interest in both being involved and in having a positive influence. With such a society, it is possible to build a nation steeped in moral principles that radiate outward to all humanity.

RELATIONSHIP AND PARENTHOOD

The psalmist opens Chapter 128 with the following words:

> A song of ascents.
>
> Happy are all who fear the Lord, who follow His ways.
>
> You shall enjoy the fruit of your labors.
>
> You shall be happy, and you shall prosper.

The chapter then proceeds to discuss a promise that seems entirely unconnected:

> Your wife is like a fruitful vine within your house;
>
> Your sons, like olive saplings around your table.
>
> So shall the man who fears the Lord be blessed.
>
> May the Lord bless you from Zion; may you share the prosperity of Jerusalem all the days of your life. And live to see your children's children. May all be well with Israel!

Apparently, a man who finds pleasure in his "labors," merits having a "wife like a fruitful vine," "sons like olive saplings," and grandchildren. The psalmist seems to draw this insight from the continuation of the story of the Garden of Eden.

As long as man's sustenance was guaranteed, he did not wish or need to have children. The birth of the next generation only appears when man is banished from the Garden: "By the sweat of your brow shall you get bread to eat, until you return to the ground—for from it you were taken. For dust you are, and to dust you shall return. The man named his wife Eve, because she was the mother of all the living" (Genesis 3:19–20). When he steps out into the world and confronts his new challenges, man's relationship with his wife is strengthened and transformed. They now share a joint goal—to survive and thrive in an unfriendly world. The woman has also been altered. She now has a name, Eve. She is no longer merely a helper; she has responsibility, and this responsibility endows her with a status: "the mother of all the living."

From this perspective, there is a natural progression of events after Adam and Eve leave the Garden. The existential urge is not muted or subdued and therefore:

> Now the man knew his wife Eve, and she conceived and bore Cain, saying, "I have gained a male child with the

help of the Lord." She then bore his brother Abel. Abel became a keeper of sheep, and Cain became a tiller of the soil. (4:1–2)

Adam and Eve sire a new generation, their living legacy, their posterity. The sons take on different roles: Cain turns to agriculture and Abel to herding. This, once again, conveys the message that the purpose of humans is to innovate, cultivate, and create on the stage that God has given them.

Biblically, siring children and having grandchildren is a direct result of working and creating which brings us back to UBI and old-new winds of stagnation. I realize that the topic of having children has somehow become charged in parts of Western society, a topic that I will cover somewhat more in the next chapter. However, I think eternal values, the fundamental tenets of economic growth and the preservation of cultures, religions, and values strongly mitigate in favor of having children and UBI puts that value at risk. Strikingly, many twenty-first century political leaders, including the Chancellor of Germany, the President of the French Republic, the President of Russia, and the Prime Minister of England, had no children. At a point when the European birthrate is close to negative or zero, Finland is seeking to establish UBI, which will enable people to live without working. Both UBI and falling birth rates are governed by the same values: a life that is comfortable and secure without unnecessary responsibilities.

In the human psyche, comfort generates boredom, and the composite effect prevents people from thinking about continuity of the world and their family. When a person lives a worry-free life and does not need to work hard, they incorrectly feel that they are invincible and eternal. When the government provides, one does not feel that they need to provide for the other and the ultimate level of giving and providing is to children. They do not consider who will work in their factory to produce food for the coming generations because people are already being provided for. In contrast, a person who works hard will ensure that someone faithfully and devotedly continues their life's mission. A person who plants fruit trees anticipates that the next generation will carry the torch and build a world that is more just, advanced, and healthier for generations that follow.

> Rabbi Ḥiya bar Ami said in the name of Ula: One who benefits from his own work is greater than one who fears Heaven, for with regard to one who fears Heaven it is written "Happy are all who fear the Lord," whereas with regard to one who benefits from his work it is written, "You shall enjoy the fruit of your labors. You shall be happy, and you shall prosper" (Psalms 128:2). "You shall be happy" in this world, "and you shall prosper" in the next world. Regarding one who fears Heaven though it is not written "and you shall prosper." (BT *Berakhot* 8a)

2
Parashat Noaḥ

THE FRUSTRATED INVENTOR: TECHNOLOGICAL INNOVATION AND MORAL INNOVATION

A New Beginning

Noah is best known as the builder of the ark that carried the remnants of Earth's human and animal life through the flood to a new world. But before and after he saved humanity, he had an equally important identity as an inventor and entrepreneur.

In the aftermath of the flood, upon leaving the ark, Noah embarked (*va-yaḥel*) on a new endeavor. According to Genesis 9:20, "Noah, the tiller of the soil, became the first to plant a vineyard." Although this action marked a new beginning for mankind, Noah was already known as "the tiller of the soil." This is an appellation that needs to be understood properly.

According to the sages in the midrash, Noah invented the plow. For the farmers of antiquity, Noah's invention brought tremendous relief and gave them the technology to work the cursed, harsh soil in the aftermath of Adam and Eve's sin. But how did the sages determine this? Was it merely homiletics, or did they deduce it from the narrative itself?

History is replete with doomsday prophets. One was Thomas Malthus, who predicted in 1798 that the world would be unable to provide enough food for its expanding human population. Malthus formulated his argument as follows: "The power of population is indefinitely greater than the power in the earth to produce subsistence for man."

In his view, man was not sophisticated enough to adequately cope with the gap between natural population growth and the earth's ability to support it. Only moral restraint or natural catastrophe can repress such growth. Malthus argued that this threat had emerged multiple times throughout human history.

In the time of Noah, a similar worldview seems to have prevailed. In fact, this approach had apparently taken root two or three generations before him. A close reading of the lineage of Seth and his descendants allows us to trace the origins of Malthus's ancestor and spiritual father.

The lineage presented in Chapter 5 of Genesis lists not only the names of fathers and sons, but also the father's age at the time of his son's birth. The biblical list maintains a very precise structure: It states that the father lived for a certain number of years and begot a son whose name was such and such. For example: "Jared lived for 162 years and begot Enoch"; "Methuselah lived 187 years and begot Lamech."

Within this rigidly structured list, though, the age at which each father begot his son fluctuates. We can examine these changing numbers to understand the message hidden in this list:

Name of Father	Age at Which He Begot His Son
Adam	130
Seth	105
Enosh	90
Kenan	70
Mahalalel	65
Jared (Yered)	162
Enoch	65
Methuselah	187
Lamech	182
Noah	500

Initially, we see a clear trend of fathers begetting children at an increasingly younger age. From Jared's time, however, this trend reverses. Within four generations, the age of fathers having children increases by more than 700 percent: from the age of 65 to the age of 500. Enoch is the exception who proves this rule: "he (Enoch) walked in the way of God" and begot children at a young age. For this reason, it is written about Enoch: "Then he was no more, for God took him." In other words, he was completely disconnected from the prevalent culture of his generation.

Postponing children is a symbol of hardship and indicative of a generally pessimistic culture. For a modern example, researchers are suggesting that European and US births dropped by hundreds of thousands of children during the COVID-19 pandemic. Other doomsdayers suggest to cease or limit bringing children into the world because of climate change. It is possible that Jared's name ("Yered" in Hebrew) indicates a downward trend (*yeridah*) in belief in God and divine providence and hope for the future, and perhaps even a decline in agricultural output. Perhaps Jared was the first doomsday prophet of antiquity: the Malthus of his generation, who sought to slow the world's birthrate lest humanity run out of food. Jared practiced what he preached, waiting 100 years beyond the age at which his father sired him, to have children of his own.

A close look at the genealogy of Cain, which parallels the genealogy of Seth, strengthens the case that there was a shift in the age at which people had children. Cain's lineage list does not include years, but the biblical description presents an identical picture. Jared is the fifth generation in Seth's lineage (Seth, Enosh, Kenan, Mahalalel, Jared), and he was born when Adam was 622 years old. It is probable that Jared's time coincided with the generation of Lamech on Cain's side since Lamech was the sixth generation after Cain (who was born before Seth). Lamech had three sons: Jabal, who "was the father of those who dwell in tents and amidst herds"; Jubal, who, "was the father of all who play the lyre and the pipe"; and Tubal-Cain, "who forged all implements of copper and iron."

These descriptions indicate that humanity was advancing in many different directions. Consequently, we can conclude that in this period, the old agrarian economy could not sufficiently provide for the needs of man, who had multiplied exponentially. It is possible that in order to deal with this crisis, people simultaneously turned to new food sources, such as herding sheep, and sharpened their swords to fight over the earth's limited food resources. Rather than bringing children into a world that suffered from hunger and warfare, people postponed having children. They saw this as the order of the day, as noted in the Talmud: "It is forbidden for a man to engage in sexual relations in years of famine, as it says: 'Before the years of famine came, Joseph became the father of two sons'" (BT *Ta'anit* 11a).

It should be noted that early plows were made of flint. It was only at a later stage that flint was substituted with copper, bronze, and eventually iron. Since Cain and his descendants were wiped out in the flood while Seth's survived, it is possible to contrast the ironsmith who forges instruments of death with the tiller of the soil who sows the seeds of hope.

As noted above, the biblical genealogy from Adam to Noah is rigidly structured. The break in this structure that comes with Noah's birth is therefore noteworthy.

> When Lamech had lived 182 years, he begot a son. And he named him Noah, saying, "This one will provide us relief from our work and from the toil of our hands, out of the very soil which the Lord placed under a curse." After the birth of Noah, Lamech lived 595 years and begot sons and daughters. All the days of Lamech came to 777 years; then he died. When Noah had lived 500 years, Noah begot Shem, Ham, and Japheth. (5:28–32)

Lamech has "a son." This son initially does not have a name. From the outset, this "son" conformed with the prevalent culture and did not bring children into a world that lacked sufficient resources. As the table above indicates, he waited 500 years. It is possible that this ongoing hardship intensified with time. As the population continued to increase, it was finally determined that people should not have children at all.[1] This may have been on account of a calculated economic analysis or the gloomy predictions of the Malthusian prophet of the day, who endlessly repeated the divine curse: "Cursed be the ground because of you; through suffering shall you eat of it all the days of your life" (3:17).

However, unlike his forefathers, Noah did not allow the pessimistic spirit and sorrowful state of the land to discourage or defeat him. Instead, he searched for a solution—and invented the plow. This is typical of entrepreneurs. Rather than capitulate, they think of creative solutions to vexing practical problems and challenges. The obstacles and fears they face are transformed into creative energy that pushes them to overcome adversity.

After he invented the plow, his name was changed to "Noah." He no longer is just "son" or whatever his previous name was. He is now called Noah, the "one who will provide relief from the hardship of tilling the land" (Genesis 5:29). In fact, the strange structure of this naming suggests that his father even blessed him at the launch of this new and exciting piece of technology: "And he named him Noah, saying, 'This one will provide us relief from our work and from the toil of our hands, out of the very soil which the Lord placed under a curse.' (Genesis 5:29). From this point on, Noah was known for his innovation: "Noah—the tiller of the soil."

The celebrations of the first crop soon followed. Increased food production, augmented by the widespread use of Noah's plow, and decreased competition over fertile agricultural lands showed that the doomsday prophets were wrong. Optimism prevailed: "And they shall beat their swords into plowshares and their spears into pruning hooks. Nation shall not take up sword against nation, they shall never again know war. But every man shall sit under his grapevine or fig tree with no one to disturb him" (Micah 4:3–4).

At this point, at a very advanced age, Noah could finally break with the zeitgeist and sire children. The rigid structure of the genealogy is disrupted yet again to emphasize this dramatic change. Rather than simply listing the names of the father and his eldest son, the biblical account mentions Noah's name twice and includes the names of all three of Noah's sons, who will in turn become the progenitors of the seventy nations of the world: "When Noah was 500 years old, Noah begot Shem, Ham, and Japheth" (Genesis 5:32).

This deviation marks the beginning of a population upsurge, as indicated by the very next verse: "And it was when men began to increase on earth" (6:1). The development of the plow significantly increased the food supply. Overnight, the twin curses administered to Adam and man—"in suffering shall you eat" and "in suffering shall you bear children"—no longer applied.[2]

The Downside of Invention?

Noah's great invention led to new prosperity and growth. But it may also explain the social, moral, and economic decline, as well as the sexual decadence, that ultimately led to the flood. A culture of abundance leads to hedonism, which quickly degenerates into sinful behavior. As immorality spread, God became angry and vowed to wipe humanity off the face of the earth: "God said to Noah, 'I have decided to put an end to all flesh, for the earth is filled with lawlessness (*ḥamas*) because of them'" (6:13).

The Hebrew word *ḥamas* indicates a slow but steady decline in social and economic relations. It is not a sudden wave of violent thefts but of small, often hidden deceits and scams in which one person takes advantage of another. *Ḥamas* is the erosion of trust between manufacturers, between partners, between longtime business associates. It is the attrition of reciprocity and fair-trade practice, and over time, it causes a society to self-destruct: "He has stripped [*vayahmos*] His booth like a garden" (Lamentations 2:6). Slowly but surely, the booth, the structure that provides shade and protects people, is consumed by bankruptcy, just like the worm that attacked Jonah's castor plant (Jonah 4:7) and the prophet's use of the verb root "H-M-S." The Jerusalem Talmud likewise characterizes *ḥamas* as the slow crumbling of law and order:

> It was taught in a *baraita*: What would they steal? A man would go out and load a basket full of lupines, and they would intentionally take less than a penny's worth [in addition], an amount that cannot be retrieved through judges.[3]

People would take inconsequential amounts of additional lupines (a small legume) without remitting payment in order to evade the law. Over time, these minor amounts accumulated into significant unsettled bills, causing great financial distress to the merchant. Ultimately, merchants stopped selling lupines, crippling the entire industry and stifling commercial productivity. According to Professor Dan Ariely's research, people lie because they don't consider petty theft to be either criminal or deceitful. Practically speaking, dishonesty slowly erodes confidence levels and can destroy societies from within.[4]

Noah's world was a world without trust. In biblical terms, regulation and division into independent political entities only occurred after the Tower of Babel, and guidelines for enforcing social norms had not yet been formulated. Social norms, boundaries, and trust must exist in commerce and intercaste relationships. However, as the Torah describes: "The divine beings saw how beautiful the daughters of men were and took wives from among those that pleased them" (Genesis 6:2). The strong of civilization, the "divine beings," breached social norms and trust, taking women as they saw fit.

When plows were first invented, only a handful of early adopters and wealthy people had access to them. Like any technological breakthrough that improves productivity, the plow gave a tremendous competitive advantage to its inventors and those who knew how to use and leverage its power.

Noah's innovation brought great prosperity, but the farmers did not know how to deal with it. Instead of building a healthy society with a strong economy, based on trust, limited regulation, and effective enforcement, they devolved into sexual decadence, overindulgence, and a negative competitive spirit in which "the ends justify the means." In the face of unmoored prosperity and abundance, humanity failed.

Innovation brings many blessings and good to the world. It is the key to breaking barriers, overcoming poverty and hunger and it gives us the ability to meet new challenges and grow our economy. At the same time, innovation undermines the foundations of the old economy and disrupts its socioeconomic balance. An educated society leverages technological developments to improve the lives of its citizens. Such a society teaches and instills principles alongside innovations. It must impart moral values alongside economic growth so that the new equilibrium is reflected not only in the economy, but in a prevailing spirit of trust, fairness, and justice. At times, however, innovation improves efficiency and competitiveness before the larger society is ready to deal with the implications.

Noah apparently made a fortune marketing his new invention (which he would eventually use to build the ark). He was the wealthiest man of his generation. He was also "a righteous man," pure in his generation. And he was a moral man, although apparently, he did not publicize his principles together with his mechanical invention.

In contrast to Noah, the Torah does not call Abraham a righteous man. This is puzzling. Why isn't Abraham, the father of the nation and of monotheism itself, described or identified as "righteous"? At any rate, it seems that the term "a righteous man" is an excellent description of Noah. Noah was important, moral, good, and decent. But he was a wealthy, important, decent man who kept to himself and for himself, making Noah a righteous recluse. But Abraham was also a wealthy and important man: "You are a prince of God among us" (23:6). And yet, when the Torah explains why God chose Abraham as the father of the nation, it states: "For I have singled him out, that he may instruct his children and his household after him.... to do what is just and right" (18:19).

There are righteous, saintly men who keep to themselves like Noah, and there are people who become princes of God, perform righteous acts for other people, and teach values to their families, progeny, and those who surround them. A righteous man earns salvation for himself and his family, but Abraham attempts to save entire nations and societies despite their dubious pasts and contemporary sins. "Abraham becomes a prince of God," a spreader of a message, "maker of souls," and father of many nations. If Noah was a righteous recluse, Abraham was a juggernaut of justice.

Was Noah selfish? Perhaps. It is entirely possible, though, that Noah was merely frustrated. He saw his groundbreaking discovery change the face of humanity, feed an entire world, and lead to exponential population growth, but it also caused the moral corruption of the world. Feelings of guilt, perhaps even melancholy, overwhelmed him. When he entered the ark and said goodbye to the world that he knew, it was a world that had changed beyond recognition.

Alfred Nobel, the chemist who invented dynamite, underwent a similar experience. Nobel had hoped that his invention would help people to lead better lives. He intended for dynamite to be used to explode mountains and rocks and aid in the construction of railway tunnels and roads as well as the drainage of rivers. Nobel established a chain of factories in different countries to produce dynamite. When he realized the deadly dynamite that he had invented was primarily being used for military purposes, he fell into a deep depression. At the end of his life, he left his native Sweden and moved to San Remo, Italy. He did not have any children, and in his will, he requested that his wealth be placed in a trust that would fund Nobel Prizes in five different fields. He saw this as a way to atone for the death caused by his invention.

Following his invention of the mechanical plow that had led both to great prosperity and the devolution of society, Noah established a similar foundation to save both humanity and animal. He invested a century of his life and applied his abilities to the construction of an ark. Noah, like Nobel, felt responsible for the continuation of life on earth.

A Second Beginning

After surviving the flood, Noah changed direction. Noah had sought to share his first invention—the plow—with the entire world in the hope that everyone would benefit from it. Post-flood Noah, however, turned inward.

Noah, the responsible adult, had to begin reinventing the world. That would have been a princely calling. Instead, he planted himself a vineyard. The vineyard became fertile ground for industrial experiments and, in fact, it appears that Noah invented wine, which could have replaced the water that had turned lethal and destroyed the world. The discovery of the fermentation process and the production of fine wine from raw grapes was a natural progression from the invention of the plow. Noah had rolled up his sleeves once again and returned to the field of innovation and creativity. He seemed poised to share his discoveries and his research with his family, promoting renewal and progress for all of mankind.

The lesson that Noah had learned from inventing the plow, however, was that he should not share his discoveries with others. He could not even reveal his secret formula to his closest relatives. Noah marketed his first invention to everyone: "This one will provide *us* relief from *our* work and from the toil of *our* hands...." In contrast, regarding his second invention, the Torah states: "He drank of the wine and became drunk" (9:21). In other words, he kept his groundbreaking chemical discovery to himself. He drank alone in his tent, isolated in his melancholy and misery.

Noah seems to have learned the wrong lesson from the flood. Noah is called "the tiller of the soil" because he returned to the pessimistic attitude, first adopted by Adam, that the land beyond the Garden of Eden was full of thorns and thistles and was an accursed land where one can only eat in pain and misery. He should have learned that technology and innovation provide great things for the world when they are accompanied by principles, trust, and intelligent use. Rather than educating the next generation towards greater responsibility, Noah chose to seclude himself. He may have thought that humanity was not yet ready for additional discoveries and that it was impossible to promote a fair, moral, and positive use of new technologies. Since in his new worldview, it was not wise to share his innovations with others, his only choice was to withdraw to his tent and drink himself into a stupor.

Nothing symbolizes this more than the invention of wine. Wine gladdens the heart of people when they drink responsibly. Wine's ability to remove barriers can be productive and helpful, provided that drinking occurs in an appropriate social context. When Noah became drunk in his tent, however, the removal of barriers resulted in his indecent exposure and the corruption of his family.

Noah's son Ham, the father of the nation of Canaan, came in and saw his father indecently exposed. He ran to tattle to his other brothers, Shem and Japheth, who responded by covering their father. Because Ham horrified and embarrassed Noah, Noah cursed Ham so that he and his descendants would be slaves to his brothers.

However, the homiletical exegetes suggest that this incident was far more traumatic than the literal reading of the text depicted which only says that Ham saw his father's nakedness. The exegetes suggest that Ham either sodomized his drunken father or castrated him. The righteous Noah, degraded by his appetites and reduced by his melancholy, is abused by his son. His family is forever scarred by a lack of values and boundaries.

Technological innovations bring both great opportunities and great responsibilities. They can advance humanity in all aspects of life. However, without taking responsibility for how our inventions are used or cultivating an environment that provides the moral framework for dealing with technological change, it will be difficult to take long-term advantage of their benefits. Worse yet, these developments can slowly erode society's moral integrity.

Thomas Malthus prophesied that population growth would lead to critical food shortages. Despite being an Anglican priest, he was not optimistic about the future of the world and its ability to reinvent itself through technological innovation. Noah, a righteous man with two remarkable inventions to his name, lacked the determination to lead a moral revolution, as well as the leadership and optimism to imagine a better and more prosperous future that was driven by innovation. Only ten generations after Noah, Abraham would enter the stage, call out in the name of God, lead others, and preach righteousness and morality.

Today, in an age of groundbreaking discoveries in physics, biology, chemistry, economics and computing, we confront a similar challenge. Correct use of innovations, such as analyzing troves of data, artificial intelligence, and synthetic biology, can help solve problems such as ongoing access to food and water, disease and aging. This will undoubtedly lead the way to new health and medical solutions. However, these same inventions can also be exploited for negative purposes. Invasions of privacy, unethical cloning, and other practices are liable to become modern-day Towers of Babel or lead to moral debasement. We must therefore build a moral framework that will support innovation and create a healthier society and a better collective future.

3
Parashat Lekh Lekha

WEALTH: TRIAL AND ERROR

Wealth as a Social Challenge

Our father Abraham, of blessed memory, was tested with ten trials and he passed them all, to demonstrate the greatness of Abraham's love of God.

—Mishnah Avot 5:3

The sages understood many of the stories from the end of Parashat Noaḥ (Genesis 11:27) until the middle of Parashat Lekh Lekha (14:24) as a depiction of Abraham's ten trials, which the Mishnah mentions but does not enumerate. Leaving his homeland and journeying to the land of Canaan was one trial, and the famine he encountered upon reaching Canaan was another. Sarah's abduction in Egypt was an additional trial, as was the capture of his nephew Lot during the first world war in the ancient Near East that involved nine separate kingdoms, pitting four against five. The commentators adopted this approach and formulated different lists of trials that God tested Abraham with.[1]

A straightforward reading of the text suggests a different interpretation from that proffered by the sages. In my interpretation, every episode, from "Go forth from your native land" until Lot's rescue in the aftermath of the war of the four kings against the five kings, constitutes one continuous trial. This trial serves as a template for the rest of the Torah, its principles, and the core values of the Jewish state in its different incarnations.

In his famous 1889 essay "Wealth," American industrialist Andrew Carnegie wrote: "The problem of our age is the proper administration of wealth, so that the ties of brotherhood may still bind together the rich and poor in harmonious relationship." Like the challenge posed by Carnegie, the stories about Abraham and his journeys and battles teach a Jewish approach to dealing with wealth generally and, more specifically, to dealing with the blessing and wealth of the promised land. Accordingly, the theme of money, possessions, and property—gold, silver, cattle and tents—is repeatedly presented throughout the narrative. Interestingly, it appears where least expected. the theme of property and wealth that is woven into the narrative helps us to understand why, for example, Abraham's father, Terah, did not complete his journey to the land of Israel and instead stayed in Haran; Abraham and Lot had to part company; and the significance of Abraham returning property in the context of his battle against the four kings.

Abraham's father, Terah, was the ultimate progenitor of all the matriarchs and patriarchs of the Israelites, and, it seems, had the potential to be the founder of monotheism and the Israelite people. According to the verses in the Bible, Terah heads to the land of Canaan of his own volition. He set out from Ur of the Chaldeans to head to Canaan, but for some reason, which the Torah does not elucidate, he pauses in Haran, where he ultimately passes away. Something clearly went amiss on the way to the land of Canaan:

> Terah took his son Abram, his grandson Lot the son of Haran, and his daughter-in-law Sarai, the wife of his son Abram, and they set out together from Ur of the Chaldeans for the land of Canaan; but when they reached Haran, they settled there. (11:31)

Dr. Yoshi (Yehoshua) Fergun suggests that Terah's decision can be understood as choosing the good life: a life of comfort and wealth in the developed region of Haran. Notably, a similarly structured parallel verse describes Abraham's departure from Haran, though it also mentions property:

> Abram took his wife Sarai[2] and his brother's son Lot, and all the possessions that they had acquired, and the souls they had shaped[3] in Haran; and they set out for the land of Canaan and they reached the land of Canaan. (12:5)

The fact that their wealth is mentioned indicates both that they met with economic success in Haran and that the Torah deems this important. Presumably, then, it was this wealth that enticed Terah to stay in Haran. Abraham, on the other hand, went beyond his father and resolved to pack up his wealth and complete the journey to Canaan. The continuation of the story will teach us whether the acquisition of wealth in Haran was due to successful business initiatives or if it was acquired in a different capacity. That Abraham took his orphaned nephew, Lot, under his wing suggests that wealth is intrinsically connected to caring for the orphan, or in a more general sense, providing for society's weakest. Furthermore, when Abraham reached the promised land, he did not seek out a small corner of the land to develop his financial interests. Rather, he traveled around and called out in the name of God. Accordingly, he intuited another challenge of wealth: establishing a society on a foundation of righteousness and justice, in which belief in God and longing to connect to Him and other people inspires happiness and wealth. It was not enough for the wealthy Abraham to build a home with high hedges and to invest his wealth. He desired and set out to build a society that would work for others.

The stories that follow consistently foreground wealth and property. The very next episode describes Abraham's enrichment when he descended to Egypt to escape the famine that has ravaged Canaan. Abraham's decision to leave his home, the land of Canaan, for economic reasons was not without trepidation. The Torah relates that he was primarily concerned that upon seeing her beauty, the all-powerful Pharaoh of Egypt would take his wife Sarah for himself and kill her husband. Abraham therefore suggests to his wife that they call themselves brother and sister. This was not entirely untrue since Sarah was Abraham's niece, the daughter of his brother. Upon reaching Egypt, his "sister" (per 12:13) was indeed taken to Pharaoh's home. As a result, Abraham increased his wealth as a businessman of stature in the royal court:[4] "And because of her, it went well with Abram; he acquired sheep, oxen, donkeys, male and female slaves, female donkeys, and camels" (12:16).

Lot, Abraham's nephew, also became rich in Egypt through his ties to the royal court. This represents a different path to material riches, one based on alliances and connections to the ruling class. Unlike in Haran—where we do not know the source of wealth but can assume it was earned in business—the wealth that Abraham acquired in Egypt also had an element of power and authority.

When he eventually left Egypt, Abraham proved once again that establishing a new society in the land of Israel was of the utmost importance to him.[5] This episode further highlights Abraham's success: "Now Abram was very rich in cattle, silver, and gold" (13:2) This emphasizes that wealth and the challenge of using it properly are the central concerns of the story. The challenge that Abraham is about to encounter—dealing with wealth within the family—is foreshadowed by a close reading of two different verses. Abraham's departure from Haran and journey to the land of Israel is described thus: "Abram took *his wife Sarai* and his brother's son *Lot*, and all the *possessions* that they had acquired" (12:5). In contrast, his return to the land of Israel is described as: "From Egypt, Abram went up into the Negev, with his *wife* and all that he *possessed*, together with *Lot*" (13:1).

The subtle change of order suggests that Lot had grown distant from Abraham and that material wealth had come between them. Lot seemingly traveled with Abraham because he was a successful person. Abraham understood that his success derived from heeding God's commands and placing justice and concern for others above everything else: "Because Abraham obeyed Me and kept My charge: My commandments, My laws, and My teachings" (26:5). Through the years, Abraham acted responsibly and provided for his orphaned nephew. He supported "the persons that they had acquired in Haran" and generously provided for all who visited his tent.

After they left Egypt, Lot began to think of himself as a successful man in his own right. The story continues: "Lot, who went with Abram, also had flocks and herds and tents" (13:5). However, while Abraham viewed money and possessions as a divine gift that enabled him to "acquire" people in Haran, build altars to thank God, and help others, Lot loved wealth in and of itself and sought to cultivate his assets. As it is written: "A lover of money never has his fill of money" (Ecclesiastes 5:9).

This debate about the source and purpose of wealth intensified until it could no longer be contained: "The land could not support them staying together; for their possessions were so great that they could not remain together" (13:6). This painful decision brought the challenge of wealth to a new climax, and Abraham nobly conquered this peak, too. The sharpness of their disagreement comes to light in Lot's decision to travel eastward:

> Lot looked about him and saw how well watered was the whole plain of the Jordan, all of it—this was before the Lord had destroyed Sodom and Gomorrah—all the way to Zoar, like the garden of the Lord, like the land of Egypt. So Lot chose for himself the whole plain of the Jordan, and Lot journeyed eastward. Thus they parted from each other. (13:10–11)

In short, Lot elected to go to a fertile and well-populated area where he could easily flaunt his wealth. The description of the Jordanian plain returns us to the Garden of Eden, where wealth grew on trees, and to the land of Egypt, where Abraham and Lot amassed great fortunes. In other words, as far as his worldview is concerned, Lot did not really leave Egypt.

In Deuteronomy, the Torah contrasts the land of Israel with the land of Egypt:

> For the land that you are about to enter and possess is not like the land of Egypt from which you have come. There the grain you sowed had to be watered by your

> own labors, like a vegetable garden; but the land you are about to cross into and possess, a land of hills and valleys, soaks up its water from the rains of heaven. (Deuteronomy 10:10–11)

In Egypt, the Nile overflows and irrigates the entire land. One can succeed without divine intervention leading to boastful declarations of the Pharaoh such as: "My Nile is my own; I made it for myself" (Ezekiel 29:3).

Worse yet, Lot sought out a place where wealth was unlimited and rich people bore no responsibility. The Torah states, "The inhabitants of Sodom were very wicked sinners against the Lord" (Genesis 13:13).[6] The prophet Ezekiel further develops this point: "Only this was the sin of your sister Sodom: arrogance! She and her daughters had plenty of bread and untroubled tranquility; yet she did not support the poor and the needy" (Ezekiel 16:49). In Sodom, wealth came with no strings attached and led to excessive pride and egoism. Sinfulness thus became a way of life.

Abraham continued his travels, calling out in the name of God and preaching righteousness and justice. Lot, on the other hand, believed that success was his and his alone. Rather than appreciating that God can endow a person with wealth or enable a person's ability to earn a fortune anywhere, Lot settled in a place where "riches are hoarded by their owner to his misfortune" (Ecclesiastes 5:12). Lot chose to live in the self-centered society of Sodom and Gomorrah, the place that was most similar to Egypt, where self-worship was part of the local culture. Unlike in Carnegie's vision of a brotherhood between rich and poor, it did not demand that he assume responsibility for others:

> Lot, who went with Abram, also had flocks and herds and tents, so that the land could not support them staying together; for their possessions were so great that they could not remain together. And there was quarreling between the herdsmen of Abram's cattle and those of Lot's cattle. The Canaanites and Perizzites were then dwelling in the land. Abram said to Lot, "Let there be no strife between you and me, between my herdsmen and yours, for we are kinsmen." (Genesis 13:5–8)

This then was the argument between Abraham's and Lot's herdsmen: What is the source of property and material wealth? Who generated it and for what purpose? The worldview that Lot constructed for himself had the capacity to destroy the vision and principles that Abraham stood for, as well as sabotage the message that he was trying to impart to his progeny. Thus, as a last resort, Abraham parted company with Lot.

As we would expect from Abraham, the separation between him and Lot was merely physical; despite their distance and estrangement, Abraham's feelings of responsibility and compassion towards Lot, his orphaned nephew, were unaffected. Thus, when Lot was seized in time of war, Abraham acted immediately to free him from his captors. This alone would be an adequate analysis of Abraham's concern. However, just as in the previous story in Egypt and the coming story of the war, the Torah raises the issue of wealth and property and develops this theme far beyond its apparent relative importance to the story.

The war of the four kings against the five kings was, in a nutshell, about property:[7] "They seized all the possessions of Sodom and Gomorrah and all their provisions and went their way" (Genesis 14:11). This verse is indicative of the attitude of the leader of the four kingdoms, the imperialist king Chedorlaomer, as well as that of his allies: property above all. The next verse continues in this vein, describing what Abraham deems most important and valuable: "They also took Lot, the son of Abram's brother, and his possessions, and departed; for he had settled in Sodom" (14:12).

Abraham was most concerned about saving his nephew Lot. Therefore, he joined the war. He took 318 soldiers and chased the four kings all the way north of Damascus. Ambushing them at night, Abram, as he was still called then, defeated the kings, retrieving both his nephew and the possessions of the five kingdoms, including those of Sodom.

But if saving Lot from captivity is what compelled Abraham to join this war, why is material wealth mentioned at all?

To complicate matters further, in the ensuing narrative, the priorities are completely reversed: "He brought back all the possessions; he also brought back his kinsman Lot and his possessions, and the women and the rest of the people" (14:16). Not only is the property mentioned before Lot and the rest of the people, but the statement "he *also* brought back his kinsman Lot and his possessions" makes Lot appear to be an afterthought, ancillary to the primary object of recovering the looted property. Thus, in the eyes of Scripture, the war was about wealth. The king of Sodom reaches the same conclusion when he says: "'...Give me the persons and take the wealth for yourself'" (14:21).

The verses seem to suggest that Abraham went to battle the four kings for a greater cause than saving his kinsman. When Abraham set out, he risked all the material possessions and spiritual achievements that he had worked so hard to attain. Why would he jeopardize everything? Because "his kinsman had been taken captive." Precisely when property and achievement were on the line, his concern for family is highlighted as a supreme value, as well as a lesson that morality is not measured by material or monetary value.

Yet with his astounding victory, a new message was added. In the aftermath of the war, the verses first note the possessions that Abraham restored before mentioning Lot. Though Abraham had rescued Lot, he could not rest on his laurels. With victory, he came into possession of all the wealth that had been despoiled from the peoples of the region, and this confronted him with a new type of trial and responsibility. He passed this challenge too when he resolutely declared in front of the King of Sodom: "I swear to the Lord, God Most High, Creator of heaven and earth: I will not take so much as a thread or a sandal strap of what is yours; you shall not say, 'It is I who made Abram rich'" (14:22–23).

Abraham became wealthy on account of his talent, faith, connections, and hard work. Not only is there nothing unsavory about this, but from the Torah's perspective, Abraham's wealth was an asset, a tool that enabled him to set a hierarchy of values for his descendants. Specifically, the wealthy Abraham, who acquired wealth and possessions in a myriad of ways, was tested to build a hierarchy of values for others in both his time and in future generations. He became an archetype of a society builder. In the future, when the Israelites, Abraham's descendants, would fight and capture the land from the Canaanites, these choices would be put to the test. During and after these battles, the Israelites would find great wealth among the spoils: "houses full of all good things that you did not fill, hewn cisterns that you did not hew, vineyards and olive groves that you did not plant" (Deuteronomy 6:11).

In short, Abraham bequeathed to his children a proper attitude towards the wealth that they would acquire in wars of conquest and after establishing an independent kingdom. He wanted his descendants to know that all the good in this world derives from God and is destined to serve the needs of a just society. His hard earned wealth enabled him to do just that.

A single trial, appearing in various guises, challenged Abraham throughout his travels.[8] The Hebrew word for material possessions, *rekhush*," recurs throughout these chapters. Typical of *leitwörter*—guide words of a particular passage—it appears seven times in the episode of the four kings, from "and all the possessions [*rekhush*] that they had acquired [*rakhashu*] in Haran" through the statement of Sodom's king many years later: "give me the persons, and take the possessions [*rekhush*] for yourself."

Abraham withstood the test that Moses warned of in his parting poem hundreds of years later: "So Jeshurun grew fat and kicked" (Deuteronomy 32:15). Moses fears that Jeshurun, an appellation for the people of Israel which means "the straight", would buck its moral path if and when they became fat and happy. Abraham did not allow wealth to erode his values just as on the eve of their entry to the Land, Moses would warn the Israelites not to abandon their values due to the wealth they would accrue when they settled the Land. Abraham also withstood the other side of wealth's challenge: the tendency to say, "My own power and the might of my own hand have won this wealth for me" (Deuteronomy 8:17). Unlike his father, Terah, Abraham did not stay in exile on account of the wealth that he had amassed nor did he become vain and arrogant like Lot. His way of life expressed the importance of righteousness and morality and of concern for the orphan, the poor, and society's weakest.

As Andrew Carnegie wrote:

> This, then, is held to be the duty of the man of Wealth: First, to set an example of modest, unostentatious living, shunning display or extravagance; to provide moderately for the legitimate wants of those dependent upon him; and after doing so to consider all surplus revenues which come to him simply as trust funds, which he is called upon to administer, and strictly bound as a matter of duty to administer in the manner which, in his judgment, is best calculated to produce the most beneficial results for the community—the man of wealth thus becoming the mere agent and trustee for his poorer brethren, bringing to their service his superior wisdom, experience and ability to administer, doing for them better than they would or could do for themselves. ("Wealth.")

Carnegie envisioned a society in which the surplus wealth of the affluent would be transferred to those who need it more. Carnegie proposed a mechanism whereby the rich, with their "superior wisdom, experience, and ability to administer," would manage these funds on behalf of the poor to the benefit of the greater community:

> There remains, then, only one mode of using great fortunes; but in this we have the true antidote for the temporary unequal distribution of wealth, the reconciliation of the rich and the poor—a reign of harmony—another ideal, differing, indeed, from that of the Communist in requiring only the further evolution of existing conditions, not the total overthrow of our civilization. It is founded upon the present most intense individualism, and the race is projected to put it in practice by degree whenever it pleases. Under its sway we shall have an

> ideal state, in which the surplus wealth of the few will become, in the best sense the property of the many, because administered for the common good, and this wealth, passing through the hands of the few, can be made a much more potent force for the elevation of our race than if it had been distributed in small sums to the people themselves. Even the poorest can be made to see this, and to agree that great sums gathered by some of their fellow-citizens and spent for public purposes, from which the masses reap the principal benefit, are more valuable to them than if scattered among them through the course of many years in trifling amounts. ("Wealth.")

Like UBI, Carnegie's proposal aimed to solve the problem of poverty, but it did not address the challenge of poor people and their dignity. Moreover, Carnegie did not suggest why such a transfer ought to take place. Given that the wealthy worked hard and succeeded in a competitive market, it is hard to understand why they should part with the fruits of their labor. A utilitarian would answer that a more egalitarian society provides better protection for everyone, including the wealthy. None of us are safe until all of us our safe.[9] One can also argue that as the general population becomes wealthier, their ability and desire to purchase consumer goods expands; therefore in essence, those who give their wealth to others will become even wealthier. Nevertheless, one gets the sense that such an approach to sharing wealth will not establish real social resilience for ultimately, the entire system is based on self-interest.

Another approach to this problem is advanced by legendary investor Warren Buffet, who has declared time and again that he won the DNA lottery—he did not choose when he was born, his parents, or his IQ:

> I won the lottery the day I emerged from the womb by being in the United States instead of in some other country where my chances would have been way different.
>
> Imagine there are two identical twins in the womb, both equally bright and energetic. And the genie says to them, "One of you is going to be born in the United States, and one of you is going to be born in Bangladesh. And if you wind up in Bangladesh, you will pay no taxes. What percentage of your income would you bid to be the one that is born in the United States?" It says something about the fact that society has something to do with your fate and not just your innate qualities. The people who say, "I did it all myself," and think of themselves as Horatio Alger—believe me, they'd bid more to be in the United States than in Bangladesh. That's the Ovarian Lottery.[10]

In effect, Buffet concluded that he was the recipient of an extraordinary stroke of good luck and has therefore decided to distribute most of his assets to charity. That said, Buffet's pledge is based on a personal belief and does not really explain why we too ought to share our wealth with others less fortunate. It is not scalable beyond his personal feelings and example. In any event, Buffet is not pursuing a higher vision of a strong and moral sovereign entity.

What Abraham stood for is the belief that man's wealth is not merely an outgrowth of his toil and efforts but of his faithful adherence to God's commandments.[11] It follows, then, that the purpose of wealth is to confer good upon another person who was also created in the image of God. It is not "good" to do so because this person benefits from the superior managerial skills of the wealthy. Rather it is "good" because it respects each person by virtue of them being created in the same image of God, thus also creating a dignity-infused society and community.

Only people who understand that their wealth is not fully of their own making can understand that the purpose of success is to take responsibility for others. This wealth was entrusted to them to benefit "his brother" who are so much more than just "the needy." We are all part of a society comprised of those created in God's image. Just as a person sees no personal indignity or weakness in the fact that God has helped them to obtain what is needed, they will not show contempt for a disadvantaged person who needs handouts or another opportunity to succeed. Thus, by walking in the way of God, Abraham withstood the challenge of wealth in all its different forms and blazed a dignified, scalable, and repeatable path for all who came after him.

POLITICAL ADDENDUM

Above, we presented the dispute between Abraham and Lot as being about the source and purpose of wealth. Here, we seek to deepen our understanding of the argument that split the family.

Abraham had "shaped souls in Haran" and continued his mission in the land of Israel, calling on everyone to unite around faith in the one and only God. Against this backdrop, parting company with Lot, his nephew and adopted son, is incongruous, even inconceivable. The Torah's brief description of the reason for Lot's departure intimates that it is just the tip of the iceberg. We must therefore examine their relationship more closely and garner greater insight from the stories of when they traveled together, as well as events they experienced separately. The Torah states in brief:

> The land could not support them staying together; for their possessions were so great that they could not remain together. And there was quarreling between the herdsmen of Abram's cattle and those of Lot's cattle—and the Canaanites and Perizzites were then dwelling in the land. (Genesis 13:6-7)

Rashi explains that the Canaanites and Perizzites caused a shortage of pastureland. But this explanation seems puzzling given Abraham's mission to bring everyone closer to God. Shouldn't he have given up on his flocks—which could easily be converted into other assets—before or instead of giving up on a family member? This family, after all, consisted of only three people living in a foreign land. Rashbam differs from Rashi but does not offer an alternative explanation. It is further unclear why the text twice repeats that the land could not support them and why the Canaanites and the Perizzites are first mentioned at the end of the verse instead of the beginning.[12]

Additionally, a comparison between this verse and two similar verses in Genesis shows that "possessions" (*rekhush*) and "livestock" (*tzon uvakar*) are not interchangeable terms:

> And he drove off all his livestock and all the possessions that he had acquired, the livestock he owned, which he had acquired in Paddan-Aram, to go to his father Isaac, to the land of Canaan. (31:18)

> And they took their livestock and the possessions that they had acquired in the land of Canaan. Thus Jacob and all his offspring with him came to Egypt. (46:6)

In these two verses, "livestock" (*mikneh*) is listed separately from "possessions" (*rekhush*). *Rekhush* refers to assets and property that are not livestock. Thus, when the Torah specifically states that the land could not support Abraham and Lot because their "possessions" were so great, it indicates that the shortage of pastureland was not the cause of estrangement.

Earlier, we suggested that Abraham withstood a single, multifaceted challenge relating to wealth. First, he disengaged from the successful businesses that Terah had built in Haran and emigrated to the land of Israel. Upon his arrival, he was tested again: weary from his physical journey and his itinerant wanderings, Abraham should have settled down, reestablished his business, and restored some stability to his life. This could have even been seen as a perfect fulfillment of God's imperative and blessing: "Go forth from your native land and from your father's house to the land that I will show you. I will make of you a great nation, and I will bless you; I will make your name great, and you shall be a blessing" (12:1–2).

Abraham, however, chose a different path. Immediately upon arriving in Canaan, he began to travel its breadth, constructing altars and calling out in the name of God. A close reading of the verses indicates that Lot was elsewhere. Their departure from Haran and arrival in the land is described thus:

> Abram took his wife Sarai and his brother's son Lot, and all the possessions that *they* had acquired, and the souls *they* had shaped in Haran; and *they* set out for the land of Canaan and *they* reached the land of Canaan. (12:5)

Abraham traveled to the land with his possessions, his people, and Lot, his orphaned nephew. Their departure and arrival are described in plural form, "they." Then there is a shift, and

Abraham continued his travels alone; henceforth, "they" is replaced by the singular.

> Abram passed through the land as far as the site of Shechem, at the terebinth of Moreh. The Canaanites were then in the land. The Lord appeared to Abram and said, "I will assign this land to your heirs." And *he* built an altar there to the Lord who had appeared to him. From there *he* moved on to the hill country east of Bethel and pitched his tent, with Bethel on the west and Ai on the east; and *he* built there an altar to the Lord and invoked the Lord by name. (12:6–8)

These verses describe Abraham traveling alone. God appeared to him, and he built altars and pitched his tent by himself, indicating that Lot did not join Abraham's spiritual mission. He did not construct altars with Abraham nor did he travel with him along the central mountain ridge.

Thus Lot joined Abraham on his sojourn to the land, but not in his spiritual and moral mission. Upon arriving in the land, Lot apparently chose to engage in something that is most natural—he set himself up in a specific place and attended to his family's property and business interests. At the conclusion of Abraham's spiritual mission, he returned to the Negev and rejoined Lot and the other members of the traveling party: "Then Abram journeyed by stages toward the Negev" (12:9). As noted above, Abraham and Lot continued south to Egypt on account of the famine that was then ravaging the land of Israel. There, Abraham became extremely wealthy, and eventually returned: "From Egypt, Abram went up into the Negev, with his wife and all that he possessed, together with Lot. Now Abram was very rich in cattle, silver, and gold" (13:1–2).

Upon entering the land, Abraham visited the site of his altar—alone again, it seems: "And *he* traveled on his journeys from the Negev as far as Bethel, to the place where *his* tent had been formerly, between Bethel and Ai, the site of the altar that he had built there at first; and there Abram invoked the Lord by name" (13:3–4). Abraham thus returned to the Land and to that spiritual landscape of altars, calling out in the name of God and traveling amongst the inhabitants. The word "formerly" indicates that Abraham had returned to this origin, to the roots of his worldview. The money and wealth that he accumulated were tethered to the values of the altar, the call to monotheism, and the understanding that he was not the only true cause of his own tremendous wealth. Someone else, however, had reached a different conclusion: "Lot, who went with Abram, also had flocks and herds and tents" (13:5). Lot, too, became wealthy in Egypt. He was not "very rich" like Abraham; he had no silver and gold, only "flocks and herds and tents." Yet he did not join Abraham at the altar nor did he share Abraham's worldview that one's wealth is dependent on God. To the contrary, Lot was convinced that he acquired his wealth on account of his talents and his connections to wealthy, powerful people.

It stands to reason that Abraham and Lot, like the other residents of Canaan, were deeply affected by the famine, and their assets dwindled significantly. Perhaps Lot, who had focused his energies on consolidating the family's wealth, was disappointed by the promised land and lost faith in divine providence, leading him to the conclusion that accumulating wealth is necessary to withstand tough times. Thus he eventually chose to live in a place that was "well-watered" and less susceptible to famine.

Lot "went with Abram," but he did not join him on his journeys: "And he traveled on his journeys from the Negev as far as

Bethel, to the place where his tent had been formerly, between Bethel and Ai." Abraham's journeys (*masa'av*) are expressed in the singular form. They were spiritual journeys to the site of the altar where he called out in the name of God. On his journeys, he was alone. Lot did not join him. Blinded by the natural wealth of Egypt, business dealings with the king's inner circle, and a society that appreciated wealth, Lot viewed the sojourn in Egypt as "professional training," whereby he mastered the skill of accumulating sheep, cattle, and tents while cultivating relationships with local officials. That was his takeaway. Eventually, it became his business.

In sharp contrast, Abraham understood that God is the source of material wealth, including the wealth that he had amassed by his efforts in Egypt. At this point, the disagreement that had been brewing between Abraham and Lot exploded. The verse repeats itself to indicate that this problem was intractable: "The land could not support them staying together; for their possessions were so great that they could not remain together" (13:6).

A comparison between the parting of Abraham and Lot and the parting of Jacob and Esau sheds light on what motivated the separation, especially given the textual similarity:

> Esau took his wives, his sons and daughters, and all the members of his household, his cattle and all his livestock, and all the property that he had acquired in the land of Canaan, and he went to another land because of his brother Jacob. For their possessions were too many for them to dwell together, and the land where they sojourned could not support them because of their livestock. (36:6–7)

When Jacob and Esau parted company, "their possessions" (*rekhush*) are distinct from "their livestock" and are a reason they could not coexist. Additionally, the land could not support them because of their livestock. In other words, there was a dual cause.

Medieval Exegete, Talmudist, and poet Rabbi Yosef Bekhor Shor of Orléans, France explores the double causality that necessitated the separation of Jacob and Esau:[13]

> He went to another land because of his brother Jacob—he knew that the blessing of Abraham, the inheritance of the land of Canaan, had been given to Jacob and his children, and he withdrew from it. Additionally, the land could not support them, so he went and settled in Seir.

According to this interpretation, Jacob and Esau could not coexist for one primary reason: the idea that the blessing stands behind financial success. Isaac transmitted the land to Jacob in a prophetic-spiritual sense. His ideological goal was not to deny Esau his physical existence; he even thought to bless him with "abundance of new grain and wine" (27:28). Later, after Isaac realized that the first blessing had gone to Jacob, he blessed Esau: "Your abode shall enjoy the fat of the earth and the dew of heaven above. Yet by your sword you shall live" (27:39–40).

However, when he transmitted the "blessing of Abraham"—not the "stolen" blessing of 27:28–29, but the blessings he freely and openly gave Jacob in 28:1–4—Isaac understood that the people and its civilization have a political and economic ethos. This ethos was not and would not be upheld by Esau, who had married Canaanite women to the chagrin of his parents (26:34–35).

Likewise, the ideological debate about the land, possessions, and the relationship between them caused Abraham and Lot to separate and explains why they could not coexist. Nineteenth century German rabbi, philosopher, and leader Samson Raphael Hirsch makes this point, though not in the exact same way:

> The land could not support them staying together. Why not? The text does not state: "Their 'cattle' was too abundant and the grazing grounds in the land were insufficient." If they would have joined forces and combined all of the cattle into one large flock and lived as one household, the land would have been sufficient for them. The land could not support them "for their possessions were so great," because their material wealth—their silver, their gold, and all of their other assets—were far too abundant. When there is disunity and a lack of mutual trust—there is a need for tents, closets, treasure boxes, and for each person to administer their wealth independently. Because they were so wealthy, and because they could not get along with one another, the land could not support them. If Abraham and Lot had been more personally compatible and were able to live together—there never would have been a need for additional grazing areas. But the only thing that mattered in Lot's home was wealth and success, while Abraham's home was concerned with more lofty things. They did not use their possessions in the same way (the difference between man and his fellow is not the way in which he makes his fortune, but in the way in which he uses it). Therefore, the land could not support them. Lot needed his own grazing grounds, so that not even one lamb would mistakenly join the wrong flock.

According to this explanation, "the land could not support [*nasa*] them," indicates a moral, ideological issue and a question of leadership. A tribal chief or a king is called a "*nasi*" in Hebrew due to their role of establishing moral standards within the community. (This is similar to the Hebrew phrase *lehasi eitzah* or "to give advice," which derives from the same root, "NSA," which connotes carrying, lifting up, bearing, or supporting.) The elders who joined Moses in leading the nation bore the burden of the people with him. Abraham is similarly called a prince of God (*nesi elokim*) because he called out in the name of God and carried the banner of monotheism.

Both Abraham and Lot aspired to the status of *nasi*, but this narrow sliver of land could not sustain two *nesi'im* with such different worldviews. Lot sought to establish a kingdom that saw money and affluence as the keys to leveraging power and influence. In contrast, Abraham sought to build a society founded on calling out in the name of God and sharing wealth with the "souls" he had shaped. But Abraham and Lot did not part company on account of their differing philosophical views of wealth and its purpose. When a disagreement is for the sake of heaven, it is possible to coexist.

Strange as it seems, their separation stemmed from their identical political views: They both wanted to acquire wealth and power in the manner of princes and world leaders. But their aspirations were completely different. Each wanted to establish a kingdom that was founded on his principles in one of the city-states of the land. The fact that they were both extremely successful enabled them to engage in a campaign to advertise their respective beliefs. In effect, they canceled each other out. They could not coexist because they were "stepping on each other's toes." This is how the Torah describes the situation: "And there was quarreling between the herdsmen of

Abram's cattle and those of Lot's cattle—and the Canaanites and Perizzites were then dwelling in the land." (13:7)[14]

These herdsmen were not simply shepherds who fought over pastureland. They were the followers of rival candidates seeking to establish themselves and their subjects in a city-state. Anyone who wants to build a society predicated on principles must have a polity where he can implement his doctrines while disseminating his teachings and worldview. This, for example, was true of Constantine, who used the Roman Empire as a vehicle for spreading Christianity. The one thing which both Abraham and Lot agreed upon was that it is impossible for one city-state to be governed by two leaders with such different social and political approaches.

The ruling Canaanites and Perizzites had their own agenda. It is possible that they would have listened attentively to Abraham's calls in the name of God, but the dispute and rift within Abraham's family precluded this possibility. Under such circumstances, "the land could not support them staying together." National priorities and the ways in which wealth serves a leader became matters of profound disagreement that ultimately undermined the ability of either to prevail.

Abraham understood that there were many provinces in Israel where he could establish his rule, and he did not want to fight with Lot. The city that would accept him or the one he would build on his own would be firmly founded on righteousness and justice. Lot's political party, which had a completely different platform, derailed the process. This was the reason Abraham wanted to distance himself—each region would have its own ideology, and time would tell which one was preferable.

> Abram said to Lot, "Let there be no strife between you and me, between my herdsmen and yours, for we are

> kinsmen. Is not the whole land before you? Let us separate: If you go north, I will go south; and if you go south, I will go north." (13:8-9)

Lot, consistent with his worldview, turned to Sodom. He believed that in the absence of the correct geographical conditions and without close connections to the king's court and a materialistic society, it was impossible to become wealthy and to gain power and prestige.

> Lot looked about him and saw how well watered the whole plain of the Jordan was, all of it—this was before the Lord had destroyed Sodom and Gomorrah—all the way to Zoar, like the garden of the Lord, like the land of Egypt. So Lot chose for himself the whole plain of the Jordan, and Lot journeyed eastward. Thus they parted from each other. (13:10–11)

The conditions of the Jordan plain reminded Lot of Egypt, where he had become rich. The memory of Egypt fired his imagination, and in his dreams he envisioned the possibility of uniting "the entire plain of Jordan." With the right relationships and clever political maneuvers, he could become a powerful and influential actor in this region that included five adjacent cities. At this point, the narrative invokes the term "and Lot journeyed" for the first time. "Journey" (*masa*) indicates an ethical quest. When Lot parted company from Abraham, he was not just leaving his geographic proximity but his value system.[15] This marked the start of Lot's "campaign" to restore and promote Egyptian values.

From the vantage point of the Torah, Lot's decision was doomed from the start since as we know, God will ultimately destroy these sinful cities. The Torah thus explains that aspiring towards wealth without a foundation of social and political morals won't succeed. Lot has yet to learn this lesson. The ideology of endless pursuit of money and power leads a society to self-destruct, as evident by both the devastation of the flood and the fiery destruction of Sodom.[16] In the absence of social cohesion, those who are connected to the wealthy and powerful will get rich, but it will bring about complete chaos.[17]

A society that is steeped in godly values, or at least aspires towards them, gains wealth and endures. The understanding that wealth derives from God leads to a willingness to work hard and to share the fruits of success with the poor and unfortunate, thus enabling and ennobling them. A society that is rooted in righteousness and justice, the way of God and Abraham, is a strong, resilient society that will endure in brotherhood and prosperity.

I will end this chapter with a story. In the aftermath of Israel's disengagement from Gaza and the dismantling of the Jewish villages of Gush Katif, the company Atzmona Potatoes reestablished itself in the settlement of Hulot Halutza, a very sandy area in the southwestern corner of Israel, close to the borders of both Gaza and Egypt ("*Hulot*" means sand dunes). I toured their facility with the owner of the company and an agronomist named Peretz. During my visit, he received a phone call from a Palestinian man who had been his foreman in Gush Katif. The Palestinian man on the other side of the line sounded downcast. I asked Peretz what was going on.

He explained that when they left Gush Katif prior to Israel's disengagement from Gaza, the company decided to leave its greenhouses to the Palestinian workers and foremen with whom they had a very good relationship. The man on the other end of the phone told him that since the Jews' departure, the harvest had plummeted more than 50 percent, and they could not understand why. I asked Peretz what he had said. "What can I tell him?" he responded. "That production is dependent on the will of God? When the Jews were in Gaza, the crop flourished. When they are not, there is a decline..." He pointed at their new fields in the sand dunes: "Look at the potato and pepper plants here in Hulot Halutza. When Prime Minister Ehud Barak went to Camp David to discuss a land exchange with Arafat, he proposed exchanging Hulot Halutza for some of the territories in Judea and Samaria. Arafat refused and said that nothing could grow in the cursed sands here. And look, peppers and potatoes are growing in the *Hulot*."

4
Parashat Vayera

AN EMBER SAVED FROM FIRE

Post-Trauma Leadership

Whatsoever therefore is consequent to a time of war, where every man is enemy to every man, the same consequent to the time wherein men live without other security than what their own strength and their own invention shall furnish them withal. In such condition there is no place for industry...no knowledge of the face of the earth; no account of time; no arts; no letters; no society; and which is worst of all, continual fear, and danger of violent death; and the life of man, solitary, poor, nasty, brutish, and short.

—Thomas Hobbes

When there is rebellion in the land, many are its rulers;
But with a man who has understanding and
knowledge, stability will last.
A poor man who withholds what is due to the wretched
Is like a destructive rain that leaves no food.

—Proverbs (Mishlei) 28:2–3[1]

The first verse cited above from Proverbs (*Mishlei*) describes a land or polity that experiences a breakdown of its value system and a collapse into crime. The verse attributes this moral decomposition to the state of "many are its rulers." Rather than the country being led by one knowing leader, who lends stability and endurance to society, the verse describes a social context where everyone lords over his fellow. There is no rule of law. Rather, an ever growing number of individuals assume power and rule irresponsibly and unjustly, each over the fiefdom he controls. The leadership becomes morally, socially, and possibly even financially bankrupt, until the entire land is governed by kleptocracy.

In direct contrast, a country guided by an understanding and knowing individual can survive and thrive. This leader knows the troubles of others. He understands the challenges that face the citizens of every region, stratum, and persuasion. In his wisdom, he will give expression to everyone's interests and needs, building bridges among the different sectors of society and establishing a just society that is founded on the principles of law and righteousness.

The second verse describes the mirror image in which there is no understanding, knowledgeable leader, leaving the polity to descend into mob rule or the assumption of power by local rulers and opportunists. Such leaders exacerbate the social gaps and rifts between favored classes and the lower classes, who are exploited. Such regimes oppress society's weakest and exploit public trauma and distress. Every crisis and economic downturn becomes a tool to cement control, causing further social deterioration. As American theologian and ethicist Reinhold Niebuhr writes: "Man's capacity for justice makes democracy possible, but man's inclination to injustice makes democracy necessary."

According to the verses in Proverbs, this crisis becomes irreversible to the point that even heavy rain, which provides sufficient water to irrigate the crops, will not yield bread. When everyone is consumed by his own personal war of survival, nobody builds infrastructure to benefit society as a whole. Bureaucratic corruption consumes any just distribution and prevents economic recovery.

In the end, the abysmal social situation will defeat any prospect for improving the situation and rehabilitating the country. This analysis is similar to the thesis presented by Thomas Hobbes in his groundbreaking political work *Leviathan*: man is a wolf to man unless he chances upon another responsible leviathan.

Sodom—Sin and Punishment

In the previous chapter, I suggested that, for reasons of personal ambition, Lot chose to live in a region that was rich in natural resources and had a thriving agricultural economy. To realize his dream of establishing his wealth and political influence throughout the district, he chose an area that had five cities in close proximity.

The Torah describes Sodom and Gomorrah as the garden of God and the land of Egypt:

> Lot looked about him and saw how well watered was the whole plain of the Jordan, all of it—this was before the Lord had destroyed Sodom and Gomorrah—all the way to Zoar, like the garden of the Lord, like the land of Egypt. So Lot chose for himself the whole plain of the Jordan, and Lot journeyed eastward. Thus they parted from each other; Abram remained in the land

of Canaan, while Lot settled in the cities of the Plain, pitching his tents near Sodom. (Genesis 13:10–12)

Lot's encampment was "near" Sodom (13:13), so at this stage, it seems that he was not actually a resident. He was simply a nomad who had set up his tents in close proximity to the city (similar to Abraham's practice in the different places where he traveled and operated).

After Lot's move to the area of Sodom and his apparent move into the city (14:12), the Torah tells of the war of the kings and its causes as well as the political context of Sodom and its neighbors. For a period of twelve years, the kings of the plain paid tribute to Chedorlaomer and his allies—Mesopotamian kings of major powers. That is, Sodom and Gomorrah, cities endowed with great natural resources, paid a tax to the mighty armies of the region, who subjugated and exploited them.

The Torah emphasizes that the people of Sodom were "were very wicked sinners against the Lord." We can suggest, then, that the enslavement and exploitation of the people of Sodom was a form of punishment for their own crimes. The prophet Ezekiel compares Jerusalem to Sodom and declares: "Only this was the sin of your sister Sodom: arrogance! She and her daughters had plenty of bread and untroubled tranquility; yet she did not support the poor and the needy" (Ezekiel 16:49). It follows that the sins of Sodom were mostly social; people were unwilling to share their wealth. Their subservience to greater powers fits their crimes perfectly.

It is unclear if Lot was affected by this servitude. Perhaps, as an outsider, he was not required to pay taxes. It is also unclear if Lot regarded the exploitation of Sodom as an appropriate platform for realizing his political aspirations. Perhaps him viewing the entire plain as a single political unit was the basis for the alliance between the five kings and their decision to join forces in a synchronized rebellion against the greater powers.

After twelve years of servitude, the kings of the plain rebelled against the powers and threw off the yoke of tribute and subjugation.[2] In response, Chedorlaomer and his allies went to war to root out all pockets of rebellion:

> In the fourteenth year Chedorlaomer and the kings who were with him came and defeated the Rephaim at Ashteroth-Karnaim, the Zuzim at Ham, the Emim at Shaveh-Kiriathaim, and the Horites in their hill country of Seir as far as El-Paran, which is by the wilderness. On their way back they came to Ein-Mishpat, which is Kadesh, and subdued all the territory of the Amalekites, and also the Amorites who dwelt in Hazazon-Tamar. Then the king of Sodom, the king of Gomorrah, the king of Admah, the king of Zeboiim, and the king of Bela, which is Zoar, went forth and engaged them in battle in the Valley of Siddim: King Chedorlaomer of Elam, King Tidal of Goiim, King Amraphel of Shinar, and King Arioch of Ellasar—four kings against those five. Now the Valley of Siddim was dotted with bitumen pits; and the kings of Sodom and Gomorrah, in their flight, fell there, while the rest escaped to the hill country. [The invaders] seized all the possessions of Sodom and Gomorrah and all their provisions and went their way. They also took Lot, the son of Abram's brother, and his possessions, and departed; for he had settled in Sodom. (14:5–12)

The redundancy in the verses—that the kings took "all the possessions of Sodom and Gomorrah and all their provisions and went their way" and then (after they had seemingly left) seized Lot and his possessions—indicates that Lot was not part of Sodom or the rebellion. Yet, given his proximity to the battlefront, Lot was captured too.[3] At the end of the war as well, Lot and his possessions are mentioned separately from the possessions of Sodom: "He brought back all the possessions; he also brought back his kinsman Lot and his possessions..." Lot and his wealth are not included in the tally of people and possessions that Abraham returns to the king of Sodom.

The devastation that Chedorlaomer's soldiers left in their wake was, presumably, terrible. Twelve years earlier, Chedorlaomer had subjugated the region, recognizing its financial potential. The conquerors therefore left the residents in place so that they could benefit from their hard work. This time, it was impossible to trust the rebellious citizens of the plain. Chedorlaomer's army exiled the women and the surviving men and plundered whatever they could—their possessions and "all their provisions"—before leaving.

In effect, this was the first destruction of Sodom and Gomorrah, whose evil inhabitants had not internalized the message that God has sent them via their oppression by the four kings.[4] Though the natural potential of this fertile region remained intact, their entire economy was in shambles. The war marked the loss of their labor force, as well as the tools and industry that had enabled them to flourish.

The second part of the story introduces a significant turnabout:

> A fugitive brought the news to Abram the Hebrew, who was dwelling at the terebinths of Mamre the Amorite, kinsman of Eshkol and Aner, these being Abram's allies. When Abram heard that his kinsman had been taken captive, he mustered his retainers, born into his

> household, numbering three hundred and eighteen, and went in pursuit as far as Dan. At night, he and his servants deployed against them and defeated them; and he pursued them as far as Hobah, which is north of Damascus. He brought back all the possessions; he also brought back his kinsman Lot and his possessions, and the women and the rest of the people. When he returned from defeating Chedorlaomer and the kings with him, the king of Sodom came out to meet him in the Valley of Shaveh, which is the Valley of the King. And King Melchizedek of Salem brought out bread and wine; he was a priest of God Most High. He blessed him saying, "Blessed be Abram of God Most High, Creator of heaven and earth. And blessed be God Most High, Who has delivered your foes into your hand." And [Abram] gave him a tenth of everything. Then the king of Sodom said to Abram, "Give me the persons, and take the wealth for yourself." But Abram said to the king of Sodom, "I swear to the Lord, God Most High, Creator of heaven and earth: I will not take so much as a thread or a sandal strap of what is yours; you shall not say, 'It is I who made Abram rich.' For me, nothing but what my servants have used up; as for the share of the men who went with me—Aner, Eshkol, and Mamre—let them take their share." (14:13–24)

As victor, Abraham became the owner of the cities of the plain, including their citizens and possessions. The king of Sodom went to greet Abraham and requested, "Give me the persons and take the wealth for yourself" (14:21).

The other four kings in the coalition are not mentioned at all. Indeed, it seems that the king of Sodom is the lone survivor of the war.[5] He thereupon seized control of the entire region. Until this point, he was exploited by Chedorlaomer, but immediately upon being liberated, he became the new Chedorlaomer.[6] His authoritarian regime began when Abraham refused to take the possessions of those who fell in battle, returning the booty to the king of Sodom. The opportunist leader thus held all the money and land.

In other words, a new political and economic reality emerged, wherein one individual king owned the wealth of the five cities. Vested with total control of the region, this king was able to resettle the survivors and begin rebuilding the local economy.

The Day After

God was displeased with what transpired in Sodom in the aftermath of the war: "Then the Lord said, 'The outrage of Sodom and Gomorrah is so great, and their sin so grave! I will go down to see whether they have acted altogether according to the outcry that has reached Me; if not, I will know" (18:20–21).

The word "outcry" (*tze'akah* or *ze'akah*) recalls the plight of the Hebrews in Egypt and indicates that the people were suffocating under their enslaver. Thus: "I have marked well the plight of My people in Egypt and have heeded their outcry (*tze'akatam*) because of their taskmasters; yes, I am mindful of their sufferings.... Now the cry of the Israelites has reached Me; moreover, I have seen how the Egyptians oppress them" (Exodus 3:7-9). Likewise: "When Mordecai learned all that had happened, Mordecai tore his clothes and put on sackcloth and ashes. He went through the city, crying (*va'yezak*) out loudly and bitterly" (Esther 4:1).

The root "know" (*yada*) appears both here and in the verse in Proverbs that discusses a leader who knows how to regulate society and deal with economic injustice (cited earlier in this essay). In both cases, the word "know" (*yada*) indicates a political-economic understanding of the situation on the ground.

On 19:5, 13th century Catalan philosopher, physician, kabbalist, and exegete Ramban (Nahmanides) explained:

> Their intention [the people of Sodom] was to stop guests from [coming] among them,[7] as the Rabbis say (BT *Sanhedrin* 109a), for they thought that because of the quality of their land, which was "like the garden of God," many would come there [to settle and share their wealth], and they found charity repugnant.

According to Ramban, the sin of Sodom and Gomorrah was xenophobia, a conclusion that fits with the description of the attempted lynching of Lot's guests. When Lot took the messengers to his home, a mob gathered outside and demanded to lynch or sodomize them. To protect them, Lot strangely offered up his virgin daughters to the angry xenophobic mob.

Nevertheless, the prophet Isaiah's comparison of the sins of Sodom and Gomorrah with those of Judea, in the final century of the First Temple period, indicates something else since xenophobia had not been an issue there. In his indictment of the Judean kings, Isaiah declared: "Hear the word of the Lord, you chieftains of Sodom; Give ear to our God's instruction, you folk of Gomorrah!" (Isaiah 1:10).

For starters, Isaiah addressed the chieftains of Sodom—the leaders, not the masses. Additionally, as Isaiah continues, it becomes evident that there is a difference between Sodom and Gomorrah. "Chieftains of Sodom" are the rulers of Sodom, which is a different designation than "folk of Gomorrah." Similarly, Jeremiah differentiates between Sodom and Gomorrah. The rulers of Jerusalem—"the prophets"—

are likened to Sodom while the nation itself is compared to Gomorrah:

> But what I see in the prophets of Jerusalem is something horrifying: Adultery and false dealing. They encourage evildoers, so that no one turns back from his wickedness. To Me they are all like Sodom, and [all] its inhabitants like Gomorrah. (Jeremiah 23:14)[8]

This difference underscores the fact that the king of Sodom took control of the entire region. The chieftains resided in Sodom, while Gomorrah and the other cities were home to the masses who followed them.

For twelve years, Sodom and the other cities of the plain had been exploited by Chedorlaomer. It now appears that they were waiting not only for the day when they would be free from this oppression, but for the opportunity to become powerful and exploit those of lesser stature themselves—whether nearby cities or visitors like the messengers without a local support network. Abraham's victory in the war enabled the chieftains of Sodom to carry out their plan against the masses of Gomorrah and all other foreigners; they thus transformed themselves from oppressed to oppressors.[9] Their true ethos of greed and alienation of others, the very offenses that had caused their servitude in the first place, reappeared.

The popular ethos of the wicked, sinful people of Sodom became enshrined as a method of governance. Instead of a sensible rehabilitative process that would make intelligent use of the resources left after the war, the king of Sodom focused on seizing control of the entire plain. He incited the different parts of the populace against one another and against foreigners. He took control of the "folk of Gomorrah" and all the other cities of the plain, exploiting society's weakest. Rather than distributing means of production and encouraging people to build a respectable livelihood, the king and his close associates exacerbated the situation by appropriating the little that was left.[10]

The king of Sodom treated Lot well; after all, he was the nephew of the savior who had restored him to power and gave him all the recovered possessions. Thus, though initially described as "pitching his tents near Sodom"—a foreigner in a xenophobic place—Lot was now allowed to camp at the city's gate, having effectively become a member of the ruling class. As the residents would later resentfully say of him: "[He] came here as an alien, and already he acts the ruler!" (19:9).

It is possible that the king of Sodom expressed his gratitude to Abraham by assigning Lot a prominent position. The reverse might also be true. Perhaps more likely, the king used Lot to justify his takeover. With Lot by his side, he could invoke the recent memory of Abraham restoring the city's stolen wealth to the king alone. Furthermore, as we explained above, Lot also sought to amass wealth in order to generate and increase power. If Lot, a foreigner who had grown up in the home of the righteous, moral Abraham supported the king of Sodom, then the king's aspirations and behavior were clearly worthy and just.

Ultimately, the process of concentrating and distributing the city's means among a small elite was justified as a necessary measure in the aftermath of the war, though it was not necessarily a long-term method of governance. Every tyrant cultivates an elite; he offers them a small piece of the pie in order to strengthen and solidify his reign.

In the prologue, we cited a verse from Proverbs that prophesies that when multiple leaders rule the masses, each of whom looks only out for himself, the masses will rebel. Ultimately, however, the masses mimic the standards set by their leaders.[11] Therefore, when they rebel, the frenzied mob takes revenge against its leaders, justices, any institution regulated by law, and even commercial enterprises. A society that has been exploited by leaders, who foment infighting in order to divide and rule, will ultimately degenerate into chaos, and the masses will rise up against the leadership.

This is precisely what happened when a pair of angels, disguised as common messengers, arrived at Lot's home to warn him about the city's impending destruction.[12] As indicated above, unlike Abram, who welcomed these same angels into his tent, when Lot approached them, he offered them a one-night stay and told them to leave the next morning. The angels responded that they preferred to sleep in the street, but ultimately, Lot prevailed upon them to come into his home. Upon Lot welcoming them in, the mobs of Sodom surrounded Lot's house and demanded that he evict the guests and let the mobs "take care of" them.

It is unclear when the people or government of Sodom instituted this unwelcoming policy. It is unclear whether it is official government or municipal policy or simply an understanding among the commonfolk or, perhaps just the culture of the town. What is clear is that Lot was aware of it, and it seemed quite commonplace for mobs of people to turn up on a moment's notice. Lot's door is analogous to the gates of the city—it represents the place of justice or the place where every passerby is meant to affirm his commitment to local rules and etiquette.[13]

The masses gathered and furiously protested the breaking of Sodom's ironclad policy of not accepting guests. By deviating from the norm and taking the law into his own hands, Lot exposed the alienation between society's elite and its commoners. Lot stepped on a landmine and incurred the wrath of the masses, who sought to not only break down his front door, but to overthrow the entire governmental system.

When the people who encircled Lot's home demanded, "Bring them out to us[14] that we may know them." they intended to subject the guests to Sodom's well-known standard practice. For Abraham, the phrase "and I will know him" refers to the values of righteousness and justice. Proverbs also pins great hope on "the man who has understanding and knowledge." In Sodom, this same root word (*yada*) reflects the very different values of rape and exploitation.[15] In sum, the political system corrupted both itself and its subjects, and its double standards led to self-destruction.

Politically Incorrect

God disclosed to Abraham that He intended to destroy Sodom in order to contrast the political values of Sodom—political insiders looking out for themselves—with Abraham's divine principles of righteousness, justice, hospitality, and willingness to forgo both wealth and political power.

Upon hearing the terrible decree, Abraham beseeched God to spare the cities of the plain:

> Abraham came forward and said, "Will You sweep away the innocent along with the guilty? What if there should be fifty innocent within the city; will You then wipe out the place and not forgive it for the sake of the innocent fifty who are in it? Far be it from You to do such a thing, to bring death upon the innocent as well as the guilty, so that innocent and guilty fare alike. Far be it from You! Shall not the Judge of all the earth deal justly?" And the Lord answered, "If I find within the city of Sodom fifty innocent ones, I will forgive the whole place for their

> sake." Abraham spoke up, saying, "Here I venture to speak to my Lord, I who am but dust and ashes: What if the fifty innocent should lack five? Will You destroy the whole city for want of the five?" And He answered, "I will not destroy if I find forty-five there." But he spoke to Him again, and said, "What if forty should be found there?" And He answered, "I will not do it, for the sake of the forty." And he said, "Let not my Lord be angry if I go on: What if thirty should be found there?" And He answered, "I will not do it if I find thirty there." And he said, "I venture again to speak to my Lord: What if twenty should be found there?" And He answered, "I will not destroy, for the sake of the twenty." And he said, "Let not my Lord be angry if I speak but this last time: What if ten should be found there?" And He answered, "I will not destroy, for the sake of the ten." (18:23–32)

Abraham, the progenitor of a heritage of righteousness and justice, attempted to resolve a leadership and political crisis. His pursuit of fifty righteous people in the city was a search for individuals with leadership potential. Perhaps these were the "captains of fifty" who currently filled government positions in the cities of the plain, as Isaiah later called the leaders of Jerusalem "captains of fifty" when comparing it to Sodom.[16] Or perhaps they were the "captains of ten"—the senior leadership of each of the five cities.

Abraham, who understood that the city's corruption was caused by its leadership, lowered his bid from fifty righteous people to forty-five to forty. Thereafter, he continued to lower his bid by ten each time. This change is significant. It is possible that Abraham initially went to the top—namely, the five rulers of the five cities—and argued that even if the most senior leaders were sinners, the secondary tier might not have been corrupt. Abraham may have hoped that God would only destroy the top brass of the city. The leaders' deputies, who were next in line in local government, would have then assumed control and ushered in a new order of righteousness and morality.

When God did not respond positively, Abraham implored Him to save the cities on account of forty righteous people. Abraham understood that Sodom and its king were a lost cause. They were the instigators and provocateurs of evil. They were the ones who had seized the spoils of war and exploited the common folk of Gomorrah and the other cities. So Abraham gave up on Sodom and its leadership, the "captains of ten." Thus, the early verses state: "If I find within the city *of Sodom* fifty innocent ones, I will forgive the whole place for their sake." But subsequent verses state: "If forty should be found *there*."

God did not agree to Abraham's request of forty. This suggests that God refused to save four entire cities, so Abraham petitioned Him to save three. This was provided that they would find thirty righteous people, meaning three groups of "captains of ten" who exhibited proper leadership in their respective locales.

Abraham understood that the social divisions in Gomorrah, the close ally of Sodom, were irreparable. He therefore also gave up on Gomorrah, the second most important city of the fertile Jordanian plain. Eventually, Abraham understood that all the cities had internalized the perverse value system of Sodom. Even the furthest city, Zoar, which was located at the edge of the plain that abutted the mountain, had absorbed these values; indeed, Ezekiel called the cities "Sodom and her daughters" (Ezekiel 16:49).

The king of Sodom had established political hegemony over all the cities of the plain and fomented social rifts, and this led to a dead-end and ultimately a deadly end. The cities had not mended their ways after their servitude, the war, and their experience of collective captivity. To the contrary, their behavior worsened, and corruption and exploitation was brought to an entirely new public level. Their overthrow was therefore inevitable.[17]

Political leaders who divide society and exploit its wealth to establish their own authority sow the seeds of destruction with their own hands. It is possible to recover from a period of servitude or from the misguided quests of weak leaders like Sodom's and Gomorrah's, who fled in time of war. However, a society that destroys its shared interests, sense of mutual responsibility, concern for the weak, hospitality, and principled laws is beyond repair, both in the eyes of God and the eyes of man.

The Final Battle

The end of the story seems to shed light on its beginning. Lot asked the angels to allow him to flee to Zoar. The city was geographically separate and apparently smaller than the cities of the plain, though it was still part of the alliance. Despite this, the angels agreed to Lot's request and changed the original plans for destruction:

> When they had brought them outside, one said, "Flee for your life! Do not look behind you, nor stop anywhere in the plain; flee to the hills, lest you be swept away." But Lot said to them, "Oh no, my lord! You have been so gracious to your servant and have already shown me so much kindness in order to save my life; but I cannot flee to the hills, lest the disaster overtake me and I die. Look, that town there is near enough to flee to; it is such

> a little place! Let me flee there—it is such a little place—and let my life be saved." He replied, "Very well, I will grant you this favor too, and I will not annihilate the town of which you have spoken. Hurry, flee there, for I cannot do anything until you arrive there." Hence the town came to be called Zoar. (19:17–22)

As noted, God had intended to destroy Zoar, too. Lot's arrival at Zoar, however, cancelled the decree. De facto, only four of the cities of the plain were destroyed—for now.

The narrative does not describe much about Lot's activities in Zoar. It does not tell us if he attempted to inspire the people to repent or if he tried to rebuild his business interests. We do not know whether he assimilated into the city or if the people of Zoar held a grudge against him because of his close association with the king of Sodom.

Lot likely stood out. He was new to the town. Moreover, we can assume that Lot was well-known. He was a judge in Sodom, and his uncle had saved the people of all five cities of the plain and was the hero of that time. From what the Torah tells us, though, we get the impression that Lot did not feel safe in Zoar:

> Lot went up from Zoar and settled in the hill country with his two daughters, for he was afraid to dwell in Zoar; and he and his two daughters lived in a cave. And the older one said to the younger, "Our father is old, and there is not a man on earth to consort with us in the way of all the world." (19:30–31)

Lot's daughters, who had just fled Zoar for the safety of the cave, contended that "there is not a man on earth to consort with us." This demands explanation.

It seems that after Lot left Zoar, the city was destroyed. Lot's daughters looked eastward and saw that the last remaining city of the plain was now in ruins.[18] Apparently, the people of Zoar did not learn from the destruction of the other cities. They did not understand that they were spared by a miracle nor did they learn the larger lesson—that a society built on greed, corruption, and violence is transient. In the end, nothing remained of the regime that was predicated on aggression and exploitation and based on the values of xenophobia, egoism, and amassing wealth for its own sake.

Epilogue

In the aftermath of the 1948 War of Independence, Israel found itself with limited resources and little foreign currency as it faced a massive wave of immigration. A large number of Jews—about 800,000—had been expelled from the surrounding Arab and North African countries. Their communities, some of which were very ancient, were uprooted and destroyed, and they decided to seek refuge in Israel.

In order to provide for these newcomers—whose language, appearance and customs were vastly different from those of the existing, mostly Ashkenazic and European Israeli settlement—David Ben-Gurion adopted a series of austerity measures. Ben-Gurion understood that a nation must be built upon the ethics of mutual responsibility and sacrifice. It is no less important—and perhaps even more so—than a nation's physical structure. Ben-Gurion, who saw in the Bible a blueprint for life, fulfilled this biblical injunction: "For I have singled him out, that he may instruct his children and his posterity to keep the way of the Lord by doing what is just and right, in order that the Lord may bring about for Abraham what He has promised him" (18:19).

Over the course of the 1990s, Israel absorbed another large influx of immigrants from the former Soviet Union. This wave actually began in the late 1980s when Mikhail Gorbachev, a relatively liberal Soviet leader, opened the gates of the USSR. This wave of immigration brought hundreds of thousands of people to Israel. In 2000, Israel welcomed its millionth immigrant from the former Soviet Union.

During that same period, Israel also welcomed the long-lost tribe of Ethiopian Jews to Israel. Again, despite debate among some rabbis about their "Jewishness" and their obviously different appearance and skin color, they were welcomed openly. My eldest son's army commander is a descendent of those early Ethiopian immigrants, a hallmark of the mosaic of mutual responsibility that the army creates.

On a national level, the increased demand for housing to accommodate these immigrants caused apartment prices to skyrocket, which in turn led to widespread social protests. At the same time, given that many were not halakhically Jewish, people saw them as a threat to the delicate balance of the different sectors of Israeli society. Despite the challenges, Israel opened her gates, pocketbook, and, most importantly, her heart. With a spirit of brotherhood and responsibility, the State of Israel stepped up to the task.

5

Parashat Ḥayei Sarah

GAME THEORY AT THE CAVE OF MACHPELAH

Values Generate Value

With the death of his wife Sarah, Abraham sought to purchase burial grounds, where he would one day be buried as well. A close reading of the complex and multipart story shows that Abraham conducted an intricate negotiation. An examination of his methods divulges his hierarchy of values as he completed his first land purchase in the land of Israel. This is the story in its entirety:

> Sarah's lifetime—the span of Sarah's life—came to one hundred and twenty-seven years. Sarah died in Kiryat Arba—now Hebron—in the land of Canaan; and Abraham proceeded to mourn for Sarah and to bewail her.
>
> Then Abraham rose from beside his dead, and spoke to the Hittites, saying, "I am a resident alien among you; sell me a burial site among you, that I may remove my

dead for burial." And the Hittites replied to Abraham, saying to him, "Hear us, my lord: you are the prince of God in our midst. Bury your dead in the choicest of our burial places; none of us will withhold his burial place from you for burying your dead."

Thereupon Abraham bowed low to the people of the land, the Hittites.

And he said to them, "If it is your wish that I remove my dead for burial, you must agree to intercede for me with Ephron son of Zohar. Let him sell me the cave of Machpelah that he owns, which is at the edge of his land. Let him sell it to me, at the full price, for a burial site in your midst."

Ephron was present among the Hittites; so Ephron the Hittite answered Abraham in the hearing of the Hittites, all who entered the gate of his town, saying, "No, my Lord, hear me: I give you the field and I give you the cave that is in it; I give it to you in the presence of my people. Bury your dead."

Then Abraham bowed low before the people of the land.

And spoke to Ephron in the hearing of the people of the land, saying, "If only you would hear me out! I paid the price of the land; accept it from me, that I may bury my dead there." And Ephron replied to Abraham, saying to him "My Lord, do hear me! A piece of land worth four hundred shekels of silver—what is that between you and me? Go and bury your dead." Abraham accepted Ephron's terms. Abraham paid out to Ephron the money

> that he had named in the hearing of the Hittites—four hundred shekels of silver at the going merchants' rate.
>
> So Ephron's land in Machpelah, near Mamre—the field with its cave and all the trees anywhere within the confines of that field—passed to Abraham as his possession, in the presence of the Hittites, of all who entered the gate of his town. And then Abraham buried his wife Sarah in the cave of the field of Machpelah, facing Mamre—now Hebron—in the land of Canaan. Thus the field with its cave passed from the Hittites to Abraham, as a burial site. (Bereishit 23:1–20)

The motif of bowing, which occurs twice in the story, divides the narrative into three distinct sections. It seems that these three stages are essential in clarifying Abraham's priorities and exposing the message of the entire affair.

For the sake of comparison, when Jacob purchases a field in Shechem later in Genesis, the Torah provides the bottom line without any details about the negotiations: "The parcel of land where he pitched his tent he purchased from the children of Hamor, Shechem's father, for a hundred *kesitah*" (33:19). At the same time, different inflections of expressions like "among you," "with you," and "in your midst" appear throughout the story. This theme also forms a central axis, whose decoding can lead us to the meaning of the story.[1]

Land is Not Subject to the Laws of Price Gouging[2]

Ramban (23:15) explores the meaning of this episode:

> According to the opinion of Onkelos [second century Aramaic translation of the Torah], the explanation of the phrase "land of four hundred silver shekels," is that

> the field was worth that amount. Perhaps he wants to say that the price of the field was fixed in that locale, for this is the usual practice in most countries, that there is a standard price for a field according to its size..."[3]

Ramban quotes Onkelos's translation, which states that 400 silver shekels was the standard price for the field that Abraham wished to purchase. Indeed, three different antique land deeds that date back to the thirteen through fourteenth centuries BCE describe real estate transactions that were priced at 400 shekels.[4] According to this finding and Onkelos and Ramban,[5] the negotiations between Abraham and Ephron were not about the monetary value of the field.

Ramban himself takes a similar line in his explanation: "land of four hundred silver shekels' means that Ephron or his forebears had bought it for that [amount]." This indicates that Abraham reimbursed Ephron for the money that his family had paid for the estate. According to this explanation, the price was not the focal point of the negotiations; the price that Ephron demanded was the fair price.

Nevertheless, the negotiations that Abraham conducted with the Hittites, and Ephron specifically, must be analyzed from Abraham's point of view. From Abraham's perspective, given his great wealth, the price was low. Prior verses indicate that this was not an excessive payment for Abraham:

> And Abimelech said, "Here, my land is before you; settle wherever you please." And to Sarah he said, "I herewith give your brother one thousand pieces of silver; this will serve you as vindication before all who are with you, and you are cleared before everyone." (20:15–16)

Abimelech, king of Gerar, gave Abraham sheep, cattle, servants, and maidservants, as well as 1,000 pieces of silver. These gifts were added to Abraham's already enormous wealth. From Abraham's vantage point, paying 40 percent of Sarah's bride price to purchase burial her grounds was an easy deal to make.[6]

Game Theory—The Next Generation

To model both how Abraham conducted the negotiations based on his interest and wealth and the advantages of the broader strategy of the impact of values on value, I want to discuss game theory, one of the leading economic models of our era. A great deal has been written about how people make decisions under uncertain conditions according to negotiation frameworks and the decisions of other players. This is in contrast with Adam Smith's theory, which views each player as acting alone and independently to maximize his or her benefit. Game theory develops models for complex negotiations in situations where strategies are impacted by the results that my rival and I are both simultaneously striving toward. I am not an expert in game theory, but since game theory has been defined as the systematic study of "*interdependent*" rational choice, few, if any, have dealt with the influence of values and principles on economic negotiations or games—let alone on closing a deal under "limitations" that are not measured by money or monetary value.

A simple game in game theory is built on four possibilities, and it includes several strategies for making a deal or maximizing benefit. The question is: What happens if one player has a non-economic principle, or perhaps one that is non-rational to the other players, on which he or she is not willing to compromise? How does it impact his or her behavior? If principles guide me and I adhere to them, then there is no price I would be willing to accept for one of the four possible outcomes. At first glance, this seems to be irrational and perhaps unpredictable behavior, and by definition, I might lose out when I refuse an offer that, from an economic perspective, is worthwhile.

The opposite conclusion can be reached by combining a principled moral stance with one of the better-known examples from game theory: the Prisoner's Dilemma.

The prisoners know all these facts but cannot communicate with one another. Each therefore faces the same dilemma: "Do I testify, or do I remain silent?" Prisoner One examines his options: "Regardless of the tactic chosen by Prisoner Two, I should testify because if I do, my punishment will be less severe than if I am silent." Therefore, "admission" seems the optimal strategy for him. Prisoner Two analyzes the situation similarly. The rational decision they reach leads them both to testify, and so each goes to jail for five years. Had they both taken the risk that the other would be silent, they would have each gone to prison for only one year.

Note that in the Prisoner's Dilemma, the rational decision to inform one's friend would not make any distinction based on whether the friend actually committed the crime. That is, to maximize one's personal benefit, one should inform on his or her friend in any case, irrespective of truth, conscience, or morality.

The paradox stems from the fact that the rational decision produces a suboptimal result. To attain the best possible result for both, they would need to cooperate (i.e., both remain silent), but since the course of action that pays off best for each player acting independently is always not to cooperate, each player chooses not to do so.

Let us now imagine a situation where the prisoners are not perfect strangers but a mother and son. Presumably, a mother would never inform on her son. She would not risk her son remaining silent on her behalf and thus spending a long time in prison while she walks free. Were that to happen, her freedom would be worthless to her.[7] She might even prefer the opposite—that her son goes free while she pays the price. Therefore, the son, even without any express communication with his mother, knows for certain that she will never inform on him. In such a case, the son would not inform on his mother, so they would both sit in prison for only a short time.

The implication is that the principled stance of one player and their ability to assume such principles (not to inform on the other regardless of the costs) does not undermine Smith's rational thinking; it even helps the players achieve the optimal result. From Smith's perspective, principles compete against pure rationality and dictate behavior that does not necessarily maximize profits. However, since the economic realm is comprised of numerous players reacting to one another, what Smith asserts as the basis of his model does not lead to market optimization. Instead the principled stance leads to the optimum.

When I was fourteen years old, during a trip to Switzerland with my grandmother Oma Els, she said to me: "No one ever got rich from tipping too little, and no one ever got poor from tipping too much." According to Smith's theory, if several friends sit at a restaurant and each contributes to a joint tip without knowing how much anyone else put in, the total tip will be zero.

This is true even if everyone agrees the waiter deserves one. If those at the table are principled and unwilling to compromise no matter what, each person will contribute their fair share of the tip to which, in their opinion, the waiter is entitled. The responsibility of "three who ate together"[8] (the Rabbinic view of a communal meal) is not individual but collective.

More fundamentally, instilling a principled norm of transparency is not only worthy on its own terms, but it is also likely to pay off for patrons of the restaurant. Sooner or later, they or their family members will be in the same place as the waiter who works hard for the wages of their labor. The Torah's view of complex negotiations is that they must be undergirded by principles in order to achieve the optimal outcome. Principles that may seem irrational actually guide the principals to better negotiating strategies and outcomes.

The Torah's excruciatingly detailed explanation of Abraham's purchase of the Cave of Machpelah, the burial cave for his wife and ultimately all the matriarchs and patriarchs, actually shows these negotiating strategies in action. It predicts and heralds that adopting principles and a doctrine of assumed or agreed principles will help families and nations make better deals.

Maximization or Sophistication

Abraham's primary goal was to purchase burial grounds. Accordingly, since Abraham was ready and willing to pay for his purchase, the transaction should not have been especially complicated. The length of the episode and the different stages of negotiations indicate that various interests other than price were at play beneath the surface.

The conflicting interests of each party necessitated carefully calculated conduct. We can yield fresh insights by applying careful textual analysis aided by the principles of game theory and the insights described above.

Unlike in the case of the Prisoners' Dilemma described above, one of the ways to prevail in complicated, multiparameter face-to-face negotiations is to allow your opponent to progress and turn over their cards so that you can better understand their strategy. In a similar manner, Abraham considered his steps carefully and did not play his cards immediately.

In this negotiation, the Hittites had two goals. They sought to absorb Abraham, his wealth, and his family into their society and also to obtain as much compensation as they could in the short term.[9] Although Abraham was familiar with the Hebron real estate market and had identified the specific property he wanted, he could not approach Ephron directly. Instead, he had to turn to the Hittites collectively and ask for their public intercession. This indicates that the issue of selling tribal lands to a foreigner was very much on the table.

From the Hittites' perspective, the natural solution was Abraham's total assimilation into their society. This would yield two obvious benefits: the foreigner would no longer be foreign, and the local economy would get a serious boost from the wealthy immigrant who had come to live in their midst. In contrast, Abraham was not interested in assimilating, and he wanted to pay a fair price for the burial plot that he needed at that moment. Each party sought to optimize their goals through the eventual deal.

The final result would include a greater or lesser degree of assimilation and a higher or lower price. The attempt of each party to obtain the best possible result in this multiparameter negotiation constituted both a difficulty and an obstacle for the other.

In practice, the nonmonetary, principle-based aspect complicates negotiations beyond what game theory conventionally deals with. Abraham had no interest in assimilating, and the Hittites had no interest in selling tribal lands to a foreigner. In classic game theory, a solution can be agreed upon when each side has two strategies for action. However, the negotiations between Abraham and the Hittites were far more complex.

Amidst his cries and lamentations, Abraham sought to bury his beloved wife. If he were willing to pay in the currency of full assimilation into Hittite society, it is fair to assume that he would have been entitled to burial grounds, just like every Hittite tribesman. But Abraham, who was not willing to pay this price, described himself as "a resident alien" to emphasize his foreignness.[10]

His words were chosen carefully. Abraham's refusal to be considered one of the Hittites echoes his directive to Isaac not to marry a Canaanite woman, which appears immediately after the purchase of the cave of Machpelah (24:3). One generation later, Rebecca would announce to Isaac: "I am disgusted with my life because of the Hittite women. If Jacob marries a Hittite woman like these, from among the native women, what good will life be to me?" (27:46). Abraham therefore emphasized that he is "a resident alien" in order to establish the framework for negotiation and to signal what he finds most important. He added "among you" to emphasize that despite his unwillingness to assimilate, his request is still legitimate. I live amongst you. I bear status as an unofficial resident. I am not a foreign nomad who has just arrived in town.

The Hittites answered that no one would deny him the right to bury Sarah in their family's ancestral burial grounds, in accordance with their customs.[11]

> And the Hittites replied to Abraham, saying to him, "Hear us, my lord: you are the prince of God in our midst. Bury your dead in the choicest of our burial places; none of us will withhold his burial place from you for burying your dead." Thereupon Abraham bowed low to the people of the land, the Hittites. (23:5–7)

They called Abraham a "prince of God" because they know (and let him know they knew) of his wealth and political status. They denied that he was "a resident alien" because their goal was to have Abraham completely assimilate to their community, not just live amongst and alongside them. They thus intentionally changed Abraham's wording "amongst you" to "in our midst." In short, they were prepared to grant him the burial grounds of his choice provided that he became part of the extended Hittite family.

Abraham, having achieved his first goal of agreeing to receive a burial plot, bowed down before the Hittites. In doing so, he effectively ended the initial stage of negotiations and declared his first victory.

He then proceeded to the next stage of this negotiation. Abraham was aware that he might have to forfeit one of his goals for according to game theory, if one uses a maximalist strategy, they may be left with nothing. Abraham did not want to reject the Hittites' basic willingness to allocate burial grounds for him, but nor was he willing to pay their maximalist price.

Complete assimilation was Abraham's primary fear, and avoiding it was his ultimate goal. He was therefore willing to make financial concessions. More to the point, he would have paid to avoid being obligated to them. However, he conducted the second negotiation about the value of the property in an attempt to reach both of his objectives.

Tactical Empathy

As former FBI international hostage negotiator Chris Voss explains in his book *Never Split the Difference*, one of the most effective ways to achieve an objective is tactical empathy. This is a technique in which one uses the exact words employed by the opponent to demonstrate understanding of the opponent's situation and distress. Ostensibly, there are certain things that both sides will never agree upon. Nevertheless, correctly utilizing the desires of the opponent and specifically invoking his exact words can help achieve the desired outcome:

> And [Abraham] said to them, "If it is your wish to bury my dead from before me, you must agree to intercede for me with Ephron son of Zohar. Let him sell me the cave of Machpelah that he owns, which is at the edge of his land. Let him sell it to me, at the full price, for a burial site in your midst." (23:8–9)

Abraham's use of tactical empathy began when he repeated the Hittites' commitment to allow Sarah to be buried in their land. Additionally, by repeating their exact words, "in your midst," Abraham transferred liability to the Hittites, effectively turning his request into their aspiration. Moreover, when Abraham first requested the burial grounds, he used the word "among you" to indicate that the burial grounds he sought to purchase are adjacent to their land and not actually within it. In contrast, the Hittites declared "you are the prince of God in our midst" in an attempt to integrate Abraham and his wealth.

At this stage, Abraham used their words to achieve his goal. He spoke of "a burial site in your midst" to express tactical empathy for the Hittites' request that he reside in their midst. Abraham also used the phrase "at the full price," giving formal, public expression to the Hittites' hidden wish. He thereby engendered an atmosphere that is accepting of the Hittites' conditions and gave them the sense that he was ready to fulfill their desires.

Yet Abraham had no intention of living in their midst, only in their proximity. Abraham signaled and emphasized this by remarking that the cave is "at the edge of [Ephron's] field" in order to anchor the negotiations. He did not want to live amidst the Hittites, only on the margins of their settlement at Hebron. With this clever formulation, Abraham employed and foreshadowed the tactic that Voss would develop.

At the same time, pursuant to the Hittites' promise that "none of us will withhold his burial place from you for burying your dead," Abraham chose a property that was not being used for burial. According to game theory, one strategy is to first state the top priority in order to anchor the negotiations on the principles that are most important to you. Abraham was prepared to pay "the full price." In saying so, he indicated that he was interested in this specific piece of property even if it was expensive and that he was not willing to assimilate amongst the Hittites.

On the other hand, he did not want to antagonize the Hittites by giving them the impression that he came to buy them out with his fantastic wealth. His request to the Hittites, "you must agree to intercede for me with Ephron son of Zohar," when Ephron was sitting right there, reflects the delicate balance of his status of "resident alien." On the one hand, Abraham knew the lay of the land and was familiar with the different properties in the area and who owned them. On the other, he did not know the people personally. He spoke their language well but only used it in accordance with his principles.

According to game theory, there are two ways to achieve a desired result in a simple game with four possible results: The basic strategy is to promote a package deal that secures a compromise and serves some interests while preventing the other party from realizing all of their aspirations. Another strategy is to isolate all factors and variables and to address each one individually. At this initial stage of negotiations, Abraham attempted to secure a package deal: "I will pay a lot of money, on the condition that I will acquire the burial plot at the edge of the field without incurring any further obligations to you as a community."

Freebies and Luxuries

> Ephron was present among the Hittites; so Ephron the Hittite answered Abraham in the hearing of the Hittites, all who entered the gate of his town, saying, "No, my lord, hear me: I give you the field and I give you the cave that is in it; I give it to you in the presence of my people. Bury your dead." Then Abraham bowed low before the people of the land and spoke to Ephron in the hearing of the people of the land, saying, "If only you would hear me out! Let me pay the price of the land; accept it from me, that I may bury my dead there." (23:10–12)

The Torah emphasizes that Ephron was sitting among the Hittites. This was his home turf, and this was where the Hittites tried to pressure Abraham. Ephron was apparently blindsided by Abraham's exceedingly generous offer to pay "full price," and he agreed in principle to sell Abraham the cave at the edge of his field. Abraham went all in, but Ephron "spoke in the hearing of the Hittites" and declared explicitly, "I give it to you in the presence of my people."

Until this point, the discussion had revolved around the purchase of a cave as a burial ground, but Ephron was now adding the entire field—and he offered it all for free. By mentioning the Hittites and expanding the discussion to the entire property (when Abraham only expressed interest in the cave), he hinted that it was still necessary to gain the approval of the Hittites. He thus subtly let it be known that "I am interested in selling, but instead I must give it away; for only if you accept the land for free will you indicate your willingness to assimilate amongst the Hittites, whose tribal lands these are."[12]

At this stage, after Ephron agrees to give Abraham the specific burial plot, Abraham banked his accomplishments again—obtaining the desired burial grounds—by bowing to the Hittites a second time. The act of bowing down was directed at the Hittites and not at Ephron, who has already agreed. He bowed to them because his next obstacle was ratification of the deal in the public square.

Full House

Confident that he had secured the desired property, Abraham opened the discussion of price. Once again, he used Ephron's exact words while still maintaining his own hierarchy of values:

> [Abraham] spoke to Ephron in the hearing of the people of the land, saying, "If only you would hear me out! I *paid* the price of the land; accept it from me, that I may bury my dead there." (23:13)

Abraham, who only wanted to purchase the cave at the edge of the field, "bought in" to Ephron's offer to sell the entire field. Ostensibly, Abraham repeated Ephron's offer to transfer ownership of the entire property, although he also mentioned monetary payment in order to maintain a line of demarcation. Abraham then offered to buy the entire field, presumably for much more than the original deal for the cave alone. He no longer spoke about "full price," instead referring to "the price of the land." "The price of the land" is the fair price or market value—namely, the standard price of 400 silver shekels for a field.

Ephron immediately understood the implication: "And Ephron replied to Abraham, saying to him, 'My Lord, do hear me! A piece of land worth four hundred shekels of silver—what is that between you and me? Go and bury your dead'" (23:14–15).

Abraham paid the sum immediately in hard cash. The phrase "accept it from me" indicates that Abraham had no need for a grace period or deferred payment. He was a wealthy man laden with gold and silver. This was also a "victory" for the Hittites, who wanted Abraham's money. "I paid the price of the land" is written in past tense, demonstrating that in Abraham's view, the transaction had already been completed. This negotiating tactic of saying "the deal is done" is meant to bring the deal to a close and leave no further room for negotiation. Immediately following Abraham's statement that he had paid and the deal was done, the Torah describes that he paid the 400 shekels to Ephron. Abraham's presumptuous verbal closing of the deal ended the negotiation even before he transferred the money.

Extending the scope of the transaction allowed Abraham to overcome the obstacle posed by the Hittites. The nationalists among them were convinced that a large-scale investment would tie Abraham to the region, while the greedy saw a larger sum than they imagined (compared to the price of the cave alone), infusing the local economy with liquidity.[13]

It stands to reason that Ephron's field was not in the center of Hebron but rather on the edge. It is likely that the standard price of a typical field that could be cultivated was 400 shekels, whereas a field with a cave at its edge should have been less expensive for there was less arable land (and less potential yield). Despite this, Abraham referred to the standard price as "the price of the field," and Ephron made sure to clarify this. That is, this was the standard price for a field, but for this specific piece of real estate, one with a cave, it was somewhat expensive. For Abraham, a man of great means whose primary goal was to bury his wife and avoid becoming entangled or assimilated with the Hittites, this was an excellent deal. Considering that, in principle, the field was worth its price, he had received the cave almost free of charge.

> Abraham accepted Ephron's terms. Abraham paid out to Ephron the money that he had named in the hearing of the Hittites—four hundred shekels of silver at the going merchants' rate. (23:16)

Israel thus acquired its first foothold in the land of Canaan. This was achieved for the standard price of an arable field, through sophisticated negotiations and without compromising its principles: to be near but not among the Hittites and to deal with them fairly and with mutual respect.

Epilogue: "Absolute Value"

Some transactions are simple and never enter the stage of negotiations. Buying a new car, for example, may include some element of negotiations, but it is a relatively simple process in which each side tries to maximize their respective net financial gain. The buyer is interested in lowering the price and getting more for his money, and the seller is interested in the reverse. Both relate to the same function that lies on the axis of price versus value and will ultimately reach a point of equilibrium.

In more complicated transactions, the price stands alongside a moral, ethical, or religious principle. There may also be other actors with similarly complex interests. In situations like these, the function is multivariable, and it is extremely difficult—and at times impossible—to ascertain the optimal solution. Often, the pursuit of the lowest price clashes with our values and principles. Purchasing a cheap apartment in an area with dubious neighbors may adversely affect our children's education; pressuring a seller who is in a difficult financial situation to lower their price can harm their businesses or the wages of employees; a company owner who seeks to maximize their business may decide to fire certain employees who are not able to find new jobs. In complex situations such as these, we must determine what is most important to us and act accordingly in the negotiation process.

Abraham's negotiations for the cave of Machpelah teach us that, on one hand, principles have no price, and on the other, that there is nothing wrong with trying to maximize your return. If it was necessary to compromise, it is obvious that Abraham would have paid any price than surrender his values. This did not prevent him from pursuing a fair and reasonable business deal. In Abraham's world, principles took precedence over financial considerations. These were his priorities.

That said, it is not necessary for one who charts their course on the basis of their values to surrender their business acumen. On the contrary, their business skills can help promote their values.[14] As Abraham buried his wife and partner Sarah, he established an ethical business model for his children to follow.

6
Parashat Toldot

THE BIRTHRIGHT AND THE BLESSING

Immigrant Wealth and Settler Wealth

Times change, and with them, the types of occupations that are in demand: from shepherding to agriculture and commerce; from commerce to finance and real estate. For each of these occupations, the Torah delineates rules of conduct and standards for integrity, truth, and justice.

In my childhood in the United States, most Jewish mothers wanted their sons to be lawyers, doctors, or accountants. In our generation in Israel, the high-tech industry has become predominant. Times change, and national needs change; the challenge is to embrace the ability to change, as well as the nature of change itself. The goal is to change one's own business environment and the world of business at large, while striving to ensure that new industries, occupations, and professions preserve and reflect the eternal values of truth, integrity, and justice.

In this chapter, we will explore how Esau missed this changing economic and national landscape. When the opportunity came knocking from a change in conditions, he remained in the ways of the past. Jacob was more adaptive to economic and technological changes, some of which were initiated by his father, Isaac. The Torah is most interested in the timeless values that must accompany these changes and occupations and is fully encouraging of changing the professions themselves in order to create the blessings of wealth, "of the dew of the heavens and bounties of earth."

The story of Esau and Jacob, twins who could not have been more different in appearance and approach, is one of the most intricate and intriguing stories of fraternity in the Bible. While the Bible is full of sibling rivalry—Cain and Abel, Isaac and Ishmael, Joseph and his brothers—the entanglement of Jacob and Esau is one for the ages. The second century rabbinic giant Simeon Ben Yochai postulated that Esau hated Jacob. That is, he would hate Jacob for generations. This sibling rivalry and animosity would live on forever.

The Torah tells us that Jacob was born holding onto Esau's ankle. After nine months of jostling in Rebecca's womb, the two emerged entangled and grew up as vastly different personalities. Esau was a hunter, a man of the wild. Jacob was a man of the tent.

> Once when Jacob was cooking a stew, Esau came in from the field, famished. And Esau said to Jacob, "Give me some of that red stuff to gulp down, for I am famished"—which is why he was named Edom (red). Jacob said, "First sell me your birthright." And Esau said, "I am at the point of death, so of what use is my birthright to

> me?" But Jacob said, "Swear to me first." So he swore to him, and sold his birthright to Jacob. Jacob then gave Esau bread and lentil stew; he ate and drank, and he rose and went away, and Esau spurned the birthright. (Genesis 25:29-34)

Two exegetical giants, Rabbi Abraham Ibn Ezra and Ramban, strongly disagree as to why "Esau spurned the birthright" (Genesis 25:34). Ibn Ezra vehemently contends that Esau rejected the birthright and traded it for lentil stew because his father Isaac did not have money. According to this view, Isaac was poor, even destitute, despite the vast wealth that he had inherited from his father, Abraham.[1] In contrast, Ramban argues that the divine blessing that accompanied Isaac included great wealth; all of the patriarchs, including Isaac, were affluent. In this view, Esau spurned the birthright because of "the cruelty of his heart."

Ibn Ezra was an exegete, philosopher, poet, linguist and astronomer who lived in the eleventh and twelfth century. Born in Cordova, Spain, Ibn Ezra traveled to North Africa, Southern Europe, England, France, and perhaps even India. In those places, he wandered between Jewish communities, writing poems and books. Destitute himself, Ibn Ezra never found a suitable way to earn a living but was sometimes supported by wealthy individuals throughout his travels. On our story, he comments:

> "Esau spurned the birthright"—because he saw that his father was not wealthy. Many will be astonished, since Abraham left him a lot of money. It is as if they never saw a person who was wealthy in his youth and impoverished in his old age. Witness: Isaac loved Esau on account of his hunting (25:28). If there was an abun-

> dance of food in his father's home, and Esau was a man of honor, he never would have sold his birthright for stew. And if his father ate fine food every day, why did he bring him game (27:3–4)? And why didn't Jacob have a fine set of clothing (27:15)? And why didn't his mother give him money and gold for his journey, as he says [as he embarks on his journey]: "and give me bread to eat and clothing to wear" (28:20)? If she loved Jacob, why didn't she send him off with a lot of money, so he wouldn't have to tend the flocks? The verse that states: "And the man [Isaac] grew richer and richer" (26:13)—this was before his old age.
>
> Those whose hearts are blind think that wealth is a great virtue of the righteous. But Elijah proves otherwise (Kings II 1:16). Many will ask further: Why did God cause Isaac's wealth to dwindle? Perhaps they can inform us why Isaac became blind (Genesis 27:1). Do not push away [these questions] using the broken reed of homily, for it is esoteric, and we must not seek. God's thoughts are profound, and human beings do not have the capacity to understand and know them.

Ramban, otherwise known as Nahmanides, lived after Ibn Ezra's passing. As we noted in one of the earlier chapters but it bears repeating to contrast his background with Ibn Ezra, Ramban was born in Girona, and was the towering rabbinic figure in northeast Spain and Catalonia during his time. He was a doctor and wrote on biblical exegesis, philosophy, medicine, and mysticism. He comments on our story:

> "Esau spurned the birthright"—"He who disdains something will be injured by it" (Proverbs 13:13). Esau himself

declared why he was interested in the sale, namely, that as an animal hunter, he would likely die an early death, during his father's lifetime. Given that the birthright does not have any value before the death of his father, what use did he have for it? The verse states: "He ate and drank, and he rose and went away, and he spurned," because after Esau ate and drank, he returned to the field to his hunting, and this was his reason for spurning the birthright. Fools desire nothing but to eat and drink and do as they please, without worrying about tomorrow.

And Rabbi Abraham [Ibn Ezra] is quite mistaken here in asserting that "Esau spurned the birthright because he saw that his father was not wealthy.... and human beings do not have the capacity to understand and know them."

And I am astonished. Who blinded the eye of [Ibn Ezra's] intelligence with this, that Abraham left [Isaac] a tremendous fortune, and he lost it just prior to this episode? And for this reason, Esau spurned the birthright?! For this episode took place in their youth, before Esau married, as Scripture tells us. And later, [Isaac] became rich again in the Land of the Philistines, becoming so wealthy that the Philistine nobles became jealous, but then he became poor again and desired the game and delicacies of his son!? This is nothing but a joke.

Further, the verse states: "After the death of Abraham, God blessed his son Isaac" (25:11). This blessing entailed additional wealth, property, and honor. But if he lost his father's fortune and became poor, in what sense was he blessed? Afterward, God told Isaac: "I will be with you and bless you" (26:3). Does this indicate that he became wealthy and then impoverished? While at times there

> may be righteous people who experience financial difficulties befitting evil people, this does not -- and human beings do not have the capacity to understand and know them -- befall individuals who were directly blessed by God, because "It is the blessing of the Lord that enriches, and man need not toil to increase it" (Proverbs 10:22). Rather, our forefathers were all like kings, and the kings of other nations sought them out and established treaties with them, as it is written, "They exchanged oaths" (Genesis 26:31). If Isaac indeed had bad luck and lost all of his father's property, how is it possible that [the Philistines] would say "We now see plainly that the Lord has been with you" (26:28), if he had already hit on hard times? Rather, Esau spurned the birthright because of the cruelty of his heart.

We have here quite a pointed disagreement between these two exegetical giants. Ibn Ezra insists that by this point in his life, Isaac had become destitute. Despite being bequeathed great wealth by his successful father Abraham, Isaac had squandered or lost the family wealth. Therefore, his son Esau saw no reason to maintain his birthright because there was nothing to inherit. Esau's sale of the birthright to his younger brother Jacob was thus a practical, if shortsighted, decision. According to Ibn Ezra, Esau was disrespectful of his father because he was only interested in a birthright if his father was wealthy and thereby did not admire or respect his now poor father.

In dramatic contradistinction, Ramban believes that Isaac was wealthy. Both by referencing the scripture describing Isaac's wealth and by invoking God's blessing to the forefathers, Ramban maintains that Isaac was obviously rich. Therefore, Esau's selling of the birthright was not an economic consideration but rather a lifestyle choice. Esau's role as a hunter led him to believe that he too would be hunted, dying before his father could bequeath him his wealth. Ramban thus decries the cruelty of his heart in rejecting the birthright. This was no practical consideration but rather a lack of faith and disrespect for his father, born of disregard for the family.

I believe that through careful analysis and by distinguishing between two types of wealth, at two different periods of Isaac's life, we can raise the possibility that both Ibn Ezra and Ramban are correct. We can make peace between these two exegetical giants and at the same time take away a lesson about the impact of economic changes and how we can and should react to them. More importantly, while the two scholars are arguing about Isaac's wealth, the Torah is trying to impart a more important issue: the need to navigate changing times and professional or business pursuits while maintaining eternal values.

Thematic Order vs Chronological Order

Oftentimes, the Torah is out of chronological order; alternatively, its written order can be thematic. This is the case in the coming stories that we will detail from Scripture. Hence, to develop this analysis, we must establish the chronological structure of these chapters and the order of events in Chapters 25 and 26 of Genesis.

We first deal with the end of Abraham's life and his progeny other than Isaac, who was the chosen one. The Torah tells us:

> Abraham took another wife, whose name was Keturah.... This was the total span of Abraham's life: one hundred and seventy-five years. And Abraham breathed his last, dying at a good ripe age, old and contented; and he was gathered to his kin. His sons Isaac and Ishmael buried

> him in the cave of Machpelah, in the field of Ephron son of Zohar the Hittite, facing Mamre....
>
> This is the line of Ishmael, Abraham's son, whom Hagar the Egyptian, Sarah's slave, bore to Abraham....

The Torah then moves on to describe Isaac, his wife, and their family:

> This is the line of Isaac, son of Abraham. Abraham begot Isaac. Isaac was forty years old when he took Rebecca as a wife, daughter of Bethuel the Aramean of Paddan-Aram, sister of Laban the Aramean. Isaac pleaded with the Lord on behalf of his wife, because she was barren; and the Lord responded to his plea, and his wife Rebecca conceived.... When her time to give birth was at hand, there were twins in her womb. The first one emerged red, like a hairy mantle all over; so they named him Esau. Then his brother emerged, holding on to the heel of Esau; so they named him Jacob. Isaac was sixty years old when they were born. When the boys grew up, Esau became a skillful hunter, a man of the field; but Jacob was a mild man who stayed in camp. Isaac favored Esau because he had a taste for game; but Rebecca favored Jacob.

Thereafter, we are told about the exhausted Esau exchanging his birthright for some of Jacob's red stew and how Esau spurned the birthright. However, the story is not over. As the Torah writes in the story that follows the grand deal between Esau and Jacob, there was a famine in the land.

> There was a famine in the land—aside from the previous famine that had occurred in the days of Abraham—

and Isaac went to Abimelech, king of the Philistines, in Gerar. The Lord had appeared to him and said, "Do not go down to Egypt; stay in the land which I point out to you. Reside in this land, and I will be with you and bless you; I will assign all these lands to you and to your heirs, fulfilling the oath that I swore to your father Abraham. I will make your heirs as numerous as the stars of heaven, and assign to your heirs all these lands, so that all the nations of the earth shall bless themselves by your heirs—inasmuch as Abraham obeyed Me and kept My charge: My commandments, My laws, and My teachings." So Isaac stayed in Gerar. When the men of the place asked him about his wife, he said, "She is my sister," for he was afraid to say "my wife," thinking, "The men of the place might kill me on account of Rebecca, for she is beautiful." When some time had passed, Abimelech king of the Philistines, looking out of the window, saw Isaac fondling his wife Rebecca. Abimelech sent for Isaac and said, "So she is your wife! Why then did you say: 'She is my sister?" Isaac said to him, "Because I thought I might lose my life on account of her." Abimelech said, "What have you done to us! One of the people might have lain with your wife, and you would have brought guilt upon us." Abimelech then charged all the people, saying, "Anyone who molests this man or his wife shall be put to death." Isaac sowed in that land and reaped a hundredfold the same year. The Lord blessed him, and the man grew richer and richer until he was very wealthy: he acquired flocks and herds, and a large household, so that the Philistines envied him. And the Philistines stopped up all the wells which his father's servants had dug in the days of his father Abraham, filling them with

> earth. And Abimelech said to Isaac, "Go away from us, for you have become far too big for us."

To summarize, the sequence of episodes is as follows: a synopsis of Abraham's life and his burial by Isaac and Ishmael; the progeny of Ishmael and his death; Isaac's progeny (beginning with the birth of Jacob and Esau until the sale of the birthright by Esau to Jacob in exchange for lentil stew); and a description of the famine that afflicted the land of Canaan and forced Isaac to relocate to Gerar.

It seems that Isaac initially intended to move down to Egypt, but when he reached Gerar, God intervened and prevented him from continuing, commanding him to stay in the land of Israel. Isaac told the locals that his wife Rebecca was his sister. One day, though, Abimelech looked out his window (which was apparently higher than the other homes of Gerar) and saw "Isaac fondling his wife Rebecca."

It is unclear how Isaac could have concealed Rebecca's true identity if she had already given birth to Jacob and Esau, especially if "some time had passed" and they had already lived in Gerar for a while. It is far more plausible that this episode took place before the birth of the boys. This is how the great nineteenth century Italian Jewish scholar, poet, and philosopher Rabbi Samuel David Luzzatto ("Shadal") explains it:

> "There was a famine in the land"—according to R. Wolf [Mayer], the author of *HaMe'amer*, this episode transpired before the birth of Jacob and Esau, and the Torah does not always report events in chronological order. Because it is unlikely that as time went by, the locals would not have grasped that the boys are Isaac's sons and that Rebecca is their mother.[2]

In general, the Torah often prefers thematic to chronological sequence. Units begin and end on the basis of thematic connections, not the historical order of events. Structurally, the transitional unit from Abraham to Isaac juxtaposes the death of Abraham, the progeny of Ishmael, and the progeny of Isaac (both of which use the familiar opening, "This is the line [lineage]" [*eleh toldot*]. Thus, Scripture closes the unit about Abraham's lineage while emphasizing that Isaac, as a father of children, was worthy and capable of continuing Abraham's legacy. Only afterward does the Torah go back and provide details about Isaac's life story.

A salient example is the record of the death of Terah in Haran. Abraham's father Terah actually died sixty years after Abraham left Haran, but his death is listed in the verses (11:32) that precede the command of "Go forth" (12:1) and begin the Abraham stories.[3]

Assuming this is so, from a chronological perspective, the story of the sale of the birthright happened against the backdrop of Isaac's financial situation as described in the unit on Isaac's life in Gerar. A careful analysis of Isaac's time in Gerar demonstrates that Isaac deviated from some of Abraham's standard practices. Understanding these changes sheds light on the type of wealth which God blessed Isaac with. Similarly, the argument between Ramban and Ibn Ezra about whether Isaac was wealthy takes on new dimensions in light of the analysis of Isaac's success in Gerar.

Although it is difficult to digest that the Torah tells us about Isaac without saying a word about how Abraham, who would have been alive and well, dealt with the famine (and I have not seen any commentaries addressing this), it seems that this is somewhat typical of Scripture. For example, in the story of the death and burial of Sarah, we do not hear anything about

Isaac. We do not know where Isaac was or how he reacted to his mother's death, although he was thirty-seven years old. Abraham mourned Sarah and cried for her (23:2), so it stands to reason that Isaac, mourned and cried for his mother too. Yet he is completely absent from the discussion of the burial process and the negotiations that Abraham conducted with the Hittites.

Likewise, it is not clear whether Abraham participated in Isaac's aborted journey to Egypt that left him in Gerar. Moreover, the verse "there was a famine in the land—aside from the previous famine that had occurred in the days of Abraham" gives the impression that Abraham was no longer alive. It also happens again later in the story, when Isaac's servants re-dig the wells that were dug in Abraham's lifetime and subsequently stuffed up by the Philistines. However, as mentioned above, Abraham was alive and well.

The solution is that Scripture intentionally creates this setting to emphasize that Isaac was charting his own path. The divine blessing that God bestowed upon Abraham forms the foundation, and Isaac drew from the wells dug by Abraham, but ultimately, the Torah shows us that by carefully tracing Isaac's activities and possessions, one will discover the new approach that he took. In fact, stories that seem so similar, such as Isaac's experiences in Gerar and Abrahams travails with King Abimelech of Gerar involving his wife and wells he dug (Genesis chapters 20 and 21:22-32), are designed to highlight certain significant differences. Against the same setting, the distinction between Abraham and Isaac becomes all the more striking.[4]

Baron Rothschild in Meah Shearim[5]

Abraham's vast wealth is described by Scripture on several occasions:

> Abram took his wife Sarai and his brother's son Lot, and all the possessions that they had acquired, and the souls they had shaped in Haran; and they set out for the land of Canaan and they reached the land of Canaan. (12:5)
>
> From Egypt, Abram went up into the Negev, with his wife and all that he possessed, together with Lot. Now Abram was very rich in cattle, silver, and gold. (13:1–2)
>
> Abimelech took sheep and oxen, and male and female slaves, and gave them to Abraham.... And to Sarah he said, "I herewith give your brother a thousand pieces of silver; this will serve you as vindication before all who are with you, and you are cleared before everyone." (20:14–16)
>
> The [Abraham's] servant brought out objects of silver and gold, and garments, and gave them to Rebecca. (24:53)
>
> To Abraham's sons by concubines, Abraham gave gifts while he was still living, and he sent them away from his son Isaac eastward, to the land of the East. (25:6)

These verses describe moveable assets—silver, gold, cattle, objects, clothing, and gifts. Beginning with Abraham's journey from Haran and culminating with God's promise to him at the Covenant Between the Parts—"but I will execute judgment on the nation they shall serve, and in the end they shall go free with great wealth (possessions)" (15:14)—Abraham's wealth was in moveable assets. God's promise was also realized with moveable assets 400 years later, during the Exodus from Egypt: "The Israelites had done Moses' bidding and borrowed from the Egyptians objects of silver and gold, and clothing." (Exodus 12:35) Abraham's wealth was held in moveable assets because he was a nomad; he journeyed from Ur of the Chaldeans to

Haran and from there to the land of Israel. He embarked on several sojourns within the land, went down to Egypt, and returned to his travels in the land, carrying the banner of God and calling out in his name. Like a contemporary diamond dealer or a migrant of old, he preferred wealth that could be easily transported.

Early in his career, Isaac too was faced with a famine, and like his father, he sought to go down to Egypt. God appeared to him and told him to stay in the land of Israel:

> Stay in the land which I point out to you. Reside in this land, and I will be with you and bless you; I will assign all these lands to you and to your heirs, fulfilling the oath that I swore to your father Abraham. I will make your heirs as numerous as the stars of heaven, and assign to your heirs all these lands, so that all the nations of the earth shall bless themselves by your heirs. (Genesis 26:2–4)

Isaac understood that God expected him to chart his own course. Rather than mimicking the path of his father, Isaac realized that he must begin a process of economic transformation and settle the land in order to realize the next stage of God's promise to Abraham. Since God asked him to stay rather than travel to Egypt, he concluded that he was to begin the process of settling the land.

Unlike his father, Isaac was not a nomad, sojourner, or Canaanite merchant. He was a settler, a permanent resident of the land of Israel. The time had come to purchase fields, cultivate orchards, and strike roots. It was necessary to invest in a production force that could endure long term and not make plans to travel abroad or flee. In light of this insight, Isaac converted his moveable assets, his liquid cash and his gold, into real estate and the means of production.[6]

Orchards and large farmsteads demand a relatively large work force, and the Torah accordingly describes Isaac's wealth after his stint in Gerar during the famine:

> Isaac sowed in that land and reaped a hundredfold [*meah shearim*] the same year. The Lord blessed him, and the man grew richer and richer until he was very wealthy: he acquired flocks and herds, and a large household, so that the Philistines envied him. (26:12–14)

Abraham had servants and maidservants, whereas Isaac had "a large household" in place of the silver and gold of Abraham's lifetime. It is fair to assume that Isaac used his silver and gold to pay for the labor that was necessary for building his agricultural enterprise.

In light of the long description of Isaac and his servants digging wells, we may boldly suggest that Isaac invented technology that eased in the process of digging and developing wells:

> And the Philistines stopped up all the wells which his father's servants had dug in the days of his father Abraham, filling them with earth. And Abimelech said to Isaac, "Go away from us, for you have become far too big for us." So Isaac departed from there and encamped in the wadi of Gerar, where he settled. Isaac dug anew the wells which had been dug in the days of his father Abraham and which the Philistines had stopped up after Abraham's death; and he gave them the same names that his father had given them. But when Isaac's servants, digging in the wadi, found there a well of spring water, the herdsmen of Gerar quarreled with

> Isaac's herdsmen, saying, "The water is ours." He named that well Esek, because they contended with him. And when they dug another well, they disputed over that one also; so he named it Sitnah. He moved from there and dug yet another well, and they did not quarrel over it; so he called it Rehovoth, saying, "Now at last the Lord has granted us ample space to increase in the land." (26:15–22)

According to the verses, Isaac dug in the riverbed and found a well. In the process of digging a well, one generally looks for water from deep aquifers. Practically speaking, it is preferable to dig a well at a distance of several dozen meters from riverbeds and wadis since the water in wadis and rivers may be dirty and contaminate the well.[7] Perhaps Isaac, who needed it for agricultural purposes, developed a method to find water that was suitable for agriculture despite its proximity to riverbeds. This would have been in contrast to other farmers, who could not irrigate their fields in times of drought, when the ever diminishing well water was rationed for drinking and reservoirs of rainwater had completely dried out.

Regardless of the precise meaning of the phrase *meah she'arim* ("hundredfold"), Isaac's agricultural enterprise was a huge success. Perhaps Isaac invented something that helped him cultivate his crops, as Noah had done, or perhaps his large workforce greatly increased his yield. Perhaps Isaac purchased land, seedlings, and fertilizer at rock bottom prices during the famine and was able to resell them for great profit. Or perhaps it was the combination of all these things, together with divine blessing, that yielded success. In contrast to Abraham, who received servants and maidservants, sheep and cattle, and one thousand pieces of silver from Abimelech, the verses tell us that Isaac sowed the land and was blessed with the success of his agricultural enterprise.

Isaac purchased or leased fields and invested in agriculture during a time of economic crisis. This is in line with the famous statement of Baron Rothschild: "When there is blood on the streets, buy real estate," a declaration that he followed through on when he bought real estate in the aftermath of the Battle of Waterloo. Isaac leveraged the divine command to stay in the land to affect strategic economic change that "reaped a hundredfold."

This section concludes with Isaac's return to Beersheba—located in the land of Philistines, but far from Gerar—where Abraham planted a tamarisk (a shrub or small tree that grows in inhospitable conditions) at the conclusion of his final campaign. The significance is that Isaac, Abraham's successor, did not mimic his father's activities. He instead connected to the point where his father concluded his life's work, continued on from there, and accomplished great things.

"Esau Spurned the Birthright"

Armed with the understanding that Isaac embarked on a different economic path than his father Abraham, we return to the story of Jacob and Esau. Isaac, now a fully settled landowner and farmer, was the father of two children. These children had seen two models of economic success: Abraham the nomad with movable wealth, and Isaac the farmer with agricultural wealth.

Jacob was "a mild man who stayed in camp," a man who settled, pitched his tent, and wanted to be set in place. Jacob's way of life suited the economic change that Isaac had implemented in his lifetime: from wealthy nomadic migrant to permanent resident of the region, a real estate developer who built an agricultural enterprise.

The verses note the type of food that Jacob prepared—lentil stew—because it is an essential part of the story (25:34). Lentils are grown in cultivated fields. They are not a vegetable that can be planted and left to grow on its own; they need to be well cared for and trellised like a vine.[8] Building trellises for a lentil field is a significant investment that yields returns only in the long-term. It is not financially prudent to build trellises for only one season, and in fact, lentils are a legume and hence replenish the soil, an important feature if one has a long-term view. Abraham served the angels veal and cream, foods that reflected his moveable assets.[9] In contrast, Jacob prepared lentil stew, a dish that was made from the crops that grew in his father's fields.

As noted above, Ibn Ezra explained that Esau easily and scornfully relinquished the birthright because his father was destitute while Ramban maintained that Isaac was wealthy. The approach we presented—namely, that Isaac converted his moveable assets to an agricultural enterprise—allows us to agree with Ramban that Isaac was affluent and explain, following Ibn Ezra's approach, that Esau was not interested in the type of wealth that Isaac had. (An extended agricultural enterprise , though fruitful, included the management of many fields and workers.)

An agricultural business limits the freedom of its owner. A farmer needs to stay close to the fields and crops and must manage workers (or slaves) and provide for their general welfare and specific needs. By day, a farmer worries about plowing, sowing, watering, fertilizing, and eradicating pestilence. By night, a farmer guards the fields to prevent theft.

Esau was "a skillful hunter" who craved open space. He liked to wander far and wide with a small band of men, basing his livelihood on opportunities that came his way. During the famine, Isaac invested his fortune in agriculture, which necessitated staying close to the soil of the land of Israel. This change did not suit Esau the hunter.[10] Esau was not prepared to embrace the lifestyle of a settler rooted to his land. Thus, when he returned exhausted from the field, he scorned his father's new wealth[11]—agricultural lands.[12]

Placing the episode of the sale of the birthright before Isaac's successful agricultural stint in Gerar despite the fact that chronologically it occurs later, creates intentional ambiguity regarding the verse, "Esau came in from the field, famished." On the one hand, it seems that the "field" in question was a hunting ground, given that Esau was "a skillful hunter, a man of the field." Indeed, Isaac would later say to Esau: "Take your gear, your quiver and bow, and go out into the field and hunt me some game" (27:3). On the other hand, when Isaac was uncertain about the identity of the person standing before him, the verse states: "And he went up and kissed him. And he smelled his clothes and he blessed him, saying: 'Ah, the smell of my son is like the smell of the field that the Lord has blessed'" (27:27). This refers to agricultural fields, not hunting grounds. In fact, Rashi notes, following the midrash, that the field in question was an apple orchard.

The text's deliberate blurring between the field where crops are planted and the field where game is hunted reflects Esau's deception of his father Isaac. It allows us to understand that Esau returned home frustrated and exhausted, "at the point of death," from working the agricultural fields. It is at this point that Esau relinquished the birthright. He wanted nothing to do with an agrarian lifestyle—neither its difficulties nor its privileges.

As noted, in his blind old age, Isaac asked Esau to prepare him a dish from the game that he had hunted, so that he might bless him. This request can perhaps be understood as an expression of nostalgia for the transient, peripatetic path of his father, Abraham, which he saw reflected in his son Esau. That said, it is also possible that there was something principled within Isaac's request: "And he said, 'I am old now, and I do not know how soon I may die. Take your gear, your quiver and bow, and go out into the field and hunt me some game. Then prepare a dish for me such as I like, and bring it to me to eat, so that I may give you my innermost blessing before I die'" (27:2–4).

Before his death, Abraham bequeathed all of his assets to Isaac. For Isaac, though, the situation was far more complicated. His successor needed to also assume control of his agricultural enterprise. However, as Isaac contemplated his death and what he would leave for posterity, he knew that there would be another period of exile of 400 years, as promised to Abraham in the Covenant Between the Parts. During the Covenant Between the Parts, in which Abraham split numerous animals into two parts and walked between them, God revealed to Abraham that his descendants would go into exile but would ultimately emerge with freedom and great prosperity. That exile would be to Egypt. Therefore, quite critically, Isaac saw that striking roots in the land of Canaan (Israel) would give the future nation of Israel a fatherland to return to.

However, with the advent of exile, Abraham's family would have to move their possessions and wealth down to Egypt, and Isaac felt that Esau was best suited for this role. Thus, in the blessing that he intended to bestow upon Esau, Isaac sought to instill his values in Esau: "May God give you of the dew of heaven and the fat of the earth, abundance of new grain and wine" (27:28). Isaac wanted Esau to remain vigilantly aware that he must maintain a foothold in the land and that agriculture is the optimal way for a nation to settle its land.

When Jacob presented himself as Esau, Isaac sensed that something was amiss. After touching Jacob and repeating the question, "Are you really my son Esau?" Isaac resolved to administer the blessing based on the "smell test." If Esau had exuded the smell of a farmhand, he would have earned the blessing of an "abundance of new grain and wine." However, the smell that Isaac detected was the fragrance of Jacob, the son who identified closely with his father's agricultural enterprise. Consequently, Jacob the farmer received the blessing.

While it is true the verse notes that Isaac smelled the fragrance of Jacob's clothing, the clothes that Jacob had taken from Esau were fine, clean garments that Rebecca kept for Esau at home; Esau never wore these clothes when he headed out on a hunting expedition. It stands to reason that the smell of the field came from Jacob's clothing, not necessarily from Esau's well-preserved clothing that Jacob had placed over his own.[13]

The Second Generation

When God revealed Himself to Isaac and asked him not to go down to Egypt despite the famine in the land, Isaac understood that the time had come for the next stage of the great vision that began with the divine directive to Abraham, "Go forth!" As his father's son, Isaac also gave up on the familiar and secure forms of wealth that the family had accumulated. He exchanged his moveable assets for an investment in agriculture, striking roots in the land of Israel.

The process that Isaac courageously undertook reflects an important message: circumstances and challenges change with time, necessitating different economic strategies. Many commentators see Esau as the one who broke with tradition by marrying unsavory local Hittite women. That is just one part of the story. Esau was also the one who sought to preserve the forms of wealth that his grandfather Abraham had cultivated in his lifetime. It was Esau who ultimately left his father's home and birthplace and wandered to Edom with all of his possessions.[14]

Esau's undoing was his inability to adapt to new circumstances and to understand changes of purpose. Jacob's greatness, however, was that he understood that fulfilling the divine destiny necessitated taking things to the next level, including redirecting the family's business interests. By virtue of his flexible thinking and his attentiveness to the world around him and the divine messages that it broadcast, Jacob was able to adapt to a new occupation when he needed to escape to Haran. Accordingly, upon his return to the land of Israel, he was able to change the focus of his dealings once again.

7
Parashat Vayetzei

QUID PRO QUO

Interpersonal Trust

> *Rabbi Elai said: A person's true character is recognizable through three things: his cup [koso," i.e., when he is drunk], his pocket [kiso," i.e., when money is at stake], and his anger [ka'aso]. And some say: A person also reveals his real nature in his laughter.*
>
> *—Babylonian Talmud Eruvin 65b*

"Our distrust is very expensive," said Ralph Waldo Emerson. Numerous academic studies have shown that trust is or must be inherent in every economic transaction[1] and that trust drives economic growth. OECD Secretary-General Angel Gurria has put "trust" at the top of his organization's agenda. Years earlier, in a much cited article, economist Kenneth Arrow wrote, "Virtually every commercial transaction has within itself an element of trust, certainly any transaction conducted over a period of time."

As we will see below, the Torah tackles this issue head on. It shows how ruptures in trust, particularly due to scarcity, erode economies and values while families and businesses based on trust will lead to growth and better values.

From Fortune to Fortune

At the seam between the story of Isaac's success in Gerar and the episode of the stolen blessings, the Torah describes Esau negatively due to his marriages to two Hittite women:

> When Esau was forty years old, he took to wife Judith daughter of Beeri the Hittite, and Basemath daughter of Elon the Hittite; and they were a source of bitterness to Isaac and Rebecca. (Genesis 26:34–35)

These Hittite women were seemingly not wanted as brides, nor were they welcome in the family of Abraham, Isaac and Rebbecca because of depraved character traits which the Torah does not detail. Later, in the aftermath of the stolen blessings and the ensuing friction between Esau and Jacob, the family's aversion to Canaanite women became a pretext for sending Jacob to Haran.

The Torah begins by telling us that Esau wanted to kill Jacob. In response, their mother, Rebecca, told Jacob to flee his vengeful brother.

> Now Esau harbored a grudge against Jacob because of the blessing which his father had given him, and Esau said to himself, "Let but the mourning period of my father come, and I will kill my brother Jacob." When the words of her older son Esau were reported to Rebecca,

> she sent for her younger son Jacob and said to him, "Your brother Esau is consoling himself by planning to kill you. Now, my son, listen to me. Flee at once to Haran, to my brother Laban. Stay with him a while, until your brother's fury subsides—until your brother's anger against you subsides—and he forgets what you have done to him. Then I will fetch you from there. Let me not lose you both in one day!" (Genesis 27:41-45)

However, when Rebecca explained to her husband, Isaac, why Jacob had to leave the family's home, she used a different reason: Hittite women. This explanation likely resonated with Isaac; Abraham had sought a wife for him from outside the land because he did not want Isaac marrying local Canaanite women. The Torah continues:

> Rebecca said to Isaac, "I am disgusted with my life because of the Hittite women. If Jacob marries a Hittite woman like these, from among the native women, what good will life be to me?" So Isaac sent for Jacob and blessed him. He instructed him, saying, "You shall not take a wife from among the Canaanite women. Up, go to Paddan-Aram, to the house of Bethuel, your mother's father, and take a wife there from among the daughters of Laban, your mother's brother. (Genesis 27:46-28:4)

Isaac's blessing to Jacob upon his departure almost foreshadows the challenges that Jacob would face in the house of his deceitful Uncle Laban.

> "May El Shaddai bless you, make you fertile and numerous, so that you become an assembly of peoples. May He grant the blessing of Abraham to you and your off-

> spring, that you may possess the land where you are sojourning, which God assigned to Abraham." Then Isaac sent Jacob off, and he went to Paddan-Aram, to Laban the son of Bethuel the Aramean, the brother of Rebecca, mother of Jacob and Esau. (28:3-5)

The Torah then returns to the negative traits of Canaanite women by telling us that Esau, who had already married some of these local women, subsequently took a wife who was a descendent of his grandfather Abraham.

> When Esau saw that Isaac had blessed Jacob and sent him off to Paddan-Aram to take a wife from there, exhorting him, as he blessed him, "You shall not take a wife from among the Canaanite women," and that Jacob had obeyed his father and mother and gone to Paddan-Aram, Esau realized that the Canaanite women displeased his father Isaac. So Esau went to Ishmael and took [a] wife, in addition to the wives he had, Mahalath the daughter of Ishmael son of Abraham, sister of Nebaioth. (27:41–28:9)

Jacob was blessed and told to avoid these unprincipled Canaanite women and families. He left his family behind to go to his uncle's home, but what happened to him is anything but principled. Upon arriving in Paddan-Aram, Jacob met Rachel, who he discovered was the daughter of his uncle Laban. Jacob fell in love with Rachel at first sight and desires to marry her. His uncle Laban suggests that Jacob work for seven years in order to marry Rachel. However, in his first act of deceit, which will foreshadow many more, Laban switched Rachel for his older daughter, Leah, sneakily marrying her off to Jacob in the middle of the night. Jacob, after working seven long years for the love of his life, was deceived by his uncle—now his father-in-law—and ended up marrying the "other" sister. After Jacob confronted him, Laban offered up a mealymouthed excuse that in their land of Paddam-Aram, it is not customary to marry off the younger daughter before the older one.

Ironically, Jacob, who listened to his parents and traveled to Haran to marry into Laban's family, was compelled to marry a woman he did not desire. Not only did Laban switch Jacob's wife, he then extracted a further concession from Jacob, seven more years of dedicated labor in Laban's family enterprise. As for his wages, despite two decades of hard work, Jacob continued to suffer from the serial deceit of Laban, who again violated their terms of agreement. Ultimately, Jacob became aware of the jealousy and hatred that Laban's sons harbored for him.

Given these descriptions of Laban and his family, the reader is left perplexed. Why would anyone assume that a daughter of Laban would be better than a Canaanite woman? Laban's house was hardly a bastion of values, good character, or morality. It preyed on the unsuspecting and was deceitful. Later, the Torah will tell us that the house revolved around idolatry, superstition, and luck. It would therefore seem that in such an environment, the chance of finding good and worthy women who were superior to the women of Canaan, was slim. As the Talmud states, the rotten date grows among fruitless trees, and as Ben Sira says, "All fowl will live with its kind, and men with those like him."[2]

Rebecca's initial instructions provide a more logical explanation. Fearing the outbreak of a civil war in her family, Rebecca instructed Jacob to flee to Haran for a short period of time, after which she would call him home. "Let me not lose you both in one day!" she exclaimed. However, at Rebecca's urging, Isaac charged Jacob with the task of building his home and his family in a difficult, alien climate, far away from the ethical, moral support of Jacob's family.

My father, who is my original teacher, suggests that naïve, simple Jacob had to build resilience under his uncle, thus preparing him for real life. For twenty years in Laban's home, Jacob was subjected to Laban's mistreatment, and after all, "whatever doesn't kill you makes you stronger." According to my father, the experience in Laban's rough and tumble environment was important because it "toughened Jacob up."

With deference to my father, I would like to suggest a different approach. By analyzing the following verses that describe the forthcoming events, we can see what the Torah seeks to teach us about the importance of interpersonal trust, the contributions it can make when trust is present, and, most importantly, the damage that can be caused when trust is punctured.

Defense Mechanisms

Jacob left his father's home and traveled to Paddan-Aram. There, at the edge of the well, he met his cousin Rachel. Jacob, perhaps aided by a rush of adrenaline, removed the stone that covered the well in a display of superhuman strength. This is how most of the commentators understand the narrative: [3]

> Jacob resumed his journey and came to the land of the Easterners. There before his eyes was a well in the open. Three flocks of sheep were lying there beside it, for the flocks were watered from that well. The stone on the mouth of the well was large. When all the flocks were gathered there, the stone would be rolled from the mouth of the well and the sheep watered; then the stone would be put back in its place on the mouth of the well. Jacob said to them, "My friends, where are you from?"

> And they said, "We are from Haran." He said to them, "Do you know Laban the son of Nahor?" And they said, "Yes, we do." He continued, "Is he well?" They answered, "Yes, he is; and there is his daughter Rachel, coming with the flock." He said, "It is still broad daylight, too early to round up the animals; water the flock and take them to pasture." But they said, "We cannot, until all the flocks are rounded up; then the stone is rolled off the mouth of the well and we water the sheep." While he was still speaking with them, Rachel came with her father's flock; for she was a shepherdess. And when Jacob saw Rachel, the daughter of Laban, his mother's brother, and the flock of Laban, his mother's brother, Jacob went up and rolled the stone off the mouth of the well, and watered the flock of Laban, his mother's brother. (29:1–10)

The verses state that "the stone on the mouth of the well was large" and that it was necessary to wait for all the flocks to gather at the well to roll off the stone. However, the verses do not explain what prevented the shepherds from removing the stone. They do not indicate that the shepherds were weak, nor do they specify that Jacob, "a mild man who stayed in camp,," was any stronger than the shepherds of the three flocks. In his commentary to 29:3, Rabbi Abraham ben HaRambam (Abraham son of Maimonides) offers a different explanation for the shepherds' delay:

> "But they said 'We cannot'"—Not because they were not strong enough to lift the stone. If that were the case, Jacob too would not have been able to lift it. Rather, they could not violate the agreement that they had reached among themselves.

According to Rabbi Abraham ben HaRambam, the shepherds did not trust one another.[4] In the absence of the stone that blocked access to the well and mutual supervision, the shepherds suspected that one of the shepherds would take all the water for himself. Because the people of Haran did not trust one another, they covered the well and stipulated that the shepherds needed to wait for everyone to reach the well. Only after that would they be able to draw water. In the words of Rabbi Abraham, the shepherds' solution or "the agreement," was the classic cooperative solution to resolving the Prisoner's Dilemma, thus preventing a Tragedy of the Commons.

As we previously discussed, The Prisoner's Dilemma is a paradoxical problem in game theory first publicized in 1950 by Merrill Flood and Melvin Dresher of the RAND Corporation. The dilemma presents a situation where completely rational behavior, from the perspective of the individual who is looking to maximize his personal success, will lead to a non-optimal aggregate benefit for all the players in the game. The paradox derives from the fact that each player stands to gain more by not cooperating with the others. However, in order to reach the optimum result for all the players, they actually need to cooperate with one another.

One factor that can influence the players to cooperate is the iteration of the game (or "Repeated Prisoner's Dilemma"), wherein the game is played many times. In an iterated game, the decision about whether to act in accordance with personal, narrow interests or to cooperate with the other players is impacted by the critical consideration of "the next game." In other words, the player who betrays in the first game will likely be betrayed the next round, and the cycle will continue.

The shepherds in Haran faced an iterated Prisoner's Dilemma. A shepherd could take all of the water for himself, only to discover a day or two later that a different shepherd beat him to the well, leaving him and his flock with an empty trough. The shepherds' collective fear of a bad (or selfish) actor—who would not only undermine economic stability and security but potentially send the entire system spiraling out of control—led them to institute a measure that protected the interests of the locals. This defense mechanism included three layers of protection: technological, legal, and social.

The stone was a basic technological solution. The next layer of protection was strict obedience to the rules that provided security to everyone, so that no individual intruded on another person's water supply. The third level of protection was the threat of ostracization; thus, even three flocks would not dare form a cartel. Consequently, the defense mechanism was successful, and the shepherds patiently awaited the arrival of the rest.

Such protective measures preserve stability, barring the arrival of a new player who has not been playing the game continuously and who is therefore not worried about counter betrayal on the next day. (This is also true of a player who decides to disobey the rules for a different reason.) When Jacob approached the well to roll off the stone, he was acting like any other player who has not been playing an iterated game; he maximized his profit at the expense of the other players, namely, the shepherds. Jacob, who was not bound by their stipulations, did not fear their betrayal because he did not have his own flocks that he would need to water the next day. Unlike the shepherds gathered there, Jacob had no reason to wait. When he saw Rachel and her sheep, he had what economists call a "trembling hand." Jacob looked only at the short-term benefits and maximized his (and his cousin's) profits immediately.

Jacob's critique of the shepherds' misuse of resources—they waited to open the well together instead of using the time more effectively by grazing the flocks—is the classic price paid by a society that lacks interpersonal trust. That is, the entire protective mechanism, even when it is warranted and necessary, comes at a price. In the words of Francis Fukuyama:

> People who do not trust one another will end up cooperating only under a system of formal rules and regulations, which have to be negotiated, agreed to, litigated, and enforced, sometimes by coercive means. This legal apparatus, serving as a substitute for trust, entails what economists call "transaction costs." Widespread distrust in a society, in other words, imposes a kind of tax on all forms of economic activity, a tax that high-trust societies do not have to pay.[5]

Water Pressure

Understanding the microeconomic and macroeconomic background to a given situation is critical to understanding the behavior of different biblical characters as well as people's behavior today. For example, children who were born in the 1920s and 1930s were greatly impacted by the Great Depression. Throughout their lives, they were more frugal than people who were born into the post–World War II boom. Studies show that children of the 2008 global recession bear economic scars as they reach the age when they assume financial responsibility and enter the job market.[6]

Accordingly, we can decode the root cause of the lack of trust among the shepherds by comparing it with a similar incident that occurred several decades earlier in the same locale.

This was when Abraham's servant arrived in Haran in search of the most suitable bride for Isaac:

> "Here I stand by the spring as the daughters of the townsmen come out to draw water; let the maiden to whom I say, 'Please, lower your jar that I may drink,' and who replies, 'Drink, and I will also water your camels'—let her be the one whom You have decreed for Your servant Isaac. Thereby shall I know that You have dealt graciously with my master." He had scarcely finished speaking, when Rebecca, who was born to Bethuel, the son of Milcah the wife of Abraham's brother Nahor, came out with her jar on her shoulder. The maiden was very beautiful, a virgin whom no man had known. She went down to the spring, filled her jar, and came up. The servant ran toward her and said, "Please, let me sip a little water from your jar." "Drink, my lord," she said, and she quickly lowered her jar upon her hand and let him drink. When she had let him drink his fill, she said, "I will also draw for your camels, until they finish drinking." Quickly emptying her jar into the trough, she ran back to the well to draw, and she drew for all his camels. (24:13–20)

Rebecca, then a maiden, drew water without waiting for anyone to roll a stone off the mouth of the well. She simply lowered her jar and filled it. The spring flowed and was open to all. Rebecca said to the servant of Abraham: "There is plenty of straw and feed at home." There was wealth and abundance. The water flowed, so there was plenty of food—even enough for a caravan of thirsty camels that had traveled from far away. In times of economic prosperity, people are more willing to share their wealth with others, and there is no pressure to protect resources. At that time, Laban and his father Bethuel were not concerned about bringing a stranger into their home; they were gracious to Abraham's servant, as was Rebecca. She had grown up in Bethuel's hospitable home, which was perfectly aligned with Abraham's values of hospitality and giving. All of this was based on trust, which was itself predicated on a strong economy and healthy society.

In the years between the servant's visit to Haran and Jacob's arrival there, Isaac faced a terrible famine in the land of Canaan; according to Ibn Ezra, this famine led to the loss of all his wealth and caused him to live out his final days in abject poverty.[7] During this same time period, in the parallel universe of Haran, water grew scarce and food resources became limited. The famine brought dramatic economic decline to Haran. Laban's home was no longer a place of abundance and wealth; his financial abilities had become quite limited. The home that Abraham's servant visited a generation earlier was no longer described as a place with plenty of straw and feed, a place to lodge, or a place to sleep. The contrast drives home the sense that Laban's resources had dried up.

The differences between a spring and a well are also telling; it demonstrates that, as a society, Haran was fighting over every drop of water. They developed wells to reach groundwater (just as Isaac did in the Negev during this same period). The evolution of cooperation, a phrase coined by Robert Axelrod, is influenced by the state of deprivation. [8] In times of deprivation, the "animal spirits" of shepherds and merchants are let loose, as described by economists Robert J. Shiller and George Akerlof.[9]

As we noted at this chapter's outset, many studies show that in times of hunger and deprivation, trust is eroded. A society that seeks to endure and survive therefore moves towards regulatory practices and develops mechanisms in the public sphere (such as the well and the stone that sits atop it) to protect itself from the self-centeredness that often runs rampant in deprived societies. As the Torah states:

> He who is most tender and fastidious among you shall be too mean to his brother and the wife of his bosom and the children he has spared, to share with any of them the flesh of the children that he eats, because he has nothing else left as a result of the desperate straits to which your enemy shall reduce you in all your towns. (Deuteronomy 28:54–55)[10]

Rebecca was unaware of the ethical decline that had taken its toll on the region of Haran and the home of her brother Laban. Isaac's family had preserved its principles, while the house of Laban fell in line with the winds of change blowing in Haran. The pangs of hunger that afflicted the entire society caused these winds to intensify and fanned the flames of "worry about the future." Survival instincts governed people's behavior, leading them to "bare their teeth" towards others who competed for limited resources. Accordingly, there was a gap between the expectation that Jacob would find a wonderful woman in the house of Laban and the society and the home that Jacob actually encountered.

Laban's daughters, Leah and Rachel, somehow managed to preserve the old value system. Perhaps this was miraculous or perhaps it was on account of their surpassing righteousness and their personal experiences with Haran's lack of principles. They saw their father exploit their cousin Jacob, demanding free labor in exchange for his daughters hand in marriage. This trade is particularly galling since it was normally the role of the father of the bride to provide a dowry. They were disgusted by his behavior: "Then Rachel and Leah answered him, saying,

'Have we still a share in the inheritance of our father's house? Surely, he regards us as outsiders, now that he has sold us and has used up our purchase price'" (31:14–15). The description of Rachel tending her father's sheep, wandering in the field full of shepherds without any protection, might be the first indication of the degree to which Laban also exploited his daughters. Laban could have hired a professional shepherd, as he later did when he contracted Jacob's services or charged his sons with the responsibility.

Rachel and Leah long for the world that was: a world that was governed by generosity and integrity, without any need for protective measures. The appearance of Jacob, who came from a completely different background, awakened these dormant feelings in their hearts.

The Prisoner's Dilemma

The dissonance between the trust-based economy that Jacob knew in his parents' home and the distrustful economy that permeated Laban's home and Haran's society suggests another way of understanding the incident at the well and Jacob's years in Laban's home.

Jacob approached the stone because that was how one behaved in a society predicated on mutual trust. Given his values, it would not have dawned on Jacob to take more water than he needed or to be inconsiderate of others. The values pulsing in his veins vaccinated him against such impulses, so he was not willing to pay the price that needs to be paid in a scheming, manipulative society.

For her part, Rachel seems to have detected something refreshingly different in Jacob, entirely unlike the wolves that danced around her. Their hearts quickened to the same beat. We can imagine that for that first month, Jacob accompanied

Rachel as she tended her father's flocks; in his eyes, he was already part of the family or one of us. Laban, who was negatively affected by the lack of interpersonal trust in his environment, unapologetically laid out his philosophy:

> On hearing the news of his sister's son Jacob, Laban ran to greet him; he embraced him and kissed him and took him into his house. He told Laban all that had happened, and Laban said to him, "You are truly my bone and flesh." When he had stayed with him a month's time, Laban said to Jacob, "Just because you are a kinsman, should you serve me for nothing? Tell me, what shall your wages be?" (29:13–15)

Jacob responded in a completely different tone:

> "Jacob loved Rachel; so he answered, 'I will serve you seven years for your younger daughter Rachel.' Laban said, 'Better that I give her to you than that I should give her to an outsider. Stay with me.' (29:18–19)

Jacob did not base his relationship with Laban on business interests but on personal ones. Laban's reaction reflects his worldview—Jacob was essentially no better and no worse than any other potential suitor. This relationship was not about brotherhood or friendship. It was purely a business transaction, just as it would be with anyone else. All things being equal on the business front, it was better that Jacob was the suitor since he was not a total stranger.

Presumably, Laban mistreated Jacob just as he would have mistreated anyone else. As noted above, after seven years, he tricked Jacob and substituted Leah for Rachel. When the deception was discovered, he fell back on a legalism: "It is not the practice in our place to marry off the younger before the older" (29:26). His cynical use of the law against Jacob, a wandering relative who cannot assert his rights or protect his interests, emphasizes Jacob's helplessness as a stranger. Jacob had to accept a new deal: "Wait until the bridal week of this one is over, and we will give you that one too, provided you serve me another seven years" (29:27).

This episode, whereby Jacob had no choice but to accept Laban's betrayal given his status as something between a refugee and a prisoner, repeats itself time and again throughout the twenty years that Jacob built his family in Haran:

> As you know, I have served your father with all my might; but your father has cheated me, changing my wages time and again. God, however, would not let him do me harm...for I have noted all that Laban has been doing to you.... Then Rachel and Leah answered him, saying, "Have we still a share in the inheritance of our father's house? Surely, he regards us as outsiders, now that he has sold us and has used up our purchase price. Truly, all the possessions that God has taken away from our father belongs to us and to our children. Now then, do just as God has told you." (31:6–16)

The fact that Rachel and Leah took Jacob's side and completely estranged themselves from their father, while Laban himself did not deny these accusations, shows that the relationship between Jacob and his family and Laban and his sons lacked any element of interpersonal trust. Instead, it was controlled by Laban and his policy of ruthless exploitation. Jacob was essentially a hostage, unable to employ any strategies aside from "permanent cooperation."

There were, however, two ways for Jacob to pay Laban back for his aggressive behavior. The Torah tells us that part of the separation agreement between Jacob and Laban was that Jacob was entitled to the speckled and spotted lambs. Since this agreement was outcome based, Jacob took advantage of a loophole in the deal and placed spotted sticks in the sheep's troughs. This resulted in the birth of only spotted and speckled sheep, which meant all the sheep belonged to him. As recounted in the Torah, this was a "small blow" to Laban:

> But Jacob dealt separately with the sheep; he made these animals face the streaked or wholly dark-colored animals in Laban's flock. And so he produced special flocks for himself, which he did not put with Laban's flocks. Moreover, when the sturdier animals were mating, Jacob would place the rods in the troughs, in full view of the animals, so that they mated by the rods; but with the feebler animals he would not place them there. Thus the feeble ones went to Laban and the sturdy to Jacob. (30:40–42)

The bigger blow that Jacob dealt to Laban was in setting the time of the "endgame." As we previously noted, players' behavior in a given game is directly influenced by their concern about revenge and betrayal in the game's next iteration. This fear encourages cooperating to reap long-term profits instead of achieving short-term profits through betrayal. A long-term vision builds stability and routine, a good reputation, and the expectation of a steady and predictable pattern of conduct. Strict adherence to the rules lends confidence and enables the same strategy to be used again and again. In the endgame, however, both players could have a vested interest in betraying because they know they will not be facing their opponent again.

This is how Jacob's flight from Haran without Laban's knowledge is described:

> Thereupon Jacob put his children and wives on camels; and he drove off all his livestock and all the possessions that he had acquired, the livestock he owned, which he had acquired in Paddan-Aram, to go to his father Isaac, to the land of Canaan. Meanwhile Laban had gone to shear his sheep, and Rachel stole her father's household idols. Jacob kept Laban the Aramean in the dark, not telling him that he was fleeing. (31:17–20)

Rachel, herself a victim of her father's deceit,[11] understood that she would never see her father again. Before she left, she stole his household idols. This may have been her symbolic way of breaking the dishes of her father's home and burning the bridges to her birthplace.

With that, the Torah seems to emphasize that though he lost his daughters, grandchildren, camels, cattle, household idols, and other property, Laban was most wounded and felt cheated by Jacob's failure to tell him he was leaving: "Jacob kept Laban the Aramean in the dark, not telling him that he was fleeing." Keeping Laban "in the dark" or sneaking away under the cover of night or some other ruse defines a disengagement strategy based on mistrust. We can say that Jacob used Laban's own strategy against him; he repaid Laban tit for tat. Ultimately, Laban—who had not engaged in confidence-building measures for twenty years and had continuously violated Jacob's trust—was forced to pay the highest price of all. Jacob and his own daughters betrayed him while he was "in the dark" about their plans.

The story of Jacob's flight to Haran, his experiences there, and his return home, is devoted entirely to the importance of cultivating interpersonal trust, as well as the factors that lead to its violation and the price exacted by its absence. The Bible is teaching us the price of the lack of interpersonal trust in business and family.

To summarize, this section is framed by parallel narratives. The unit begins with the story of Jacob's arrival in Haran and focuses on his activities at the well—the rolling of the stone off the well and giving water to the sheep. This establishes that Jacob was a visitor and therefore not bound by "the rules of the game" in Haran. He did not have his own flock of sheep and did not need to worry about a counter-betrayal or even about destroying the system of protective measures that functioned there.

The unit ends with Jacob's departure from Haran twenty years later, an act that takes him beyond the game. In order to protect his livestock and the financial future of his children, he had to end his losing streak, wherein his (forced) loyalty had been repeatedly exploited and betrayed.

We may suggest more generally that like modern laws, many of the Torah's laws aim to encourage interpersonal trust and ensure that it remains in effect in all economic situations. Interpersonal trust, after all, forms the backbone of society. These rules and lessons are as valuable today as they were thousands of years ago.

Endgame

As soon as he learned of Jacob's flight, Laban gave chase in an attempt to recover his wealth:

> On the third day, Laban was told that Jacob had fled. So he took his kinsmen with him and pursued him a distance of seven days, catching up with him in the hill country of Gilead. But God appeared to Laban the Aramean in a dream by night and said to him, "Beware of attempting anything with Jacob, good or bad." Laban overtook Jacob. Jacob had pitched his tent on the mountain, and Laban with his kinsmen encamped in the hill country of Gilead. And Laban said to Jacob, "What did you mean by keeping me in the dark and carrying off my daughters like captives of the sword? Why did you flee in secrecy and mislead me and not tell me? I would have sent you off with festive music, with timbrel and lyre. You did not even let me kiss my sons and daughters goodbye! It was a foolish thing for you to do. I have it in my power to do you harm; but the God of your father said to me last night, 'Beware of attempting anything with Jacob, good or bad.' Very well, you had to leave because you were longing for your father's house; but why did you steal my gods?" (31:22–30)

It seems that Laban, whose language was the language of power, continued this pattern; if Jacob refused to return to Haran, Laban would physically assault him. God therefore needed to intervene and threaten Laban. The accusation that Laban hurls at Jacob, ("What did you mean by...carrying off my daughters like captives of the sword") attests to Laban's state of mind and explains the next part of his statement: "I have it in my power to do you harm." Likewise, Laban's declaration "but the God of your father said to me last night, 'Beware of attempting anything with Jacob, good or bad,'" intends to relay the message that Laban is not scared off by God's threat. After all, in spite of God's message, he came "to speak" with Jacob.

Ultimately, Laban changed his plan and returned home, leaving Jacob and his family to continue on their journey to the land of Israel. As we read the verses that relate this, we must ask why Laban changed his mind. As they reveal, even Laban now understood, at least on some level, the message of the importance of trust and the terrible damage that his behavior had caused through the years.

Jacob would answer each of Laban's questions in turn and finally force Laban to face the truth. It seems that Jacob's bold statement, a statement that oscillated between total despair and courage, is what caused the shift:

> Jacob answered Laban, saying, "I was afraid because I thought you would take your daughters from me by force. But anyone with whom you find your gods shall not remain alive! In the presence of our kinsmen, point out what I have of yours and take it." Jacob, of course, did not know that Rachel had stolen them. So Laban went into Jacob's tent and Leah's tent and the tents of the two maidservants; but he did not find them. Leaving Leah's tent, he entered Rachel's tent. Rachel, meanwhile, had taken the idols and placed them in the camel cushion and sat on them; and Laban rummaged through the tent without finding them. For she said to her father, "Let not my lord take it amiss that I cannot rise before you, for the period of women is upon me." Thus he searched, but could not find the household idols.
>
> Now Jacob became incensed and took up his grievance with Laban. Jacob spoke up and said to Laban, "What is

> my crime, what is my guilt that you should pursue me? You rummaged through all my things; what have you found of all your household objects? Set it here, before my kinsmen and yours, and let them decide between us two. These twenty years I have spent in your service, your ewes and she-goats never miscarried, nor did I feast on rams from your flock. That which was torn by beasts I never brought to you; I myself made good the loss; you exacted it of me, whether snatched by day or snatched by night. Often, scorching heat ravaged me by day and frost by night; and sleep fled from my eyes. Of the twenty years that I spent in your household, I served you fourteen years for your two daughters, and six years for your flocks; and you changed my wages time and again. Had not the God of my father, the God of Abraham and the Fear of Isaac, been with me, you would have sent me away empty-handed. But God took notice of my plight and the toil of my hands, and He gave judgment last night." (31:31–42)

In the middle of the conversation, Jacob gathered the strength and confidence to fight with Laban for the first time. In the furious words that follow, Laban became aware that this time, he had pushed things too far. Jacob was no longer willing to be exploited by his dictates. At this point, Laban understood that he could not turn back the clock, and he therefore did not respond to Jacob's harsh accusations. He instead changed his strategy to something between general trust and a carefully calculated threat:

> Then Laban spoke up and said to Jacob, "The daughters are my daughters, the children are my children, and the flocks are my flocks; all that you see is mine. Yet what can

> I do now about my daughters or the children they have borne? "Come, then, let us make a pact, you and I, that there may be a witness between you and me." Thereupon Jacob took a stone and set it up as a pillar. And Jacob said to his kinsmen, "Gather stones." So they took stones and made a mound; and they partook of a meal there by the mound. Laban named it Yegar-Sahadutha, but Jacob named it Gal-ed. And Laban declared, "This mound is a witness between you and me this day." That is why it was named Gal-ed; And [it was called] Mizpah, because he said, "May the Lord watch between you and me, when we are out of sight of each other. If you mistreat my daughters or take other wives besides my daughters—though no one else be about, remember, God Himself will be witness between you and me." And Laban said to Jacob, "Here is this mound and here the pillar which I have set up between you and me: this mound shall be witness and this pillar shall be witness that I am not to cross to you past this mound, and that you are not to cross to me past this mound and this pillar, with hostile intent. May the God of Abraham and the god of Nahor judge between us." And Jacob swore by the Fear of his father Isaac. (31:43–53)

Laban attempted to salvage the situation by focusing on the future. Through an ongoing family relationship, he hoped to formalize cooperation in order to recreate the dynamic of an iterated game. In this conversation, Laban predicated everything on family relationships in an attempt to obligate Jacob to return. He finally understood that this was what had kept Jacob loyal to him over the past twenty years. However, Jacob had enough and set his sights westward to his father's home and once and future homeland. He wanted his family to grow up in a land and household predicated on trust.

The final line of this story is the perfect synopsis of the entire episode: "Laban arose in the morning and kissed his sons and daughters and blessed them. Then Laban left and returned to his place" (32:1). The midrash (*Bereishit Rabbah*, based on MS Parma) comments: "They did not kiss him back."

8
Parashat Vayishlaḥ

FROM LOVE TO FEAR

Business Integrity

Upon this a question arises: whether it be better to be loved than feared or feared than loved? One should wish to be both, but, because it is difficult to unite them in one person, it is much safer to be feared than loved.

That prince who, relying entirely on the people's promises, and has not taken other precautions, is ruined; because friendships obtained by payments, and not by greatness or nobility of mind, may indeed be bought, but they are not owned. In time of need, they cannot be relied upon. Men have less scruple in offending one who they love than one who they fear, for love is preserved by the link of obligation which, owing to the baseness of men, is broken at every opportunity when their self-interest intervenes; but fear preserves you because a dread of punishment never wanes.

—Niccolò Machiavelli[1]

Scare Tactics

After twenty years in the home of Laban, Jacob made his way back to his father's home in the land of his birth. As he traveled southward, on the heels of his tense encounter with Laban in the Gilead mountains, he learned that his brother Esau was traveling towards him. Recall twenty years earlier, Esau wanted to kill Jacob for taking his firstborn blessing: "Now Esau harbored a grudge against Jacob because of the blessing which his father had given him, and Esau said to himself, 'Let but the mourning period of my father come, and I will kill my brother Jacob.'" Moreover, their father Isaac's blessing to Esau included the prediction that Esau would "live by the sword." Hence, Jacob likely feared this impending encounter with Esau even more than he feared Laban.

To mitigate the potential danger and to mollify Esau, Jacob dispensed much of his wealth to Esau in the form of gifts:

> After spending the night there, he selected from what was at hand these presents for his brother Esau: Two hundred she-goats and twenty he-goats; two hundred ewes and twenty rams; thirty nursing camels with their colts; forty cows and ten bulls; twenty she-asses and ten he-asses. These he put in the charge of his servants, drove by drove, and he told his servants, "Go on ahead, and keep a distance between droves." He instructed the one in front as follows, "When my brother Esau meets you and asks you, 'Whose man are you? Where are you going? And whose [animals] are these ahead of you?' you shall answer, 'Your servant Jacob's; they are a gift sent to my lord Esau; and [Jacob] himself is right behind us.'" He gave similar instructions to the second one, and the third, and all the others who followed the droves,

> namely, "Such and such shall you say to Esau when you reach him. And you shall add, 'And your servant Jacob himself is right behind us.'" For he reasoned, "If I placate him with presents in advance, and then face him, perhaps he will show me favor." And so the gift went on ahead, while he remained in camp that night...He himself went on ahead and bowed low to the ground seven times until he was near his brother. Esau ran to greet him. He embraced him and, falling on his neck, he kissed him; and they wept.... So Esau started back that day on his way to Seir. (32:14–33:16)

As the verses describe, after Jacob forded the Jabbok stream from north to south, he met Esau; they embraced and each then went his separate way. Jacob successfully navigated this chilling encounter, and Esau continued southward.

It seems as though Jacob should have turned west to ford the Jordan River to the land of Israel. However, he did not cross the Jordan yet. Rather, he lingered at Succoth, on the eastern bank of the Jordan, where he built stalls for his animals and a house for himself:

> But Jacob journeyed on to Succoth and built a house for himself and made stalls for his cattle; that is why the place was called Succoth. Jacob arrived intact in the city of Shechem which is in the land of Canaan—having come thus from Paddan-Aram—and he encamped before the city. The parcel of land where he pitched his tent he purchased from the children of Hamor, Shechem's father, for a hundred *kesitah*. He set up an altar there, and called it God, the God of Israel. (33:17-20)

Sandwiched between the reunion and subsequent separation of Esau and Jacob and the rape of Jacob and Leah's daughter, Dinah, this passage encapsulates the essence of Jacob's approach to economic leadership. His approach was diametrically opposed to the notorious advice of Machiavelli, who sought to intimidate the reader and his subordinates.

Niccolò Machiavelli, perhaps the greatest political theorist in history, suggested that in politics, fear is a better motivator than love. His core argument was that someone who loves will not be deterred from backstabbing or shenanigans, and in Machiavelli's worldview, it is as applicable to business as it is to politics. Without fear, human nature will take over, and Machiavelli's view of human nature is hardly inspiring.

Machiavelli's businessman, much like his politician, is steeped in contracts, sanctions, and policing agreements and is less focused on relationships and trust. He undoubtedly employed hardnosed attorneys, who would write fearsome agreements with significant penalty clauses.[2] My personal view and experience suggests that relationships matter more than fear-based contracts, particularly over the long term. Reliance on deep relationships and earning money over time through hard and honest work is deeply rooted in the biblical outlook.

Twenty Years Later

Why did Jacob, who had been exiled from his home for twenty years and commanded by God to return to the land, linger so long in Succoth?[3] Shouldn't he have entered Eretz Yisrael immediately? One would expect that specifically now, having overcome his obstacles, Jacob would want to finally realize his dream standing just across the border.

Scripture does not say much about the region of Succoth. From the sources that we have, it seems that it was rich in pastureland and good for raising cattle. In the fortieth year in the wilderness, on the cusp of their entry into the land of Israel, the Israelite tribes of Reuben and Gad approached Moses and asked to remain on the eastern bank of the Jordan because they owned large herds of cattle:

> The Reubenites and the Gadites owned cattle in very great numbers. Noting that the lands of Jazer and Gilead were a region suitable for cattle, the Gadites and the Reubenites came to Moses, Eleazar the priest, and the chieftains of the community, and said, "Ataroth, Dibon, Jazer, Nimrah, Heshbon, Elealeh, Sebam, Nebo, and Beon—the land that the Lord has conquered for the community of Israel is cattle country, and your servants have cattle. (Numbers 32:1–4)

Moses acceded to their request, and they settled on the eastern bank of the Jordan. The Book of Yehoshua further describes that Gad settled "in the Valley, Bet-Haran, Beth-Nimrah, Succoth, and Zaphon" (Yehoshua 13:27), indicating that Succoth was a grazing area in the region of Beth-Nimrah and Bet-Haran (Haram) in the territory of Gad.[4]

It follows then that Jacob's delay in the pastures of Succoth was connected to the previous episode, the encounter with Esau, in preparation for which Jacob gave Esau more than five hundred animals as a peace offering. It is impossible to know how many sheep Jacob had in total when he left Laban's home, but giving away so much livestock, including males for breeding, nursing females, and their young, must have significantly depleted Jacob's wealth.[5] In a general sense, it seems that Jacob transferred a good part of the wealth that he had accumulated from Laban to Esau.

When Jacob implored Esau to accept his offerings, he began with the word "gift" (which appeared earlier in the episode) and concluded with the word "blessing":

> But Jacob said, "No, I pray you; if you would do me this favor, accept from me this gift; for to see your face is like seeing the face of God, and you have received me favorably. Please accept my blessing which has been brought to you, for God has favored me and I have everything." And when he urged him, he accepted.

The transition from "gift" to "blessing" recalls the events of twenty years earlier, when Jacob impersonated Esau and took the blessing. Now, Jacob not only gave away the wealth he had accumulated in integrity challenged Haran, but also the blessing that he had schemed to obtain.

Before entering the land, Jacob wanted to give up the wealth he had acquired through tactics adapted to and adopted in Haran, based not on trust but aggression and a culture of suspicion. By giving away this wealth, he definitively cut ties with that world.

Therefore, Jacob decided to stay on the eastern bank of the Jordan and build up his wealth again without resorting to power struggles, fear,[6] or predatory, retributive competition.[7] He built stalls or booths (*sukkot*) because the area was unsettled pastureland. He thus returned to shepherding, which had brought him success in the house of Laban, and thereby rebuilt his economic power. He became wealthy again—this time through his own hard work, without placing rods in the troughs and waterholes,[8] an apparent loophole or breach in his agreement with Laban (a move that Jacob needed to take after Laban had reneged on their deal on numerous occasions). Jacob had used some form of "genetic engineering" or magical mating to increase his portion of the herd that would be due to him under the agreement with Laban. Upon reaching the border of the land of Israel and gifting this wealth to Esau, it is clear that Jacob was not interested in wealth amassed though dubious scheming.[9]

Jacob thus arrived in the city of Shechem "intact" (*shalem*). Some commentators understand the word *shalem* as a description of Jacob's material situation (Rashi, based on Babylonian Talmud Shabbat 33b, Ibn Ezra). Rashbam identifies *shalem* as a place near Shechem, while Ralbag understands the word as indicative of Jacob's approach to the people—namely, that he came in peace (*shalom*).

It seems that the Torah intentionally used an amorphous word that sustains several different meanings because they are all correct. Jacob arrived in the Shechem region and the land of Israel in general with his new, clean wealth and an attitude of peace and cooperation. He returned to the land of Israel in innocence, intending to walk in the footsteps of his grandfather Abraham, a prince of God in the land of the Hittites, and the footsteps of his father Isaac, an ally of the Philistine King Abimelech.

The Incident in Shechem

When Jacob and family enter the land of Canaan with their newly earned wealth, they settled outside of Shechem. However, things immediately took an apparent negative turn at the hands of the prince and namesake of the town:

> Now Dinah, the daughter whom Leah had borne to Jacob, went out to visit the daughters of the land. Shechem son of Hamor the Hivite, chief of the country, saw her, and took her and lay with her by force. Being strongly drawn to Dinah daughter of Jacob, and in love

> with the maiden, he spoke to the maiden tenderly. So Shechem said to his father Hamor, "Get me this girl as a wife." Jacob heard that he had defiled his daughter Dinah; but since his sons were in the field with his cattle, Jacob kept silent until they came home. (34:1-5)

Despite the rape of his daughter at the hands of Prince Shechem, Jacob entertained a visit from the prince's father. Notwithstanding this discussion, about which we know little, the verses immediately turn to other protagonists:

> Meanwhile Jacob's sons, having heard the news, came in from the field. The men were distressed and very angry, because he had committed an outrage in Israel by lying with Jacob's daughter—a thing not to be done. *And Hamor spoke with them*, saying, "My son Shechem longs for your daughter. Please give her to him in marriage. Intermarry with us: give your daughters to us, and take our daughters for yourselves: You will dwell among us, and the land will be open before you; settle, move about, and acquire holdings in it." (34:7-10)

The Prince re-enters the picture to plead his case to both the brothers and their father, so that he may marry Dinah.

> Then Shechem said to her father and brothers, "Do me this favor, and I will pay whatever you tell me. Ask of me a bride-price ever so high, as well as gifts, and I will pay what you tell me; only give me the maiden for a wife." (34:11-12)

Again, strangely, the verses turn the conversation away from Jacob, and the brothers surreptitiously answer the prince and his father:

> Jacob's sons answered Shechem and his father Hamor—speaking with guile because he had defiled their sister Dinah—and said to them, "We cannot do this thing, to give our sister to a man who is uncircumcised, for that is a disgrace among us. Only on this condition will we agree with you; that you will become like us in that every male among you is circumcised. Then we will give our daughters to you and take your daughters to ourselves; and we will dwell among you and become as one kindred. But if you will not listen to us and become circumcised, we will take our daughter and go." Their words pleased Hamor and Hamor's son Shechem. (Genesis 34:1–18)

The story of Dinah's rape, the seemingly disjointed interactions between the different players in this story, and the unclear thematic connections between this story and the preceding ones require close examination.

Boundless Integrity

"The people when rightly and fully trusted will return the trust."

—Abraham Lincoln

Great leaders understand that trust matters. They understand that power and fear have their limits. More deeply, they understand that societies that are founded on fear and rules are fragile. The ties that bind different populations or tribes in a given land or country must be erected on a bedrock of trust. If not, they are easily frayed.

Like Abraham Lincoln, who sought to avoid a civil war and pleaded for friendship between North and South, our forefathers stood for good neighborly relations in the land of Israel.

They understood that the successful establishment of a people on its land must be built on the foundation of an exemplary society and achieved through trust, integrity, and cooperation. Abraham's family forged alliances with the Canaanites Aner, Eshkol, and Mamrei; King Melchizedek of Salem; and Abimelech (at least after the latter came to his senses and accepted their reproach). Against this backdrop, Jacob arrived in the city of Shechem financially whole or intact (through wholesome means) and purchased a parcel of land within the city limits:

> The parcel of land where he pitched his tent he purchased from the children of Hamor, Shechem's father, for a hundred *kesitah*. He set up an altar there, and called it God, the God of Israel. (33:18–20)

The commentators suggest two alternate explanations for the word *kesitah.* Rashi contends that *kesitah* is a form of currency,[10] while Onkelos (referencing the book of Job) and Rabbi Saadia Gaon explain that "*kesitah*" is an animal.[11] The explanation advanced by Onkelos and Rabbi Saadia Gaon fits better with the general framework of the story: Jacob, who had just repopulated his herds in Succoth, traded his livestock for a parcel of land on the outskirts of Shechem.[12] Exchanging his animal herds for real estate symbolizes the transition from wandering and moveable wealth to permanence in the land of Israel. Jacob's message was that to hold the land firmly, one must buy real estate, while to build an exemplary society, one must build wealth honestly, observing the highest standards of transparency and trust.

Accordingly, purchasing real estate from the sons of Hamor was a transaction designed to cultivate good neighborly relations and build trust. In Succoth, Jacob was a homesteader;

he raised his cattle and built a temporary shelter. In the land of Israel, he bought land.[13] His actions thus cultivated upright and trustworthy neighborly relations. In the words of Ralbag (on 33:19):

> When an individual comes to live in a certain place, it is proper for him to conduct business with the important people in that place so that they will view him in a positive light, and he will thereby be better protected from the potential damage that the local population can cause him. For this reason, immediately [upon his arrival in Shechem] Jacob bought a field from the prince of the land, and Abraham too bought a field from Ephron, who was among the rulers of the land in which he lived.

Harvard Business School professor Rosabeth Moss Kanter argues that individuals and leaders are more successful in achieving cooperation when they are present, frame the discussion, espouse values, and generally cultivate an atmosphere of generous reciprocal relations. Building an enchanted circle where the giver will receive more than is put out strengthens trust between strategic players.[14]

Upon entering the land, Jacob appeared before the people of the city, spoke clearly, and conducted an important business deal with obvious benefits for the townsfolk, thus successfully cultivating a spirit of cooperation and reciprocity. By camping near Shechem, whose leaders were apparently the princes of a large region of the land of Israel, Jacob positioned himself as a person who was ready to conduct business honestly and transparently in the most central, influential region of ancient Canaan.

It is important to note that for Jacob, this approach was a way of life, not a business tactic. This is the approach that Jacob adopted after he saw with his own eyes how difficult it was to live in either the harsh, dishonest culture of Haran or under the reign of terror of Esau, who lived by the sword.

As noted, Jacob immediately purchased a field from the children of Hamor (the father of Shechem); all of the princes—the entire royal family—participated in the deal. The question remained, though, as to whether this was a purely financial deal that aimed to cultivate trust and confidence in a neighborly business relationship or a move towards assimilation and integration that would eventually lead to cultural domination.

From the way things progressed, it is apparent that the older generation, Jacob and Hamor, envisioned a healthy and mutually beneficial business relationship. The younger generation saw things differently. They did not understand the intricate approach to reciprocity that advocated self-determination for each cultural group alongside respect for one another. The "Machiavelli" in them burst forth and dominated the discourse.

Hamor's son Shechem, who permitted himself to rape Dinah as a way to take her as a wife, and Dinah herself, who went out to visit the girls of the land, saw this business transaction as a step towards assimilation. The sons of Jacob—founders of the twelve tribes of Israel—took it even further. They saw their land purchase as a bridgehead toward their ultimate goal of domination. From their perspective, now that they had survived their frightening struggles with Laban and Esau, their arrival in the land marked the advent of a new era, an epoch of prosperity and serenity. They were no longer foreigners in exile in Haran; they had assumed the status of permanent settlers of the land of their fathers. Therefore, they should act like masters of the land.

Blood Pact

Per the above, three distinct voices emerged in the discussion conducted in Shechem the day after the rape of Dinah, corresponding to the different worldviews about the unfolding events:

> And Hamor spoke with them, saying, "My son Shechem longs for your daughter. Please give her to him in marriage. Intermarry with us: give your daughters to us, and take our daughters for yourselves: You will dwell among us, and the land will be open before you; settle, move about, and acquire holdings in it." (34:8–10)
>
> Hamor proposed continued confidence-building measures and good business practice. The familial bonds that would be woven through intermarriage would be the best guarantee for ongoing business integrity and mutual cooperation.

Among the voices, Jacob's fell silent. A thick fog had descended upon the process that he had carefully devised and implemented. On one hand, the crime was committed by one lone person. On the other hand, the perpetrator was the son of the local ruler, the one described as "the most respected in his father's house" (34:19). The city itself bore his name. Jacob wanted to be a beacon of light, a respectable person who respects others and their leaders, an individual whose leadership stems from recognition and trust. But the dam had burst.

But there is no such thing as a vacuum. Jacob's children, Dinah's brothers, grabbed center stage and tricked Hamor and his son Shechem. Their words are very telling and indicative of the approach that they espoused all along:

> Jacob's sons answered Shechem and his father Hamor—speaking with guile because he had defiled their sister Dinah—and said to them, "We cannot do this thing, to give our sister to a man who is uncircumcised, for that is a disgrace among us. Only on this condition will we agree with you; that you will become like us in that every male among you is circumcised. Then we will give our daughters to you and take your daughters to ourselves; and we will dwell among you and become a single people. But if you will not listen to us and become circumcised, we will take our daughter and go." (34:13–17)

Their words, "if you will become like us" and specifically their statement of "we will...become a single people," which went well beyond Hamor's original proposition, demonstrate that Jacob's sons had envisioned conquering Shechem and taking control of its people from the very beginning. They deliberately left out Hamor's vision of economic cooperation. As noted, Hamor wanted to establish economic cooperation in order to build confidence and reciprocal business relationships: an economic détente or peaceful coexistence. The worldview and upbringing of Jacob's sons was not built on trust, and they consequently did not mention business or trade opportunities at all. The road from an absence of trust to wiping out the entire city was not long.[15] Their ultimate threat is very telling: "We will take our daughter and go." In other words, our way or the highway.

Jacob's sons were born and raised in the prickly business environment of Haran. Their manner of speech and mode of thinking was wired to be manipulative. They began their speech deviously and capped it off with a threat. They did not understand the dramatic change undertaken by their father when he gave away a significant part of his assets to Esau and subsequently tarried in Succoth to rebuild his wealth on the basis of a new and different value system. When Jacob called out in the name of God in Shechem, they heard the call of war, not a clarion call to seek closeness to Him.

The way that Hamor and Shechem presented the proposed treaty to the townsfolk is a mirror image of Jacob's sons' belligerent demand that the people of Shechem trade in their national identity. Hamor and Shechem broadcast that they would actually absorb Jacob's family, including their material wealth, by themselves invoking a beguiling strategy that encouraged them to settle in the area, assimilate, and build up their wealth. In a mirrored twist, the "single people" that Jacob's sons envisioned, though, would actually be Hivite according to the plan of Prince Shechem and his father, the chief of the Canaanite Hivite people.

> So Hamor and his son Shechem went to the public place of their town and spoke to their fellow townsmen, saying, "These people are our friends; let them settle in the land and move about in it, for the land is large enough for them; we will take their daughters to ourselves as wives and give our daughters to them. But only on this condition will the men agree with us to dwell among us and be as one kindred: that all our males become circumcised as they are circumcised. Their cattle and substance and all their beasts will be ours, if we only agree to their terms, so that they will settle among us" (34:20–23)

The violent, aggressive culture of the leadership of Shechem is indicative not only in the rape of Dinah by the crown prince of the city, but also in their speech to their subjects. They proclaimed that all of the material wealth of Jacob's family would be diverted to the people of Shechem. In all aspects, this is a terrible story of mutual deception and violence, beginning with rape and deceptive behavior and culminating with violent retribution. But it is told by the Torah unvarnished because there is an important lesson inherent in it.

Ultimately, since Jacob's sons deceived the people of Shechem in the short-term while the people of Shechem planned to manipulate Jacob's family in the long-term, the sons of Jacob prevailed. Exploiting the weakness of the people of Shechem in the aftermath of their collective circumcision, they killed them and plundered the city, murdering the males of the city. Although it is never answered with certainty whether or not this attack was warranted as an act of self-defense, was acceptable in the ancient Near East, or was a despicable act of murder,[16] it is clear that Jacob was outraged by their behavior for the rest of his life. On his deathbed, Jacob chose especially harsh words:

> Simeon and Levi are a pair; their weapons are tools of lawlessness. Into their conspiracy let my soul not enter! With their congregation, do not join my honor! For when angry they slay men, and when pleased they maim oxen. Cursed be their anger so fierce, and their wrath so relentless. I will divide them in Jacob, scatter them in Israel. (49:5–7)

While his sons schemed and secretly planned a takeover, Jacob longed for transparency and cooperation, so he did not want them to represent him. Since they did not understand his maneuvers to leave the corrupt value system of Haran behind and faced with Shechem's belligerent approach, Simeon and Levi responded violently, destroying what Jacob had worked so hard to cultivate:

> Jacob said to Simeon and Levi, "You have brought trouble on me, making me odious among the inhabitants of the land, the Canaanites and the Perizzites; my men are few in number, so that if they unite against me and attack me, I and my house will be destroyed." (34:30)

Accordingly, the story concludes: "As they set out, a terror from God fell on the cities round about, so that they did not pursue the sons of Jacob" (35:5). Jacob fled once again, and fear once again governed the situation.

Jacob, who advocated honesty and economic cooperation as he entered the land, felt that his own sons had turned on him. While it is true that Jacob betrayed Laban's confidence when he escaped from Haran in the middle of the night, he also rebuilt his wealth from scratch on better values before he entered the land of Israel, perhaps even on account of his experiences with Laban. In effect, he had "repented" and sought to build a better ethical and economic foundation for a new people—the people of Israel—in an old land.

The sons of Jacob, however, were not interested in cooperative efforts. As soon as they encountered their first setback, they took the extreme step of deceiving the leaders of Shechem and completely betrayed their trust. They destroyed and plundered the city and earned the disgraceful distinction of becoming a band of lawless nomads. For the next several years, until they descended to Egypt, the sons of Jacob remained transient shepherds. They did not establish themselves as settlers in the land; they were always on the move.

Their act was a fatal blow to Jacob's vision of a successful society predicated on mutually beneficial trust. He dreamt of commercial relationships that connected the two peoples while also respecting their cultural differences. Despite the heinous crime that Shechem, had perpetrated, Jacob understood that physical strength was not the way to build a healthy society in the land of Israel. Strength and resilience were essential but not exclusive. Trust, economic cooperation, and integrity are the critical building blocks of society. Other people (even adversaries) cannot be allowed to dictate (or tarnish) the norms on which that society is based. Jacob's only hesitation was whether it was indeed possible to build such a society in a place like Shechem, given the violent behavior of the prince.

Ultimately, Jacob fled from Shechem to Bethel. From that point on, he would have no further interaction with the inhabitants of the land. He had attempted to set in motion a process based on his own bitter life experiences. He wanted to begin building a people in its land. He envisioned a healthy society, based on a strong ethic of socioeconomic trust that would benefit all inhabitants, but his sons ruined everything, and in the end, he cursed them for it.

9

Parashat Vayeshev

LAND RESERVE

A Family Business at a Crossroads

"A strategic inflection point is a time in the life of business when its fundamentals are about to change. That change can mean an opportunity to rise to new heights. But it may just as likely signal the beginning of the end."

— Andrew S. Grove, Only the Paranoid Survive. Lessons from the CEO of INTEL Corporation

It has been said of Microsoft founder Bill Gates that he not only anticipated inflection points in technology and business but accelerated them.[1] Many great minds, innovators, and seers of a different economic and technological future have been ridiculed. Famously, Ken Olsen, CEO of Digital Equipment Corporation (DEC), the then-leader in computers, said "there is no reason to have a computer in every home." Bill Gates thought otherwise. He pursued that vision with religious zeal, investing in the supporting ecosystems of semiconductors, hardware, and applications to make his vision come true.

Gates was not an easy boss or changemaker. According to James Wallace and Jim Erickson, authors of the 1993 biography *Hard Drive: Bill Gates and the Making of the Microsoft Empire*, Gates was notorious for sending "critical and sarcastic" emails—often referred to as "flame mail"—to his employees in the middle of the night. He was frequently critical of their performance, software, code, and direction. It is challenging and sometimes unpopular to be a technological and economic innovator.[2]

However, economic and technological changemakers and accelerators are critical. They are critical for innovation in general, calcified family businesses, and nations in formation. If you do not integrate and accommodate them, you lose them to others, and your business, economy, and culture loses out.

Background

After decades of wandering, and then abruptly leaving Shechem, we next find Jacob settling in the land of Israel and setting up his family and business interests. The Torah is now transitioning to describe the evolution of the twelve sons of Jacob into the twelve tribes. Family dynamics can be challenging. A family comprised of twelve sons, born of four wives and one father, is even more so.

Jealousy divided the patriarch's family, sowing conflict within it and almost leading to the murder of one of the brothers, which is to say, one of the future tribes of Israel. Simultaneously, Jacob was involved in creating a family, laying the foundations of a nation, and building a business that could support both.

The family business was shepherding. Jacob had been a shepherd for Laban in Haran and raised his own flock in Succoth, as we saw in the previous chapter. His attempt to become a landowner and homesteader failed when he needed to pack his bags and leave following the incident in Shechem. Now settled nearly fifty miles to the south in the hills of Hebron, he launches the third episode of his family business, including integrating his sons in the endeavor.

Jacob was a thrice-successful businessman and entrepreneur. His resilience is startling. However, like many successful entrepreneurs who attempt to turn their business into a familial legacy, he ran into trouble. Jacob's business, like many family enterprises, began to unravel in the second generation.

> Now Jacob was settled in the land where his father had sojourned, the land of Canaan. This, then, is the line of Jacob: At seventeen years of age, Joseph tended the flocks with his brothers, as a helper to the sons of his father's wives Bilhah and Zilpah. And Joseph brought bad reports of them to their father. Now Israel [aka Jacob] loved Joseph best of all his sons, for he was the child of his old age; and he had made him a fine woolen tunic. And when his brothers saw that their father loved him more than any of his brothers, they hated him so that they could not speak a friendly word to him. Once Joseph had a dream which he told to his brothers; and they hated him even more. He said to them, "Hear this dream which I have dreamed: There we were binding sheaves in the field, when suddenly my sheaf stood up and remained upright; then your sheaves gathered around and bowed low to my sheaf." His brothers answered, "Do you mean to reign over us? Do you mean

> to rule over us?" And they hated him even more for his talk about his dreams. He dreamed another dream and told it to his brothers, saying, "Look, I have had another dream: And this time, the sun, the moon, and eleven stars were bowing down to me." And when he told it to his father and brothers, his father berated him. "What," he said to him, "Is this dream you have dreamed? Are we to come, I and your mother and your brothers, and bow low to you to the ground? So his brothers were jealous of him, but his father kept the matter in mind. One time, when his brothers had gone to pasture their father's flock at Shechem, Israel said to Joseph, "Your brothers are pasturing at Shechem. Come, I will send you to them." He answered, "I am ready." And he said to him, "Go and see how your brothers are and how the flocks are faring and bring me back word." So he sent him from the valley of Hebron, and he arrived at Shechem. (Genesis 37:1–14)

Intergenerational Failure

Harvard Business School has invested vast resources in studying family businesses, their internal dynamics, and the parameters that influence their short-term and long-term success. In a 2012 article, George Stalk, a partner at the Boston Consulting Group, identified three central factors underlying the findings that only 30 percent of family businesses are successful in the second generation:

1. **Family-owned firms allow *all* family members to work in the business, not only those actually qualified to manage, develop the business, and foresee changes and opportunities.**

2. **The family has grown more quickly than the business, and the business is not able to support all the family members who need it for their livelihood.**
3. **Members of the extended family differentiate themselves according to bloodline—that is, by closeness of relation—so votes and feedback do not reflect pure business interests and decisions are not made on the basis of purely economic factors.**

These three factors can all be clearly seen in the verses above.

After leaving Shechem following the rape of Dinah, the killing of its inhabitants by Simeon and Levi, and the plundering of the city, Jacob was forced to travel south towards the hilly country of Hebron and the upper Negev, where his father lived. Jacob settled in a region less suitable for shepherding,[3] but continued to rely on his livestock (after paying for the field in Shechem with one hundred animals). Jacob's sons, who had grown up in the meantime, helped the family to make ends meet and began to take over their father's business. The Torah's account divides the family into three distinct groups: "At seventeen years of age, Joseph tended the flocks with his brothers, as a helper to the sons of his father's wives Bilhah and Zilpah. And Joseph brought bad reports of them to their father." On the basis of bloodline and genetics, Joseph, his brothers, and the sons of Bilhah and Zilpah represent three distinct subgroups in the family.

The description of Joseph as one who "tended the flocks alongside his brothers" (*haya ro'eh et eḥav ba-tzon*)[4] fits the situation perfectly; he criticized his brothers, so he was *ro'eh et* (shepherded *alongside*) and not *ro'eh im* (shepherded *with*). That is, Joseph, the son of Rachel, tended the flocks and fulfilled his responsibilities as his brothers did but was not truly "with" them.[5]

In this verse, the brothers themselves are subdivided into two groups—the sons of the maidservants and "the brothers," namely the sons of Leah. Naturally, the status of the sons of Leah was stronger, given that there were six of them, as opposed to Joseph, who stood alone, and the four sons of the maidservants, who were of inferior status.

Joseph and the sons of the maidservants naturally joined forces to oppose the sons of Leah: Joseph viewed the sons of the maidservants as equals, and they backed him up so he did not need to stand alone, vastly outnumbered. It seems that the scales were tipped in favor of Leah's sons, but Jacob, patriarch and owner of the business, balanced the scales in favor of Joseph and the sons of the maidservants when he expressed unreserved support for Joseph: "Now Israel loved Joseph best of all his sons, for he was the child of his old age; and he had made him a fine woolen tunic. And when his brothers saw that their father loved him more than any of his brothers, they hated him so that they could not speak a friendly word to him."

Many commentators explain that Jacob's preference for Joseph caused the tension between the brothers. This favoritism may have derived from the fact that Joseph was the only son of Jacob's beloved wife, Rachel, or it may have been because Jacob identified Joseph's economic analytical abilities and viewed him as a worthy successor, who would do the best job developing the business further.

As we have noted, however, this preference was designed to balance the power among the subgroups and give Joseph and the maidservants' sons positions of responsibility within the family business, which would thereby benefit from their skills and wisdom and temper the criticism. The problem was that due to the intensification of the dispute between the subgroups, Joseph could no longer continue in his role in the family business. He stayed back with Jacob while the brothers decided to take their sheep to graze in the Shechem region.

Relocating to distant Shechem, a region where the family had previously experienced shepherding success, indicates that the family business was not as successful in the next generation. Initially, the brothers had tried to develop their herds in Hebron. But either the unsuitability of the area, the adoption of a less effective management style, or a combination of the two, combined with the family's growth, generated pressure to seek greener pastures back in Shechem.

In light of Simeon and Levi's actions there and the danger that the local population would try to exact revenge on Jacob's family, the choice of Shechem demonstrates the degree of pressure felt by the brothers. However, they apparently sensed that they had no choice, so they went to Shechem with their father's flocks to revive a floundering family business. This failure was reported by Joseph to his father: "And Joseph brought bad reports of them to their father."

Later in the story, Judah suggested to his brothers:

> "What do we gain [monetarily, from the word *betza*] by killing our brother and covering up his blood? Come, let us sell him to the Ishmaelites, and let us not do away with him ourselves. After all, he is our brother, our own flesh." His brothers agreed. When Midianite traders passed by, they pulled Joseph up out of the pit. They sold Joseph for twenty pieces of silver to the Ishmaelites.... (37:26–28)

The prospect of turning a profit on Joseph's disappearance proves that the brothers were preoccupied with capitalizing on any and every possible financial resource.

A Dream Interpreted

In the midst of these struggles within the family, the verses tell the story of Joseph's dreams. Analyzing them and their placement in the narrative demonstrates that Joseph had a completely different solution—not only for his dreams but for the explosive family dynamic.

As noted, Joseph worked as a shepherd like his brothers, but not "with" them. The maidservants' sons were not equal partners in the family business, so Joseph aligned with them to cultivate a coalition of "outsiders." Slowly but surely, he too became an outsider. Meanwhile he watched as the family business hit on hard times and understood that something needed to change.

The "bad reports" Joseph brought to Jacob involve the disagreement between Joseph and his brothers regarding the shepherding business. The maidservants' sons were disillusioned because they had been pushed out of the family business, and Joseph, who had begun to understand that Leah's sons were not running the business effectively, listened attentively to their critique.

The verse notes that Joseph served "as a helper to the sons of his father's wives Bilhah and Zilpah." The fact that Bilhah and Zilpah were referred to as "his father's wives" is instructive. In truth, Leah's sons were mistaken in relating to the children of Bilhah and Zilpah, as the sons of concubines or maidservants. Consequently, this led to friction. If the brothers had accepted the maidservants' sons as equals and given up their need for control based on bloodline, perhaps Joseph's harsh criticism would never have surfaced.

Also reverberating in the background was the unresolved debate about Simeon and Levi's actions in Shechem. Due to this, the family had to flee the region and thus could not enjoy the fruit of their significant investment in the parcel of land Jacob had purchased. Every step of the way, doubts arose about the managerial abilities of Leah's sons.[6] Beneath the surface, gnawing uncertainty about their flawed decision-making and questionable leadership mounted.

Joseph was in a difficult position. Though he had received his father's recognition, he was forced to watch from a distance the mismanagement of the business and its inability to support the growing family. He dreamed of a rosier future. Rabbi Joseph B. Soloveitchik has explained that while the brothers were conservative, Joseph was an innovative and forward-thinking entrepreneur, able to anticipate future trends and make the necessary changes. Joseph wanted to induce strategic change and leverage it by redirecting the family's business interests from shepherding to agriculture.[7]

In Joseph's dream, the brothers were not struggling herdsmen but successful farmers: "There we were binding sheaves in the field."[8] Moreover, all of the sons worked in the family business, not just the sons of Leah, who were older and comprised a majority.

The dream does not discuss planting or harvesting but focuses on the stage in which the wheat was being cut and bound, which is to say, prepared for distribution.[9] Joseph's dream was to switch the family business into an agricultural empire, and he apparently believed that a more organized approach to production and distribution would build the family's fortune.[10] Moreover, as Rabbi Soloveitchik and others have noted, Joseph saw that a shift towards agriculture, which is far more scalable than shepherding ,[11] was imperative given the demographic changes the family would undergo. And then: "... suddenly my sheaf stood up and remained upright; then your sheaves gathered around and bowed low to my sheaf."

In contrast to shepherding, which is nonhierarchical by its very nature, distribution chains and logistical networks demand hierarchy. The automatic outcome of transitioning to an agricultural distribution business model is that there must be one person who stands at the top. For the business to succeed, the brothers needed to recognize this and so the other sheaves bow down to Joseph's. It is the sheaves that bow, and not the brothers themselves, because the relevant factor is a structural economic change, not control or monarchy.

When Abraham purchased the cave of Machpelah, he bowed to the Hittites during the negotiation to show both acceptance of their position and gratitude that they had affirmed his request. In light of this, we can suggest that the bowing of the sheaves is an expression of the brothers' agreement to Joseph's proposed business model, not their acceptance of his assumption of power.[12] However, as the verses state, the brothers did not understand Joseph's dreams in this way.

Leah's sons instead felt threatened by Joseph's dreams. They felt that Joseph's vision jeopardized the family business as well as their status within the family. As shepherds, they were continuing the family tradition and the business interests cultivated by their father, three decades earlier. If they pursued a different line of business, the family hierarchy and natural continuity would simply collapse.

Leah's sons hated Joseph on account of his dreams, which suggested that he would lead by controlling the family's finances. They also hated him on account of "his words"—i.e., his entrepreneurial demand for economic change. In fact, the brothers' interpretation cost Joseph the trust of the maidservants' sons, his former allies. They felt that Joseph was just another "royal son" who wanted to assume control, notwithstanding his understanding of their potential to be equal partners in the new family enterprise.

Calculated Risk

Joseph dreamt another dream. According to Rabbi Soloveitchik, the heavenly bodies that appear in this second dream symbolize Joseph's understanding that it was necessary to use new knowledge and new tools, the cosmos and technology, to contend with the challenges that would confront them in a foreign land and in changing times.[13]

The verses describe how Joseph told his second dream twice. First, he told it to the brothers alone, and they did not react. Eventually, he told the dream to his father and brothers together, and his father reproached him:

> He dreamt another dream and told it to his brothers, saying, "Look, I have had another dream: And this time, the sun, the moon, and eleven stars were bowing down to me." And when he told it to his father and brothers, his father berated him. "What," he said to him, "is this dream you have dreamed? Are we to come, I and your mother and your brothers, and bow low to you to the ground? So his brothers were wrought up at him [were jealous of him], and his father kept the matter in mind. (37:9–11)

The brothers had already responded to the first dream, and since, from their perspective, there was nothing new here, they presumably did not need to respond to this one. Nevertheless, this interpretation does not explain why Joseph, who had not shared the first dream with his father, chose to share the second dream with him.

It seems that the two dreams and their interpretations differ from one another. The sun, moon, and stars symbolize the seasons (this does not coincide with how Jacob understood the dream, as will be explained). The sun is the solar calendar of years, the moon is the lunar calendar of months, and the stars reflect day and night. In other words, the dream was meant to express control over the natural processes of the calendar.

Agriculture is extremely susceptible to the seasons and the elements, so when Joseph suggested a transition to agriculture, the family rejected it, claiming that the risk was too great. Joseph shared his first dream in an attempt to persuade the others of the high potential yields, but as noted, the brothers misinterpreted the dream as an expression of his ambition to seize control. Through the second dream, Joseph explained to his brothers that his familiarity with different agricultural methods, and perhaps his technological proficiency, would enable him to devise an agricultural enterprise that would not be contingent on forces of nature and the seasons. Joseph apparently believed that he could provide sheaves of wheat, even when wheat was out of season (41:56).

In the first dream, the brothers' sheaves bowed to Joseph's sheaf and not to Joseph himself. This act expressed the structural and economic change the family business would undergo since a company that markets and distributes products needs a centralized chain of command. In the second dream, the novel concept of harvesting grain in all seasons of the year was Joseph's revolutionary idea, and the heavenly bodies bowed to him accordingly.

Ultimately, the dream would be realized on a far grander scale than Joseph ever anticipated; during the years of famine, when he guided and guarded the storehouses of food for all Egypt, he overcame the worst string of multiyear famines the region had ever endured.[14]

Joseph's vision was an economic and technological breakthrough. The brothers, though, attached to an older economic model and bogged down in the daily travails of shepherding, were stuck in the past. They could not understand what Joseph was talking about, so they did not react.

Since the brothers neither understood nor responded to him, Joseph sought his father's attentive ear. He repeated the dream to Jacob, attempting to win Jacob's approval for his business proposal. Unlike the brothers, Jacob understood the potential, for he himself had "genetically engineered" the flock's young in the house of Laban after he dreamed about it (30:37–42; 31:10–12). Early in the story, when Jacob heard from Joseph that the family business was in a state of decline, he understood that Joseph was endowed with a keen business sense and showed his support for him by giving him a special tunic. At this point, too, the scene concludes with the statement: "but his father kept the matter in mind."

Nevertheless, Jacob did not want to deepen the rift in the family. He redirected the conversation in favor of family harmony: "Are we to come, I and your mother and your brothers, and bow low to you to the ground?" Despite Joseph's troubling discoveries, Jacob put his full weight behind protecting the existing hierarchy within the family. He scolded Joseph out of genuine concern for the family dynamic, but he understood the economic implications of Joseph's innovative vision.

Earlier in the story, the verses tell us several times that the brothers hated Joseph, but only after the second dream and

Jacob's rebuke of Joseph does the Torah say they envied him. Even after Jacob made him a fine tunic, the Torah speaks of hate, not envy. One would expect the second dream to intensify their hatred, and at first glance, there seems to be no reason for Jacob's intervention on their behalf—and at Joseph's expense—to arouse their jealousy.

Jim Grote, himself a leader of a multigenerational family food processing business, suggested a psychological approach to family business succession and inclusion of family members that avers that most people seek role models to aspire to in the family business. Incompatibility between the role model and those who model themselves after them causes envy. That is, envy is produced when an individual or a group wants to model itself upon someone else. This, of course, happens in many family businesses.[15]

The first dream made the brothers hate Joseph because agriculture was alien to them. They hated him for trying to change the focus of the family business and for dreaming of standing at the top of the pyramid. Despite their precarious position in the livestock sector in Hebron, they did not know—and did not want to learn—how to farm. Joseph's critique struck them in their most sensitive and vulnerable place, fanning the flames of hatred.

However, when Joseph told the brothers the second dream, they interpreted it as relating to overcoming the obstacles that nature and the seasons pose to farmers. Deep down, the brothers knew that Joseph had an entrepreneurial spirit and the ability to foresee things. But like many people failing in business, it was difficult to admit that someone else knew better. Their desire to be like him and mimic his abilities therefore produced envy—envy of his confidence, his ability to confront and deal with challenges, reinvent himself and innovate, and be enterprising and disruptive.

The brothers' solution was to go to Shechem—a region that was familiar to them and was suitable for cattle. Their father understood that no good was happening in the business and was concerned about his children's journey to Shechem. Jacob feared the revenge of the locals. He and his family had fled in the aftermath of Simeon and Levi's massacre of the people of Shechem. At the same time, he wanted an eyewitness report. Was the journey worth the effort and the risk? When it came to the family business, Jacob trusted Joseph about everything. After all, Joseph was the one who had first made him aware of its decline. Jacob therefore sent Joseph to see if the situation had improved in line with the brothers' expectations.

> His brothers had gone to pasture their father's flock at Shechem, Israel said to Joseph, "Your brothers are pasturing at Shechem. Come, I will send you to them." He answered, "I am ready." And he said to him, "Go and see how your brothers are and how the flocks are faring, and bring me back word." So he sent him from the valley of Hebron. When he reached Shechem, a man came upon him wandering in the fields. The man asked him, "What are you looking for?" He answered, "I am looking for my brothers. Could you tell me where they are pasturing?" The man said, "They have gone from here, for I heard them say: Let us go to Dothan." So Joseph followed his brothers and found them at Dothan. (37:12–17)

Joseph is not described as wandering on the road but in a field. We can assume that Joseph expected to find his brothers in Shechem, as Jacob had told him they were there. If so, it is quite likely that they would make camp in the field that the family owned, which Jacob had purchased for the sum of one hundred *kesitah*. This field would have comprised an excellent basis for the agricultural enterprise that Joseph dreamed of developing, and he no doubt wanted to determine if it was suitable for this purpose. From a broader perspective, when Jacob asked Joseph to go to Shechem, Joseph accepted because he wanted to teach his methods and ideas to his brothers. For his father's sake, he wanted to save the family business, and perhaps for his brothers' sake as well.[16]

Without an objective or judicious mediator like his father, this was a lost cause. Grote explains that the ability to temper jealousy and improve relationships is largely dependent on bringing in a third party (preferably someone independent). As such, Jacob was able to keep the tension from bubbling over—for a while. But when Joseph faced his brothers alone, any chance of mending the rift disappeared.

The Face of the Future

Someone who can anticipate changes and economic shifts like Joseph has the upper hand in business. If you can accelerate the shifts like Bill Gates, then it can be transformational. This same phenomenon is as true for families and states as it is for individuals. Fiscal conservatism bolsters feelings of attachment to what is known and familiar, whereas Joseph's success in Egypt demonstrates that one must not remain entrenched in it. Particularly in changing times and conditions of uncertainty, those who create or anticipate technological or economic changes will have outsized impact on our future and on their families.

Entrepreneurial ventures include many unknowns. Some will fail miserably, and one must not close one's eyes to the risk. Yet any long-term enterprise must be open to innovation.

It must stride into the unknown. Determined investment in the future actually ameliorates risk and increases prosperity.

Joseph, who was charged with planning and managing the Egyptian economy, had the brilliant idea of changing the economic structure in order to overcome the impending famine and other possible future crises. As in other situations, a technological invention that supported the entire economic maneuver made this shift possible.

As we will see, Pharaoh's enthusiasm for Joseph's plan was rooted in the fact that it would not only save Egypt from the crisis, but it would also leverage it, turning the country into a regional power.

10
Parashat Miketz

CITY MOUSE

The Urban Revolution

PHARAOH'S DREAM—AND JOSEPH'S

Joseph was sold into Egyptian slavery by his brothers, who despised him for his different view of the future and their family business. Upon arrival in Egypt, Joseph served Potiphar, a senior advisor to Pharaoh. However, the anger of Potiphar's spurned wife caused Joseph to be jailed on the false charge of attempting to cavort with her.

In jail, Joseph quickly became the right hand man of the chief jailkeeper, serving all the royal inmates and particularly the senior ones. Joseph was as successful at this task as he had been with Potiphar. Everything Joseph touched was blessed and successful. While in jail, Joseph happened upon the Pharaoh's jailed baker and butler, who looked troubled after a restless night. Each had dreamt a dream that they could not understand. Patiently, Joseph interpreted their dreams, explaining to the butler that he would be returned to his job within three days while on the same day, the baker would be hanged and his flesh devoured by birds.

Joseph implored the butler not to forget him when he was reinstated. And so when Pharaoh was disturbed by a pair of troubling dreams, which none of his magicians could interpret, the royal vintner suggested that Joseph be summoned.

Joseph was hurried from his jail cell, cleaned up and brought before Pharaoh.

> Then Pharaoh said to Joseph, "In my dream, I stand on the bank of the Nile, when out of the Nile came up seven sturdy and well-formed cows and grazed in the reed grass. Presently there followed them seven other cows, scrawny, ill-formed, and emaciated—never had I seen their likes for ugliness in all the land of Egypt! And the seven lean and ugly cows ate up the first seven cows, the sturdy ones; but when they had consumed them, one could not tell that they had consumed them, for they looked just as bad as before. And I awoke. In my other dream, I saw seven ears of grain, full and healthy, growing on a single stalk; but right behind them sprouted seven ears, shriveled, thin, and scorched by the east wind. And the thin ears swallowed the seven healthy ears. I have told my magicians, but none has an explanation for me."
>
> And Joseph said to Pharaoh, "Pharaoh's dreams are one and the same: God has told Pharaoh what He is about to do. The seven healthy cows are seven years, and the seven healthy ears are seven years; it is the same dream. The seven lean and ugly cows that followed are seven years, as are also the seven empty ears scorched by the

east wind; they are seven years of famine. It is just as I have told Pharaoh: God has revealed to Pharaoh what He is about to do. Immediately ahead are seven years of great abundance in all the land of Egypt. After them will come seven years of famine, and all the abundance in the land of Egypt will be forgotten. As the land is ravaged by famine, no trace of the abundance will be left in the land because of the famine thereafter, for it will be very severe. As for Pharaoh having had the same dream twice, it means that the matter has been determined by God, and that God will soon carry it out.

Accordingly, let Pharaoh find a man of discernment and wisdom, and set him over the land of Egypt. And let Pharaoh take steps to appoint overseers over the land and organize the land of Egypt in the seven years of plenty. Let all the food of these good years that are coming be gathered, and let the grain be collected under Pharaoh's authority as food to be stored in the cities. Let that food be a reserve for the land for the seven years of famine which will come upon the land of Egypt, so that the land may not perish in the famine." (41:17–36)

Joseph's plan contained several key points:

1. **Appoint a wise man to supervise the economy.**
2. **Gather and store food[17] during the years of abundance in order to organize the land of Egypt. The word for "organize" *(ḥimesh)* has many different explanations[18]. The analysis presented here follows the interpretation of Rashi, who explains that *ḥimesh* refers to the reinforcement of Egypt's military might, relying on its strong economy, to improve its ability to vanquish enemies.**

3. **Store food reserves in cities under government supervision.**
4. **Retain the food as a "deposit" *(pikadon)* for the upcoming years of famine. A "deposit" is something that one keeps on behalf of another individual. It is not something used, traded, or consumed.[19] Below, we will consider the nature of this "deposit" and show how Joseph was able to profit from it, thereby building the Egyptian economy and transforming an impending crisis into an asset.**

Joseph succeeded where the magicians failed because he had a "contingency plan." He who had anticipated impending transformation while still in his father's home now understood that the time had arrived to realize his vision. In fact, he now accomplished the economic shift that he had devised in Canaan years earlier on behalf of Pharaoh and the entire Egyptian economy. Thus, though the brothers assumed that they had thwarted Joseph's plans by selling him into slavery, Egypt was where he was able to realize his dreams on a regional scale.

Joseph's personal dreams made all the difference. In his dreams, Joseph saw a strong executive at the top of the organizational pyramid, overseeing the collection, storage, and distribution (or sale) of produce with perfect synchronization. He accordingly determined that the first step in establishing this system was appointing such a manager.

Still, it was necessary to bridge the gap between Pharaoh's dream and Joseph's. Pharaoh's dream dealt with stalks of grain, symbolizing a time of famine, when people snatch and eat the meager food reserves. Yet Joseph dreamt of collecting heaps of wheat (*alumot*)—massive amounts of grain that were gathered together. Joseph bridged this gap by invoking his second dream, the sun and the moon bowing to him, which symbolized the harnessing of nature and technology to overcome the normal seasonal pattern. Under regular climatic conditions, grain can only be preserved for one agricultural cycle. Given that the impending famine would last for seven years, Joseph needed to develop new methods for long-term storage.

Joseph meditated upon his dreams to both devise the new methods and to construct a new, urban economic-technological plan. He remembered all too well that his father had an alternate interpretation of the dream that featured the sun and the moon bowing to Joseph: "Are we to come, I and your mother and your brothers, and bow low to you to the ground?" Jacob indicated that Joseph's dream was absurd since Rachel was no longer alive.[20]

While in jail, Joseph averred that he had been stolen from the land of the Hebrews and incarcerated for no apparent reason. Therefore, he likely had time to ruminate on his own dreams and perhaps how they diverged from what his father understood. Jacob's interpretation gnawed at Joseph for years. Now, as he stood before Pharaoh, he finally understood what his father had hinted at long ago.[21]

Joseph's dead mother, who lived in his dreams (and especially in Joseph's and Jacob's longing for her), alludes to the mummification technology at which Pharaoh and his magicians excelled. The process of mummification, designed to protect a corpse from microbial decay and preserve it for thousands of years, could be adapted and applied to agriculture. This innovative technology, well-developed and preserved in the inner chambers of the Egyptian central authorities, had the potential to change the economic structure of Egypt and preserve the regime. Long-term storage possibilities enabled a new model of storage and distribution, independent of market prices or current demand.

Alternatively, the possibility of maintaining emergency grain stores was perhaps not based on new technology in the field of chemistry but rather on the physical construction of the food storage structures. Joseph proposed collecting all of the food from the years of abundance and added "food to be stored in the cities" as a separate element of his plan. The household pantry and the regular storage facilities used in the fields and villages along the Nile were not suitable.[22] However, large structures built in the cities that were hermetically sealed and insulated against cold, heat, and damp could do the trick. Local distribution centers meant that less grain would be lost in transport, and it would be easier to enact more exact rationing for local populations. Establishing such facilities required the intervention of the central government in planning and constructing this infrastructure. It also involved enlisting the populace to build the right defenses for these facilities in the form of fortified cities.

THE KEY TO THE CITY

The first two aspects of Joseph's plan adequately provided for the impending catastrophe on a technological and organizational level. After all, the central government would be meticulously supervising this large national project. And yet, many concerns had yet to be allayed. The fact that the gaunt cows in Pharaoh's dream swallowed the healthy, full bodied cows, coupled with the fact that the cows remain gaunt—"but when they had consumed them, one could not tell that they had consumed them, for they looked just as bad as before"—left Pharaoh fearful that he had received an unambiguously apocalyptic message that no technical breakthrough could solve.

Indeed, Joseph emphasized the obvious point: the devastation of the famine would overwhelm the surplus of the years of abundance. Joseph interpreted the dream using four unambiguous expressions of impending devastation:

> Immediately ahead are seven years of great abundance in all the land of Egypt. After them will come seven years of famine, and all the abundance in the land of Egypt will be forgotten. As the land is ravaged by famine, no trace of the abundance will be left in the land because of the famine thereafter, for it will be very severe.[23]

Despite the frightful bottom line, two subtle nuances in the dream leave a sliver of hope. The opening scene found Pharaoh standing on the riverbank. Later, when Pharaoh recounted his dream to Joseph, he began by noting, in present tense, "In my dream, I stand on the bank of the Nile." In other words, according to his own dream, Pharaoh himself did not die of hunger. Nor did the starving nation rise up and overthrow him.

Furthermore, without a plan to begin storing grain from the very next crop, Egypt would have succumbed to famine in far less than seven years. The deprivation would have been noticed within a few months and would have become a full-fledged catastrophe soon after that. Even with the national effort to store food, after just a few years, the people said to Joseph: "Let us not perish before your eyes!" (Genesis 47:19). The repetition of the seven years of hardship showed that there was a way to survive the years of famine, even if the full output of the years of abundance was inadequate to meet the shortages.

Yet Pharaoh and the magicians did not know how to overcome the famine and defeat the prophetic vision. Joseph's answer was structural change, as reflected in the third and fourth elements of his plan: "food to be stored in the cities" and "let that food be a reserve for the land."

Joseph proposed a complete overhaul of the Egyptian economy. The produce would be collected in specialized cities, not only on account of the size of the storage facilities, the nature of these facilities, or the supervision they afforded. Inventing long-term food storage gave Joseph the chance to change the Egyptian way of life, their community structure, and even their professional pursuits: "And he removed the population town by town, from one end of Egypt's border to the other" (47:21).

In a different context, author Matt Ridley discusses the impact of agricultural technology on urbanization in his book *The Rational Optimist*:

> A modern combine harvester, driven by a single man, can reap enough wheat in a single day to make half a million loaves. Little wonder that as I write these words (around the end of 2008), for the very first time, the majority of the world's population lives in cities—up from just 15 percent in 1900. The mechanization of agriculture has enabled, and been enabled by, a flood of people leaving the land to seek their fortune in the city, all free to make for each other things other than food. Though some came to town with hope and ambition, and some with desperation and fear, almost all were drawn by the same aim: to take part in trade.[24]

New technology makes urbanization possible, generating opportunities for people to work and contribute to areas beyond food production. This leads to population growth and growing markets, which lends strength and stability to the empire. People from all over the country migrate to the city to conduct business with its residents.[25]

Like that of the combine which made farming less people-intensive, the invention of urban food storage—"food to be stored in the cities"—moved the populace into cities and naturally created new opportunities and interests that differed significantly from those of rural villages.[26] If the food was in the cities, then representatives of other countries would also come to the cities when they came to Egypt to purchase food: "So all the world came to Joseph in Egypt to procure rations, for the famine had become severe throughout the land" (41:57).[27]

That is how Joseph transformed Egypt's cities into international centers of commerce. The idea was that if people come from all over the world to purchase food, it would create new market interactions, activities that go well beyond the purchasing of food from government outlets. Joseph told his brothers that they could only partake in Egypt's bustling markets if they proved that they were not spies: "And bring your youngest brother to me, that I may know that you are not spies but honest men. I will then restore your brother to you, and you shall be free to move about in the land" (42:34).[28] The implication here is that most people who came to Egypt did not limit themselves to quick trips to buy food. Rather, there was a significant expansion of commercial activity and perhaps industry, as well.

Industry and trade develop in cities that concentrate different forms of expertise and a variety of skills. As the Talmud states, "Go and sustain one another."[29] With time, these cities became centers of technology, knowledge, and culture, thus generating added value to the scope of products offered and the efficiency of their production. This productivity was shared by its producers: the government, which provided the infrastructure, and the general populace, who benefitted from growth and efficiency.

"Old" Egypt, which was based on a decentralized agricultural system, could not produce enough food during the seven years of abundance in order to sustain the population through the seven years of famine. "New" Egypt, which was far more efficient and advanced and had several different sources of revenue, could survive the crisis.

Commerce is less volatile and has more economic (and political) value than agricultural production. I was once invited to participate in a discussion in the presence of the Israeli Finance Minister about the future of the economy and the high-tech industry. A representative of the Manufacturer's Association got up and shouted that hi-tech (software) is destroying Israel's competitive edge in production. He argued that the government needs to invest in manufacturing as it invested in Motorola, Intel, and others. That same day, the smartphone giant Apple had announced excellent annual results. I quickly pulled up the results and told the man that while Apple manufactures all of its phones in China, all of its earnings accrue in the United States because the services and the software are all "made there."

This is as true politically and economically as it is in the business world. The fact that Apple's headquarters are based in California brings a lot of business and political connections to California and the United States in general. In its broadest sense, then, macroeconomics sees value not only in production but also in distribution and trade. The bottom line is that the location of company headquarters is most important; that is where the profits accrue, and that is where everyone looks to or comes through. Ultimately, that is also what can bring manufacturing back. A company's headquarters, where management resides and convenes, meets with customers and partners, will also drive where new initiatives can take root.

Joseph understood that the impending famine in Egypt would not be a one-time occurrence.[30] In order to diversify[31] the Egyptian economy, he turned to a technology-based system of trade and distribution, just as he had predicted as a seventeen year old in the faraway land of Canaan.

THE FARMER'S SAVINGS BANK

After interpreting Pharaoh's dreams, Joseph speedily leapt into action to set up the infrastructure that would be needed for the coming years of plenty—and the famine that would follow.

> Joseph was thirty years old when he entered the service of Pharaoh king of Egypt. Leaving Pharaoh's presence, Joseph traveled through all the land of Egypt. During the seven years of plenty, the land produced in abundance.[32] And he gathered all the grain of the seven years that the land of Egypt was enjoying, and stored the grain in the cities; he put in each city the grain of the fields around it. So Joseph collected produce in very large quantity, like the sands of the sea, until he ceased to measure it, for it could not be measured. (41:46–49)

It is unclear in what sense the produce "could not be measured."[33] Was it difficult to record? Did they run out of numbers? It is inconceivable that someone planning absolute control to prevent anarchy during a time of shortage would permit himself such carelessness, which could in turn create theft, smuggling, and the rise of a black market. It therefore seems that the straightforward meaning of the verses is that Joseph planned, seven years in advance, the quantity of food that would be needed by the Egyptian populace and perhaps the entire region.[34] Once that quota was filled, he locked the emergency storage facilities. Anything else was surplus and could be stored in regular warehouses and under typical conditions. It is apparently this surplus, which was not under tight government supervision, that he "ceased to measure." It had been leftover once the quotas had been met.

As stated, while traveling in his chariot through land of Egypt, Joseph, with a royal golden chain around his neck, conducted a publicity campaign on behalf of the national emergency food bank in the cities. The message percolated into public consciousness, and Egypt's citizens mobilized themselves on behalf of the project. Thus, in addition to the efforts of the central government, the masses also began saving for a (non) rainy day. The next verses show that this program also had two parts:

> The seven years of abundance that the land of Egypt enjoyed came to an end, and the seven years of famine set in, just as Joseph had foretold. There was famine in all lands, but throughout the land of Egypt there was bread.
>
> And when all the land of Egypt felt the hunger, the people cried out to Pharaoh for bread; and Pharaoh said to all the Egyptians, "Go to Joseph; whatever he tells you, you shall do." Accordingly, when the famine became severe in the land of Egypt, Joseph laid open all that was within, and dispensed grain to the Egyptians. The famine, however, spread over the whole world.
>
> So all the world came to Joseph in Egypt to procure rations, for the famine had become severe throughout the world. (41:53–57)

During the first phase, even though the seven lean years had already begun, all the lands experienced famine except for Egypt. Since word of the impending famine was well-publicized (in order to build the cities and storage facilities), the Egyptian public organized itself and kept food reserves in their private homes and pantries.

In the second stage, their private food stashes were depleted, and the public protests began. It was at this point that Joseph opened the surplus warehouses, where food was stored under standard conditions. The verse therefore states: "Joseph laid open all that was within." This does not refer to the food in the special government warehouses. The first food to reach the market at the beginning of the famine was the surplus produce that was stored in the standard facilities—namely, the produce that exceeded Joseph's careful calculations for food allowances. By immediately flooding the markets with food, Joseph earned the public's trust—the government had prepared a "tool kit" for dealing with the impending crisis, using the means at its disposal to help the people. This is exactly what a "deposit" is meant to be.

It is not clear whether he sold the surplus produce that he had collected or dispensed it for free.[35] On one hand, during the later years of the famine, the verses state explicitly that the people paid for the food, suggesting that at the early stages, the surplus that had made its way into the short-term storage facilities was distributed for free. On the other hand, Joseph dispensed food to people who came to Egypt from elsewhere as well, and it does not make sense that he would have given it away. Moreover, when Joseph's brothers came from the land of Canaan, they brought money to purchase food.

The commentators disagree regarding Joseph's methods for stockpiling grain and using it later. Medieval Jewish philosopher and scholar Rabbi Don Isaac Abarbanel, who served as Portugal's finance minister in the latter half of the fifteenth century, explained that Joseph worked with market forces and "bought on the cheap." Abarbanel's explanation evokes the well-known mantra of legendary investor Warren Buffet: "Be fearful when others are greedy, and only be greedy when others are fearful." In contrast, Ramban implies that Joseph expropriated a share of the produce.

In his book *Ki Karov Elekha*, modern bible scholar Rabbi Yaakov Medan, suggests that Joseph did not exploit the nation's crisis or naivete to enrich himself or Pharaoh. Rather, Joseph was concerned that wealthy people and early adopters would exploit the crisis to enrich themselves at the expense of the poorer and less savvy. Joseph was, in effect, the first communist to work with market forces—stockpiling on behalf of the government during years of plenty when there was abundant supply and thus low prices. When the famine came, he divided the supplies equally among all of Egypt's citizens and kept prices low. Rabbi Medan notes that this is quite similar to the system of the manna[36] during the Jews' forty-year sojourn in the desert: one *omer* per capita per day.

Either way, Joseph gained the trust and dependence of Egypt and the surrounding lands. He used the grain deposits not only to distribute and monetize the food reserves but to forge alliances with peoples in the region and to gain loyalties, both within Egypt and abroad.[37] This was part of Joseph's plan to "organize the land of Egypt" ahead of the famine. Rather than invasions and political instability, the famine brought peace and security. That there was plenty of food in storage facilities, ready for use at a moment's notice, generated confidence in the commercial basis of Egypt's cities and built strong external relations. Since "all the world" came to Egypt to procure food, everyone benefited from the new urban centers and organized supply chains, and no one had any interest in initiating war.[38] Additionally, a state that stands at the center of regional commerce has separate relations with each neighboring country. Thus, any country considering an invasion would have also risked a response from Egypt's allies.

Since everyone knew that the warehouses were full of reserves that could last a long time, there was no panic or hysteria in the market that Joseph created. As the famine continued and the markets slowed down, he reinvigorated them by releasing goods or "deposits" in a calculated and precise manner, so that it could continue to function and keep prices reasonable.

THE PERSONAL STORY

Joseph's plan and its implementation sets the stage for the family drama that unfolded when his brothers traveled to Egypt to purchase food—the major plot development that culminates in the descent of the Israelites to Egypt.

In year two of the famine, Jacob sent his sons—excluding the youngest, Benjamin—from the land of Canaan to Egypt to procure food. On their first foray, they come back with food but also sans one brother, Simeon. Joseph recognized his brothers, but they did not recognize him. He treated them like intruders, jailed Simeon, and demanded that they retrieve his full-blooded brother, Benjamin.

When the brothers returned a second time with Benjamin and gifts from the land, they again bowed down to Joseph or the person they recognized as the ruler of Egypt's storehouses. Joseph now schemed to keep Benjamin with him, putting his royal silver goblet in Benjamin's sack and then arresting him for stealing. As his elder brother Judah strode forth to take responsibility for Benjamin, he told Joseph their family history, which included the "disappearance" of Joseph two decades earlier and the distress their father felt over the risk to Benjamin's life. At this, Joseph broke down and revealed his true identity to his stunned brothers. The brothers returned to Canaan with the carriages that Joseph sent for his father and family, and this, in turn, brought the children of Israel down to Egypt for what would turn into a multi-century sojourn, culminating in servitude and an eventual exodus.

But when the brothers arrived in Egypt among the teeming throngs of travelers and traders gathering to do business in the Egyptian capital—"Thus the sons of Israel were among those who came to procure rations" (42:5)[39]—they journeyed straight into Joseph's dreamscape. They traveled through cities bustling with merchants and busy marketplaces, and they were summoned to meet the finance minister, Joseph, the dispenser in chief, who stood at the head of the chain of command of the new economy. They encountered the hierarchy, the heaps of wheat that have been well-preserved, as well as things that were different and strange. They traveled along the same route taken by the Ishmaelites twenty years earlier, leaving behind their sheep and nomadic existence in the land of Canaan so they could purchase grain.

The peak fulfillment of Joseph's dreams was not only when the brothers bowed to him, but in their need to engage in commerce with him (even adding the nuts and almonds that were still available in Canaan) in order to obtain the "sheaves" that were being distributed in Egypt. Joseph's objective was to get them to adapt to commercial life—the new economy giving stability to a nation on its land.

The transition to the new commercial economy would raise the Israelites' standard of living and bring them new alliances.[40] But structural change like this comes at a price. Like learning a new profession, it generates frustration among those who cannot adapt, necessitates the allocation of resources to manage trade policies, and even raises concerns about assimilation.[41] But Joseph insisted that the benefits far outweighed the costs.[42]

Centuries later, when the Israelites left Egypt, the verse states: "And Moses took with him the bones of Joseph, who had exacted an oath from the children of Israel, saying, 'God will be sure to take notice of you: then you shall carry up my bones from here with you'" (Exodus 13:19). Joseph's last will, in which he asked to be buried in the land of Israel, can be seen as a religious instruction. However, his request also symbolizes his aspiration that the Israelites would learn to apply his economic doctrine in their own land.[43]

11
Parashat Vayigash

A WARNING SIGN

Over-Centralization and Economic Decline

THE COMPLEXITY AND FRAGILITY OF METICULOUSLY PLANNED ECONOMIES

The final verses of Parashat Vayigash give us a glimpse into life in Egypt during the years of famine and how Joseph operated during this period. These long-winded verses, seemingly out of place in the Torah, serve both as an introduction to Egyptian slavery—the theme that opens the book of Exodus—and a detailed cautionary tale about the complexity of economic systems and the negative impact of too much government intervention.

The Torah painstakingly details all the stages of the famine and the corresponding interventions. Over time, through liquidity, trade-ins, back-to-work programs, and seed money investments, Joseph's government intervention acquired more control over the economy, slowly atrophying its actors and dampening the freedom and vigor of the Egyptian citizenry and economy.

> So Joseph settled his father and his brothers, and he gave them holdings in the choicest part of the land of Egypt, in the region of Rameses, as Pharaoh had commanded. Joseph sustained his father, and his brothers, and all his father's household with bread, according to the [number of] little ones.
>
> Now there was no bread in all the world, for the famine was very severe; both the land of Egypt and the land of Canaan languished because of the famine. Joseph gathered in all the money that was to be found in the land of Egypt and in the land of Canaan, as payment for the rations that were being procured, and Joseph brought the money into Pharaoh's palace. And when the money gave out in the land of Egypt and in the land of Canaan, all the Egyptians came to Joseph and said, "Give us bread, lest we die before your very eyes; for the money is gone!" And Joseph said, "Bring your livestock, and I will sell to you against your livestock, if the money is gone." So they brought their livestock to Joseph, and Joseph gave them bread in exchange for the horses, for the stocks of sheep and cattle, and the asses; thus he provided them with bread that year in exchange for all their livestock. And when that year was ended, they came to him the next year and said to him, "We cannot hide from my lord that, with all the money and animal stocks consigned to my lord, nothing is left at my lord's disposal save our persons and our farmland. Let us not perish before your eyes, both we and our land. Take us and our land in exchange for bread,

> and we with our land will be serfs to Pharaoh; provide the seed, that we may live and not die, and that the land may not become a waste."
>
> So Joseph gained possession of all the farmland of Egypt for Pharaoh, every Egyptian having sold his field because the famine was too much for them; thus the land passed over to Pharaoh. And he removed the population town by town, from one end of Egypt's border to the other. Only the land of the priests he did not take over, for the priests had an allotment from Pharaoh, and they lived off the allotment which Pharaoh had made to them; therefore, they did not sell their land.
>
> Then Joseph said to the people, "Whereas I have this day acquired you and your land for Pharaoh, here is seed for you to sow the land. And when harvest comes, you shall give one-fifth to Pharaoh, and four-fifths shall be yours as seed for the fields and as food for you and those in your households, and as nourishment for your children." And they said, "You have saved our lives! We are grateful to my lord, and we shall be serfs to Pharaoh." And Joseph made it into a land law in Egypt, which is still valid, that a fifth should be Pharaoh's; only the land of the priests did not become Pharaoh's.
>
> Thus Israel settled in the country of Egypt, in the region of Goshen; they acquired holdings in it and were fertile and increased greatly. (Genesis 47:11–27)

Abarbanel wonders about the length of this description: "Why does the Torah recount this entire story about Egypt, including the law of the fifth [of the land], the transfer of the population to the cities, and the law [exempting] priests? This is appropriate for the chronicles of Egypt, not for God's Torah.[1]"

A careful consideration of the sequence of events sharpens Abarbanel's question.[2] The Torah first describes Joseph's activities in Egypt (Joseph's appearance before Pharaoh, the preparations for the famine, and how Joseph conducted himself vis-à-vis Egypt and other countries at the outset of the famine). It then shifts the focus to the main plot—Joseph's confrontation with his brothers, culminating in the arrival of Jacob and his family in Egypt.

At first glance, this seems like the grand finale to the entire book of Genesis: the closing of a circle that began with the Covenant of the Parts, when God told Abraham that his children would be exiled to a foreign land and return to their land 400 years later. The enslavement of the Israelites in Egypt, which opens the book of Exodus, is a direct continuation of the descent to Egypt at the end of Genesis. It describes the realization of another aspect of the Covenant of the Parts: "They shall be enslaved and oppressed" (15:13).

If the story is really about closing the circle on God's promise to Abraham then the above text is bizarre. It is a non sequitur and seems completely unnecessary. It appears after the narrative has reported that Jacob's children settled in Egypt and received an estate that enabled them to survive. The postscript—"Thus Israel settled in the country of Egypt, in the region of Goshen; they acquired holdings in it and were fertile and increased greatly"—is a natural, direct continuation of the opening description: "So Joseph settled his father and his brothers, giving them holdings in the choicest part of the land of Egypt, in the region of Rameses, as Pharaoh had commanded. Joseph sustained his father, and his brothers, and all his father's household with bread, according to the [number of] little ones."

The question, then, grows stronger: Why does the narrative return to the famine years and describe at length what happened in Egypt at that time? As Abarbanel points out, this section seems to belong in the chronicles of Egypt.

I would like to suggest a different way to analyze the structure of these episodes. The Torah does not begin with the general, geopolitical background of the story and then focus inward on Jacob and his sons. Rather, it weaves together two stories that happened at the same time and inform one another. In fact, on four different occasions, the Torah jumps back and forth between three different story pairs. After Joseph's dreams, the conflict with his brothers, and his sale into slavery, we jump to the Egyptian story, which describes Joseph interpreting the dreams of the chief butler and the chief baker, as well as the dreams of Pharaoh himself. The Egyptian story continues with a discussion of Joseph's activities in the years of abundance and at the outset of the famine. The narrative then returns to the personal story of Joseph and his brothers, which includes them confronting each other and Joseph revealing his identity.

Earlier, we expounded on the close connection between Joseph's dreams and the plan that he outlined to Pharaoh (the first story pair) and the connection between the steps that Joseph took to save Egypt and the brothers' descent to buy food supplies in Egypt (the second). The verses now move to the third story-pair: the continuation of the sons' personal story as they descended to Egypt and settled in their new homestead and the political and economic events that transpired at the same time in Egypt. Finally, the narrative returns to the personal story of Jacob's sons and concludes the book of Genesis with the blessings that Jacob bestowed upon his sons and the deaths of Jacob, Joseph, and the entire generation.

The last part of Genesis is not unique in this weaving of stories. The book of Exodus opens with the same literary technique. The narrative repeats the story of Jacob's sons' descent into Egypt and then jumps to the Egyptian Story: the new king and his decrees.

Before we dive into analyzing Joseph's management of the economic crisis in Egypt, it is useful to briefly review how Joseph treated his own family on arrival. After the first two years of famine, Jacob's sons descended to Egypt. They arrived in the only country in the entire region that had food stockpiles as honored guests and close associates of the king. The food was in the cities, but Jacob's sons, who presented themselves as shepherds in need of pastureland, were given a homestead in "the choicest part of the land" and a food allowance: "So Joseph settled his father and his brothers, giving them holdings in the choicest part of the land of Egypt, in the region of Rameses, as Pharaoh had commanded. Joseph sustained his father, and his brothers, and all his father's household with bread, according to the [number of] little ones."

There are two approaches to evaluating Joseph's economic activities in Egypt. In both, it is necessary to compare the personal story of Jacob's sons and their settling in Egypt with the story of the Egyptian economy and how it was managed during the famine years. As noted, the two stories inform and influence one another and are critical in understanding the broad meaning of Joseph's stories.

The first approach sees Joseph as an economic and political genius who presided over the Egyptian economy with ultimate authority. The length of the episode is meant to demonstrate that Joseph was a good person, who benefitted both the

Egyptians and his family. Ralbag, known as Gersonides, a late 13th and 14th century French Talmudist, mathematician, philosopher, physician and astronomer, who takes this approach, further elaborates that Joseph managed public funds with integrity and only gave his family per capita rations despite his powerful position. Joseph also transferred all of the accumulated wealth to its proper owner, Pharaoh, and kept nothing for himself. Due to his excellent planning and supervision, his agricultural and economic rescue plan was carried out with probity and wisdom. Although he collected all of Egypt's wealth from its inhabitants, the populace thanked him, proclaiming he had saved them. At the same time, he kept the political and religious elites at bay. By appeasing them at this challenging economic time, he prevented an uprising that would undermine his authority.[3]

Rabbi Samson Raphael Hirsch presents a similar approach. He suggested that Joseph's wisdom tempered the results of the edict. By organizing the people so that the residents of each city would always stay together and be relocated as a unit, their social and communal structures would remain largely intact. Therefore, this change did not lead to complete overhaul.[4]

The second approach maintains that Joseph's economic policies led to the later enslavement of the Israelites. The first commentator to adopt this approach was Rabbi Yosef Bekhor Shor of Orléans, France. In his commentary to Exodus (1:11), he avers that the pharaoh who enslaved the Israelites needed many repositories, since a fifth of all the Egyptian produce belonged to him per Joseph's edict. However, the Israelites did not need to hand over one-fifth of their produce because Joseph had given them ownership of an estate in the choicest part of the land and sustained them without demanding payment. Bekhor Shor suggests that the Egyptians started a libel against the Israelites and claimed that all the Egyptians served the king. They worked the land and turned over one-fifth of their produce and handed over half of their flocks' and herds' offspring to him. Effectively, all of the native Egyptians were sharecroppers. But since the Israelites did not serve him in this same way and the Egyptians gave them grain, the Israelites were required to build the repositories in which to store it.[5]

A socioeconomic analysis of the episode indicates a third approach. By its very nature, the economy is dynamic. Even visionary economists and ministers, equipped with the best forecasts, sometimes adopt policies that cause risk to accumulate to the point of critical mass.[6] It is difficult to anticipate the behavior of the citizenry or the economy when both are changed simultaneously. This is especially true of a centralized and planned economy.

For example, out of millions of economists and investors across the globe, very few foresaw the impending financial crisis of 2008. The interdependencies, counterparty risk, and opaque nature of leverage and the housing market were the results of a complex system—because by their nature, economies and finance are complex.[7]

In complex systems, when one thing is changed, it is nearly impossible to predict the impact that it will have, directly or indirectly. Economies are extremely complicated systems comprised of fiscal activity, both national and international, as well as impulses, psychology, and government intervention. Hidden risks suddenly appear in unpredictable ways. While it is true that Joseph successfully adapted Egypt's foreign, security, and economic policies continuously, he did not anticipate the greatest risk of all: the internal disintegration of Egyptian society.

This third approach combines Joseph's good intentions, presented in the complimentary interpretation (the first approach), with the de facto results noted in more critical interpretations (the second approach). This third approach understands Joseph as a person who tried to act for the benefit of the Egyptian people, not only for the benefit of his brothers. However, he ultimately missed something along the way, leading to bleak results. Joseph's economic reforms did not yield positive results for Egyptian society at the end of the famine, and these results may have been a significant factor in the ensuing enslavement and persecution of the Israelites.

Joseph acted with integrity, skill, and alacrity. He saved the Egyptian people, and perhaps the entire region from famine. However, even the best intentions can be foiled by complex systems, whose outcomes can be hard to anticipate. The centralized control Joseph exerted over the economy meant there was one person to blame when the complex system did not function as everyone had hoped. When things did not end well for the native Egyptians, it might have led to persecution of Joseph's family, the Israelites. The displaced and somewhat impoverished Egyptians, took out their anger by enslaving the Israelites. In retrospect, we often forget how dire the original situation was.

GOVERNMENT BALANCE SHEET EXPLOSION

In his book *The Most Important Thing*, legendary investor Howard Marks of Oaktree Capital describes the need for what he calls second level thinking (sometimes referred to as second order thinking). First level thinking resolves an immediate problem. Second level thinking looks deeper and asks probing, long-term questions. The goal is to understand the "second order" effects of what look like good decisions in the present.

As discussed in the previous chapter, Joseph worked during the seven years of abundance to grow the Egyptian economy by means of a fiscal policy that included increased government spending, investment in infrastructure (cities and food storage facilities), and the establishment of a governmental chain of command. Joseph continued these policies in the early years of the famine. Recall:

> The seven years of abundance that the land of Egypt enjoyed came to an end, and the seven years of famine set in, just as Joseph had foretold. There was famine in all lands, but throughout the land of Egypt there was bread. And when all the land of Egypt felt the hunger, the people cried out to Pharaoh for bread; and Pharaoh said to all the Egyptians, "Go to Joseph; whatever he tells you, you shall do."—Accordingly, when the famine became severe in the land of Egypt, Joseph laid open all that was within, and rationed out grain to the Egyptians. The famine, however, spread over the whole world. So all the world came to Joseph in Egypt to procure rations, for the famine had become severe throughout the world. (41:53–57)

In the first phase, the Egyptians stored food at home, since all knew about the impending famine. Therefore: "There was famine in all lands, but throughout the land of Egypt there was bread." In the second phase, Joseph "laid open all that was within," namely, the grain stored in regular facilities and under standard storage conditions (as you may remember, this grain was the surplus of what was held in long-term storage facilities in the cities). This produce was released into the market in order to preserve stable, normal economic activity. For two years, Joseph managed to prevent panic in the markets, which could have caused prices to spike and black markets to rise.

The turning point of the famine came two years later. In the third year of the famine, Joseph was extremely active in attending to the needs of the economy of Egypt and the wider region. This can be seen in the range of verbs in the verses describing Joseph's activity: "And Joseph settled"; "and he gave"; "Joseph sustained"; "Joseph gathered in"; "and Joseph brought." Economic reform was the new normal in Egypt, and in this context, Joseph collected all the money that belonged to Egypt's citizens and transferred it to Pharaoh's treasury. At the same time, Joseph provided for his brothers' physical and economic needs, although he took care to avoid anything that could bring on accusations of nepotism. Thus: "Joseph sustained his father, and his brothers, and all his father's household with bread, according to the [number of] little ones" (47:12).

This was the phase of austerity: "Now there was no bread in all the world, for the famine was very severe; both the land of Egypt and the land of Canaan languished because of the famine" (47:13). At this stage, it was necessary to open the emergency food storage facilities that were located in the cities: the storehouses that had been carefully stocked with the precise amount of food necessary, according to the number of children. Everyone received food in accordance with the specific needs of their families. There was no preferential treatment for those who were well-connected. Even Joseph's family was provided with food in accordance with this strict rationing system.[8]

The famine had intensified to a point where Joseph had to work according to very precise calculations. There was no room for error.[9] However, the very act of opening up the emergency warehouses and the transition to an austerity regime naturally produced tension in the cities. Everyone huddled by the warehouses and demanded more emergency rations. People did not know how long the food reserves would last. Since there was no population registry with the number of persons per family—unlike when it came to his own family, whose needs he could assess precisely—there was no way for Joseph to stem the tide. Joseph's solution to stabilizing demand was to charge money for the food.

The government's investments began to yield significant returns. Joseph had invested in technology ("and Joseph gathered grain") in a local distribution system and in sophisticated infrastructure ("stored the grain in the cities") that transformed Egypt's cities into international centers of commerce. As second-in-command to the king, Joseph controlled the most in-demand consumer product as well as its channels of distribution. During the first two years of the famine, Joseph had proven that he could successfully manage the economy that was in a state of crisis. He had earned the confidence and trust of the Egyptians, and nobody entertained the possibility of a rebellion. They all accepted Joseph's careful calculations of food allowances, namely, his formula of "according to the [number of] little ones,," and acted in accordance with his instructions to preserve quotas by charging for food. Joseph let them experience the intensity of the famine, and then responded each time. Everyone cooperated, fearing total collapse. Thus, all of the money that Pharaoh's regime had invested in Joseph's economic reforms generated nice returns:

> Now there was no bread in all the world, for the famine was very severe; both the land of Egypt and the land of Canaan languished because of the famine. Joseph gathered in all the money that was to be found in the land of Egypt and in the land of Canaan,[10] as payment for the

> rations that were being procured, and Joseph brought the money into Pharaoh's palace. (47:13-14)

The words "Joseph gathered" give the impression that Joseph sold the grain easily, as part of the regular business cycle and at reasonable prices. The Egyptians and the Canaanites willingly parted with their money to buy food, and Joseph simply collected the money. That the grain was sold at fair prices (as suggested earlier—the price was only instituted to regulate demand) is demonstrated later in the story. At this moment, Joseph seemed surprised to learn the Egyptians had exhausted all their money, and this caused him to find a solution for when "the money is gone":

> And when the money gave out in the land of Egypt and in the land of Canaan, all the Egyptians came to Joseph and said, "Give us bread, lest we die before your very eyes; for the money is gone!" And Joseph said, "Bring your livestock, and I will sell to you against your livestock, if the money is gone." So they brought their livestock to Joseph, and Joseph gave them bread in exchange for the horses, for the stocks of sheep and cattle, and the asses; thus he provided them with bread that year in exchange for all their livestock. (47:15–17)

When the money ran out and the economic depression became more severe, the bartering phase commenced. The Egyptians bartered their animals for bread. Horses, which are mentioned in the Torah for the first time here, were apparently an expensive animal and a fine source of business travel for the international traders involved in Egypt's emerging commercial centers.[11] Perhaps horses were hot commodities, and perhaps they were shipping vehicles. The Torah lists the various types of animals that were bartered for bread to demonstrate that the entire population, the full Egyptian socioeconomic spectrum, bartered their belongings for Joseph's bread. In the absence of money,[12] anything can be bartered. In 1970s Ireland, people resorted to the bartering system to survive due to the banks' extended closure and the lack of liquid assets.[13]

When the money was gone, economic activity that was not related to the government and food purchases took a hit because barter is not sophisticated enough to conduct regular business deals. Ultimately, diverting all of Egypt's money to Pharaoh's treasury not only enriched the king; it also unintentionally exacerbated the dependency of Egypt's citizens on him. In the absence of currency that could be used to buy and sell goods and services, it became increasingly difficult for citizens to conduct their own affairs.

The people turned to Joseph and demanded bread. Joseph initiated a bartering system in order to maintain normal business procedure to the extent possible. Perhaps, Joseph detected the possibility for additional fiscal gains; it may have become necessary for the government to expand its operations and employ more personnel to take care of all these animals collected through barter. With time, however, Joseph would realize his mistaken understanding of human nature.

Joseph emphasized that he was willing to accept cattle as payment only "if the money is gone," since something with an accepted value, like cash or silver, was preferable to an animal that consumes feed[14] and whose value is not accepted by all. Additionally, unlike animals that become a drain on resources in times of famine, money or silver has an infinite shelf life.[15] In order to save Egypt from hunger and death by starvation, these were obvious risks that Joseph was prepared to assume when there was no other alternative.

But there was another hidden risk: psychological impact. It is hard for people to part with their animals—especially if the animals in question were not part of large herds but individual beasts of burden that put on mileage with their owners. Even if the situation demanded the sale of these animals and they were sold at fair market value, when Joseph reluctantly agreed to purchase all of Egypt's livestock, the Egyptians still felt that he stole the "poor man's lamb."[16] Joseph may have expanded the economy by increasing government spending on care of animals it owned, but in actuality, the citizens had given the viceroy and his officers all the capital that they had allocated to industrial production. That is, they gave up their "machines."

Until this point, Joseph provided only his family with "bread." At this stage, we are first told that Joseph provided the people with bread, that is, prepared food. On previous occasions, Joseph dispensed "rations" (*shever*), which is identified with "grain" (*bar*). Joseph was forced to provide bread for the populace because the beasts, who now belonged to the king, had done threshing, milling, and other labors. People had no way to make bread without their animal machines, so Joseph had to intervene at a higher resolution and provide bread for them from government bakeries.

Centralized government grabbed another slice of the economy at the expense of its citizens. Joseph did not realize it at the time, but he paid the terrible price of emptying citizens' lives of any productive activity and increasing their dependence on him. Expanding the scope of government intervention and regulation is like using antibiotics—necessary in order to overcome the catastrophic famine, but weakening for society's individuals. As with antibiotics, the dosage is critical.

In the fifth year of the famine, after two years of injecting food into the markets and another two years of collecting the

Egyptians' money and animals and transferring them to government ownership, the people remained empty and deflated. They had barely passed the halfway point of the famine, and they were already starving and destitute.

> And when that year was ended, they came to him the next year and said to him, "We cannot hide from my lord that, with all the money and animal stocks consigned to my lord, nothing is left at my lord's disposal save our persons and our farmland. Let us not perish before your eyes, both we and our land. Take us and our land in exchange for bread, and we with our land will be serfs to Pharaoh; provide the seed, that we may live and not die, and that the land may not become a waste." So Joseph gained possession of all the farmland of Egypt for Pharaoh, every Egyptian having sold his field because the famine was too much for them. (47:18–20)

Joseph did not propose buying the land. The people suggested parting with the only source of production they still had: their land. Joseph, it seems, understood that demanding land crossed a line. A person cannot wake up in the morning, look out at his ancestral lands, and accept that he has transferred his family's property and estate to the government. Furthermore, Joseph already controlled the distribution channels and machinery. If he were to take the "plant" as well—the food production system—ordinary citizens would no longer have any means of independence, and the economy would become overcentralized.

But Joseph had no other solution, at least at this point. Thus: "Joseph gained possession of all the farmland of Egypt for Pharaoh, every Egyptian having sold his field because the famine was too much for them." Joseph understood that the

Egyptians were desperate, for they had suggested, "Take us and our land." At this stage, though, Joseph purchased only the lands. Inevitably—much like in the case of Esau and Jacob where Esau hastily made a deal because he was starving and later repudiated it—here, too, the Egyptian commoners turned their current and future assets over to a Hebrew foreigner and later attempted to undo it through servitude.

Joseph understood that in a time of famine, if the government were to transfer payments for free, the people would lose their will to work, and the economy would not flourish again. A person needs to make an effort to obtain his bread.[17] Under conditions of famine and desolation, the only productive activities that can be conducted by the general public are real estate transactions. Remaining active is crucial for life and for the individual's self-image. It is even more important for the economy as a whole.

Once this burst of activity exhausted itself, Joseph introduced a new initiative: "Thus the land passed over to Pharaoh. And he removed the population town by town, from one end of Egypt's border to the other."

In addition to increasing economic activity, transferring the population purported to address a different problem and contains the beginnings of the post-famine plan. As mentioned above, Joseph understood that leaving people to wake each morning and weep over the loss of their ancestral lands[18] would destroy them on the inside.[19] Warning bells went off when Joseph heard the Egyptians say, "Nothing is left at my lord's disposal save our persons and our farmland. Let us not perish before your eyes, both we and our land. Take us and our land in exchange for bread, and we with our land will be serfs to Pharaoh." All day long, as Joseph was doing whatever he could to save Egypt's life and wealth, the public was sink-ing into depression and despair. The one point of light was the statement: "Provide the seed, that we may live and not die, and that the land may not become a waste." But it was too early for that. There was no sense in wasting seeds in the fifth year of the seven year famine.[20] Joseph ultimately bought time by trading in real estate and transferring the people to cities across the country.

At this phase, Joseph understood that he had concentrated too much power and means of production in his hands, leaving the economy and society extremely fragile. But it seems that the nation and its people were no longer economically active. It was too little too late. In the sixth year of the famine, when Joseph already held all of Egypt's assets, he was forced to buy the Egyptians as slaves. In the seventh year, he introduced a privatization initiative to restart the Egyptian economy:

> Then Joseph said to the people, "Whereas I have this day acquired you and your land for Pharaoh, here is seed for you to sow the land. And when harvest comes, you shall give one-fifth to Pharaoh, and four-fifths shall be yours as seed for the fields and as food for you and those in your households, and as nourishment for your children."

Joseph built a new urban economic plan as though it were Lego. From his perspective, the people would reside in the cities and the fields would be located outside of the cities. As the people had been transferred from their lands to new cities, Joseph seems to have redistributed the land so that the nation would plant, trade, and pay taxes. It is quite possible that Joseph was ahead of his time.[21] In his time, however, risk accumulated beneath the surface.

On one hand, the tax regime benefited the people, even generously. Both researchers and the Talmud are quite familiar with a socioeconomic structure of sharecropping, in which tenants divide the yield with the landlord. Typically, a tenant would receive half, a third, or a quarter of the harvest. Joseph, however, instituted the reverse. The people were taxed at a rate of only one-fifth.[22] The 20 percent income tax rate gave the farmers breathing room, enabling them to invest working capital and still have surplus to trade. By emphasizing "your children," Joseph sent the message that he wanted them to live normal lives, not the lives of slaves.

But other voices murmured under the surface. The people had been transferred from one place to another and were not connected to their new locales or to their new urban lifestyles. All of their money had been handed over to Joseph, making commerce difficult. Since their animals, had been turned over to Joseph, the people were forced to work the harsh land that had lain fallow for six years with their own bare hands.

The verses describe how all of the land in Egypt was transferred to Pharaoh—with one exception: "Only the land of the priests he did not take over for the priests had an allotment from Pharaoh, and they lived off the allotment which Pharaoh had made to them; therefore they did not sell their land."

By noting that the priests did not sell their lands, the Torah demonstrates the importance of ancestral lands. Anyone who could survive the famine (i.e., the priests by virtue of their allowance from Pharaoh) did not sell their land. People only sold their lands to the king as a last resort, a life-saving measure that takes precedence over the whole of the Torah.[23] Thus, the frustration of those who were tilling strange and foreign soil grew; the dissonance was enormous, for they may have even known the person who had been transferred to their ancestral lands. Excessive centralization and absolute control over the lives of ordinary citizens became a ticking time bomb.

Worse yet, the fact that the priests did not sell their lands, while the general populace sold their lands and moved to the cities, caused a disconnection between the priests and the people. There were many facets of the disconnection between the government and the emerging city culture, who made up one category, and the religious establishment, who made up another. It was impossible to estimate the impact that this move would have on society.

On one hand, the priests may not have been needed to the same degree in the cities, given that urban environments tend to be less religious than outlying areas.[24] The Egyptians' socio-economic decline may have made them more susceptible to religious and nationalistic extremism.[25] In light of this, the government had a vested interest in keeping the priests away.

On the other hand, people who had been disconnected from their ancestral lands and needed to develop new careers in unfamiliar cities would have experienced daily frustration. The public looked at this highly centralized economy, where all the resources were controlled by a foreigner,[26] a Canaanite-Hebrew who was appointed as second-in-command to the king, and hatred rose in their hearts. The people were well aware that the religious establishment, which was ostensibly close to the regime, had retained its ancestral lands, and their frustration mounted.

Given this context, the nation's estrangement from religion likely included harsh feelings of widespread confusion and palpable social danger. Religious figures, who received a regular food allowance from the regime, could have functioned as the regime's trustees and ambassadors. They could have helped explain the difficult situation that was decreed upon the people and been a voice of moderation, an attentive ear for the daily struggles of the nation. As noted, however, due to the framework of the urban planning, they remained detached from the people.

Practically speaking, only two groups "grew and flourished" outside of the cities: the Egyptian priests and the Israelites of Goshen. Rabbi Yosef Bekhor Shor (47:27) makes this comparison:

> "They acquired holdings in it"—because all of the land belonged to Pharaoh, and he gave it to them, and it became their holding, because they did not need to sell anything. Just like the priests did not sell [their land], because they had an allowance from Pharaoh, so too, Joseph sustained his brothers, and they did not sell anything, so the land was a homestead for them.

This comparison alludes to the fact that these two groups lived under markedly better circumstances than the rest of the populace, thanks to their close relationship with the regime. The Egyptians in the cities saw that the Israelites were fruitful and increased in the land of Goshen. It is impossible to see the growth of the Israelite population in Egypt without placing it in a wider context: In suburban Goshen, the birthrate rose while the Egyptians, the new city dwellers—like city dwellers throughout history—were having fewer children.[27]

All along the way, the variables that accumulated within the complex economic system—including lack of land ownership; a vibrant, rapidly reproducing immigrant group that became entrenched on the periphery, on land that had belonged to Egyptians; and a depressed and weakened society that had absolved itself from all personal responsibility and began to rely on the state to bail them out—were a recipe both for a crumbling society and an attendant wave of xenophobia.[28] The public has a short memory, and the Egyptians quickly forgot how Joseph had saved them. In their lack of gratitude and patchy memory, they were like Chief Butler: "Yet the chief butler did not think of Joseph; he forgot him" (40:23). The Egyptians felt that the Canaanite minority was increasing and taking over, rendering them foreigners in their own land.

THE UGLY DUCKLING

A Black Swan event, an economic term coined by Nassim Nicholas Taleb, aptly describes the situation in Egypt under Joseph. Joseph's risk management and economic forecasting models broke down. His faith in his own planning expertise blinded him to the surprises that lurked beneath the surface.

Upon hearing Pharaoh's dreams, Joseph relied on his interpretation of his earlier dreams and the economic plan that he had devised in order to save Egypt. He did not critically examine his paradigm or how it would be applied practically to the economy and a citizen society. At the end of the seven years of famine, it became apparent that despite careful and proper management of the crisis, a problematic social structure had emerged in Egyptian society, inadvertently and unforeseen.

Many small details did not align with the grand plan, and social conditions turned on Joseph and ultimately, his family. If one does not think too deeply about the social ramifications of their plan, carefully monitor the mood on the street, and reframe or adapt due to spreading risks, even genius and accurate economic predictions can yield unanticipated negative results. In Egypt, these hidden risks were hardly marginal; they were substantial risks that could completely reshuffle the deck and tear society apart. Black Swans can be massively impactful.

Joseph overlooked this dynamic risk in a complex system. When it came to averting risks and threats that were part of his vision and economic calculations, Joseph handled them expertly. In Mark's terms, this was classic first level thinking. What was absent was second level thinking, which would have considered longer term effects and more pernicious outcomes for an immigrant population living among the Pharaoh's empire.[29] By two or three generations later, Egyptians could deny that Joseph had saved them from famine. Instead, the enemies of the Hebrews could tell the story in the same vein as Rabbi Yosef Bekhor Shor and other exegetes.

According to the Egyptians' story, Joseph showed concern only for his own family and callously trampled on the rights of native-born Egyptians. This was a second order effect of Joseph's innovations and their built-in limitations. The children and grandchildren of the famine's survivors heard about how Joseph, in times of plenty, had forced the people to build cities and storage facilities and then filled them with produce that the people themselves had cultivated. They were told how, during the famine itself, the greedy Joseph, bought land from their hunger-stricken parents and grandparents for pennies on the dollar, paying them with the same grain that they had previously deposited in his storehouses.

The cynicism was rampant. At the outset of the famine, large amounts of grain hit the markets (there was enough to even support people from distant lands), but when his family arrived, Joseph gave them all food for free. The Egyptians, meanwhile, had to sell themselves into slavery to obtain basic foodstuffs. It was not long before the Egyptians implemented a cruel tit for tat: just as Joseph had engineered the enslavement of the Egyptians, the Israelites would also be enslaved. Joseph's family would be tasked with the backbreaking labor of building storage cities—"just deserts" for Joseph's urban revolution.

To summarize, Joseph saved the Egyptian economy from catastrophic famine and the threat of external enemies. He strove to create alliances and good business relations with the other people in the region, allowing them access to the food he had stockpiled. Here, too, his political strategy boomeranged against the Israelites. After Joseph's death, the threat of external enemies became an important element in the fearmongering campaign against the Israelites: "Let us deal shrewdly with them, so that they may not increase; otherwise in the event of war they may join our enemies in fighting against us and rise from the land" (Exodus 1:10).

Joseph had overcentralized and significantly raised the level of vulnerability to the unseen risks that had accumulated within the system. In a less centralized system, the risks themselves are less systemic and can be managed on the edges. They do not cause the system to fail with catastrophic consequences. Often, it is possible to identify these risks ahead of time and to even solve the problems that they present. Private initiatives can identify needs and generate ways to address them, making decentralized systems more resilient against the buildup of residue.

In the face of the pressure generated by Pharaoh's ominous dreams, Joseph undertook the centralization of powers. In tandem with his efforts, the economy and society became extremely fragile and susceptible to tragic risks. One might say that in the form of these hidden, unforeseen risks, Pharaoh's dreams about the seven years of famine that would completely consume all of the good that preceded them came true—including "one could not tell that they had consumed them."

Would it have been preferable for Joseph to sit with his arms folded and not take the steps that he took to save Egypt? It is hard to say. Was it wise to separate his family geographically from the rest of Egypt? It is impossible to know what the price would have otherwise been. Man's best laid plans do not always pan out in a world that is engineered by the divine. It is impossible to anticipate all the risks that lurk around the corner. Historical counterfactuals are also impossible to substantiate.

No one is wise like one with experience, and the wisest of all learns from the experiences of others. All we can do to hedge against uncertainty is learn from the wisdom of and lessons of history and cleave to the values that undergird human society. By broadening the foundations of social existence and improving its durability, we can provide protection against threats—even if they cannot be completely foreseen.

12
Parashat Vayeḥi

THE LAND AND THE SEA

Entrepreneurship and Management

ISRAEL'S BIBLICAL ECONOMY

The Washington Post asked the following: How can Israel—with only 7.1 million people (its population at the time of the article's publication), no natural resources, enemies on every border, and in a constant state of war—produce more start-up companies than Japan, India, Korea, Canada, or the United Kingdom? (Washington Post Book Review of *Start-up Nation* by Saul Singer and Dan Senor).

Broadly, we can answer that a lack of natural resources forces people to work harder and to innovate more. Challenges and constraints drive ingenuity, and partnerships between different tribes and countries can create meaningful impact. A close reading of the Torah shows that in this case, the modern Israel draws its inspiration from the Torah in and, more specifically, from the tribes of Issachar and Zebulun and the blessings they received.

At the end of Genesis, we find Jacob gathering his children to "bless" them. In this blessing (or foretelling), the patriarch of Israel's twelve tribes described their strengths, weaknesses, opportunities, and perils. These descriptions and prescriptions are sometimes personal, as in the case of Reuben but are mostly tribal. The tribal blessings and prescriptions relate not to their present circumstances in Egypt, but rather to the time, centuries in the future, when their spiritual and genetic descendants will settle in the land of Israel and become the nation of Israel.

Later, in the book of Numbers, tribal parcels in land of Israel would be apportioned in a lottery to each of the tribes, based on their size. Despite that, Jacob already seemed to know where different tribes will be located, and he addressed the perils, challenges, and opportunities of building a successful and diversified economy—from agriculture to ranching to global imports and exports. He envisioned economic relations among the tribes and their neighbors and steadfastly insisted that they not become corrupt.

Alongside economic opportunities and enchanting marketplaces, realpolitik can present challenges to values, and Jacob foresaw these issues and addressed them head-on in these blessings. At the end of the Torah, Moses also blessed the tribes, focusing on similar challenges and opportunities.

On these two different occasions—the blessings of Jacob and Moses—the tribes were the beneficiaries of blessings that expressed their distinct characters. The singular character of each tribe is not merely a biographical-historical fact but a critical component of the mosaic that constitutes the people of Israel. Accordingly, the blessings do not only confer bounty; they also map out each tribe's unique destiny and their interactions with one another. The whole would also be greater than the sum of the parts.

Jacob was the first of the patriarchs to gather his sons together and assign roles for inheriting the land and establishing an independent commonwealth: "And Jacob called his sons and said, 'Come together that I may tell you what is to befall you in days to come. Assemble and hearken, O sons of Jacob; Hearken to Israel your father.'" (Genesis 49:1–2)

The establishment of a country demands political leadership, and an extended family's leadership usually emerges from the oldest children.[1] Jacob, however, criticized his three oldest sons, and explained why they were not worthy of the mantle of leadership:

> Reuben, you are my first-born, my might and first fruit of my vigor, exceeding in rank and exceeding in honor. Unstable as water, you shall excel no longer; For when you mounted your father's bed, You brought disgrace—my couch he mounted! Simeon and Levi are a pair; their weapons are tools of lawlessness. Let not my person be included in their council, Let not my being be counted in their assembly. (49:3–6)

Here, Jacob was referring to Reuben sleeping with Jacob's concubine Bilha, while also admonishing Simeon and Levi for slaying the people of Shechem.

He then came to Judah, the fourth son and Jacob's anointed leader: "The scepter shall not depart from Judah, nor the ruler's staff from between his feet...." (49:8). Jacob then connected leadership with developing an independent economy based on agriculture, especially viniculture—for which the soil of the Judean Hills is well-suited—and shepherding, which was suitable for the desert areas of Judah's territory. Thus, the verses read: "He tethers his donkey to a vine, his donkey's foal to a choice vine; he washes his garment in wine, his robe in blood of grapes. His eyes are darker than wine; his teeth are whiter than milk" (49:11–12).

Knowing his sons as he did, Jacob foresaw the eventual split of the Hebrew kingdom into the kingdoms of Judah and Israel with Joseph ("the shepherd" "the elect of his brothers") as the leader of Israel's kingdom. Here, too, leadership is linked to economic blessings. This is apparently out of recognition that the economic power of a commonwealth is important for its establishment:

> Joseph is a wild ass...the shepherd of the Rock of Israel—the God of your father who helps you, and the Almighty Who blesses you with blessings of heaven above, blessings of the deep that couches below, blessings of the breast and womb. The blessings of your father surpass the blessings of my ancestors, to the utmost bounds of the eternal hills. May they rest on the head of Joseph, on the brow of the elect of his brothers.

Some three centuries later, on the eve of the entry into Eretz Yisrael, Moses blessed the tribes again, also shortly before his death. Many commentators have compared these two sets of blessings.

Here, we will specifically focus on the blessings of Issachar and Zebulun, two tribes who walked side-by-side in the desert for forty years[2] and dwelt adjacent to one another in their ancestral home in Israel.[3] What makes them particularly interesting is that they are the only partnership among the tribes. Moreover, unlike Judah and Joseph, Issachar and Zebulun did not have natural resources in their parcels. Additionally, the peculiarity of the textual reference does not seem to comport with the realities they encountered when they actually arrived at their parcel of land. In analyzing their connection, my goal is to reveal other foundational principles of the Israelite economy, especially the commercial and service infrastructure with which these two tribes were charged.

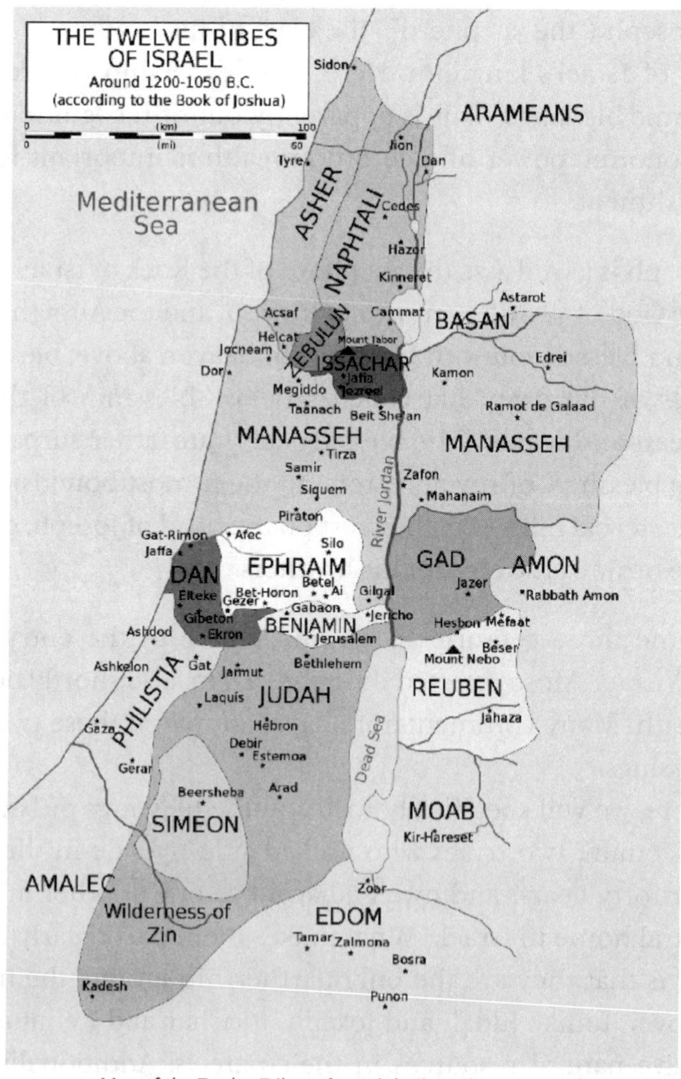

Map of the Twelve Tribes of Israel. (Wikimedia Commons)

FORTUNE TELLER

Jacob blessed Zebulun as follows:

> Zebulun shall dwell by the seashore; he shall be a haven for ships, and his flank shall rest on Sidon. Issachar is a strong-boned donkey, crouching among the sheepfolds. When he saw how good was security (rest) and how pleasant was the country, he bent his shoulder to the burden, and became a toiling serf. (49:13–15)

And in the words of Moses:

> And of Zebulun he said: Rejoice, O Zebulun, on your journeys and Issachar, in your tents. They invite their kin to the mountain, where they offer sacrifices of righteousness. For they draw from the riches of the seas and the hidden hoards of the sand. (Deuteronomy 33:18–19)

With a quick glance at the above map, readers will note that Zebulun's territory does not, in fact, border the sea. This seeming anomaly will be explained below.

Jacob placed the blessings of Zebulun and Issachar side by side, and Moses actually combined them, explicitly prophesying a shared future. It is noteworthy that the age order of Zebulun and Issachar is reversed in both Jacob's and Moses's blessings, thus making them a "duo."

The midrash (also cited by Rashi) addresses the connection between these two tribes and the reversal of their birth order. The role of the seafaring trader Zebulun was to support Issachar's Torah study while the spiritual and judicial leadership of Israel came from Issachar, who dwelled in the tents that the midrash understands as tents of Torah. The seafaring Zebulun paid for this through his commercial journeys.[4] In addition, the midrash essentially avers that the blessing of Zebulun preceded Issachar's because Zebulun's success in business was a prerequisite of his support for Torah study: "Without flour, there is no Torah" (*Avot* 3:17).

This midrash gave rise to much interpretation and many practical halachic (Jewish law) discussions about the Issachar–Zebulun relationship. In certain communities, even today, married men spend their days studying Torah in *kollel* with the support of donors under an Issachar-Zebulun agreement. It is enshrined in *Shulḥan Arukh* (*Yoreh De'ah* 246:1), the standard halachic code:

> Every Jewish man is obligated to study Torah, whether he is poor or wealthy, physically fit or suffering, young or very old. Even a poor man who goes begging at the doorsteps, even a husband with children, is obligated to allocate time for Torah study by day and by night, as it is stated: "You shall contemplate it day and night..." One who cannot study, because he does not know how to study at all or because he is preoccupied, should support others who study.
>
> Gloss [of Rema]: And it is considered as though he himself studied. And one can stipulate with his fellow that one will engage in Torah study and one will provide for his livelihood and they will divide the reward. However, if one already engaged in Torah study, he cannot sell his portion for money that will be given to him.[5]

The above homiletical approach presents a compelling view of the importance of Torah study. However, it is also quite difficult to reconcile with the straightforward meaning of Scripture and the clear socioeconomic message of Jacob's blessings.

SETTING BOUNDARIES

As noted in the verses cited above, Zebulun "dwells" by the seashore,[6] and his seafaring ways bring him to Sidon, an international commercial center developed by the Phoenicians.[7] Issachar, on the other hand, is compared to a strong ox who crouches "among the sheepfolds." Targum Yerushalmi ("Targum Pseudo-Jonathan"), a western Aramaic translation and exegesis of the Torah which was composed according to scholars anywhere between the 4th century and the 14th century, explains: "Issachar will be a strong tribe whose territory will be between two territories/ridges." That is, this verse alludes to the character of Issachar's territory, through which a branch of the ancient international trade route, the Via Maris, passed. The Via Maris ("sea road" or "way of the sea") passed through the land of Israel along the sea before forking north along the sea and east through the Jezreel valley, linking Egypt to Syria and Anatolia to Mesopotamia This popular and crucial trade route is a crucial geographic feature in numerous biblical narratives.[8]

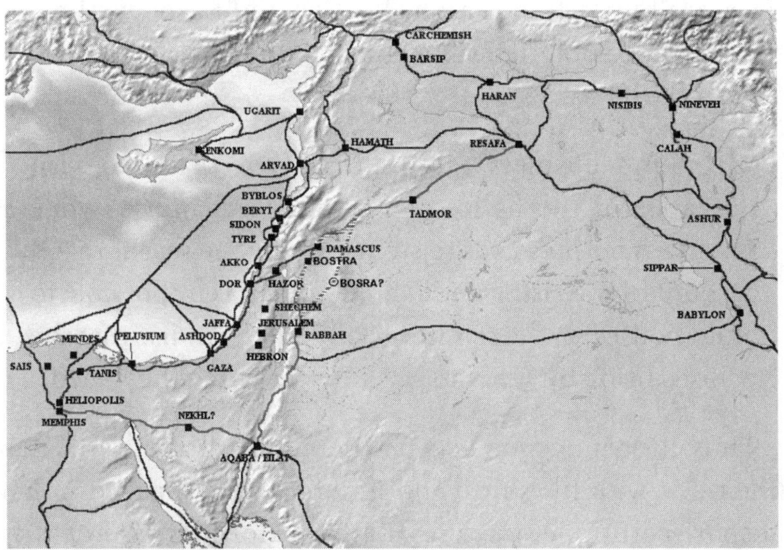

Trade routes in the Middle East, c. 1300 BCE. (Wikimedia Commons)

Unlike Zebulun, who sails to distant lands, the strong-boned "donkey" Issachar takes advantage of the major commercial artery that traversed his territory as it forked east. His beasts of burden provide transport for goods, and his personnel, who use their shoulders to load and unload merchandise, make excellent porters.[9] Accordingly, the "good security" mentioned in the verse does not describe a state of idleness and is rather a contrast to Zebulun: Issachar benefits from the land routes passing through his territory and establishes service centers, lodgings, and encampments for travelers. The contrast between Zebulun and Issachar is evident on a linguistic level as well—the use of the word "shoulder" (*shechem*) as opposed to "flank" (*yerekh*), as we will discuss later.

For Issachar, the land was indeed pleasant. With his strong-boned donkey, Issachar oversaw the distribution of Zebulun's merchandise along land routes. The people of Issachar crouched among the sheepfolds—the markets and the shops—selling services and merchandise along the route that passed through the Jezreel Valley, which was located between two mountain ridges. Malbim, a 19th century Russian and European linguist, exegete and Rabbi, describes the activities of Issachar somewhat similarly:

> "Zebulun's business was to trade overseas and visit the lands of the nations with his merchandise...while Issachar's business was to sit in tents by the seashore (on account of the rising and falling tides, it is impossible to build houses on the seashore), buy merchandise that the nations bring by sea, and sell seafarers what they need...

Thus, the connection between Zebulun, who mastered maritime trade with his ships, and Issachar, who engaged in land transport and trade, was only natural. However, the description of the seafaring tribe of Zebulun presents a geographical conundrum that is clearly visible on the map of the tribal territories (above).

As noted above, the borders of Zebulun, as described in the book of Joshua, did not have any maritime border—and certainly not a coastline or natural harbor.[10] Indeed, the description of the borders of Manasseh demonstrate beyond doubt that Zebulun's territory was landlocked; Manasseh was bordered by Asher to the north, and the two tribes together covered the entire northern coastline.

> The region of Tappuah belonged to Manasseh; but Tappuah, on the border of Manasseh, belonged to the Ephraimites. Then the boundary descended to the Wadi Kanah. Those towns to the south of the wadi belonged to Ephraim as an enclave among the towns of Manasseh. The boundary of Manasseh lay north of the wadi and ran on to the Sea. What lay to the south belonged to Ephraim, and what lay to the north belonged to Manasseh, with the Sea as its boundary. [This territory] was contiguous with Asher on the north and with Issachar on the east. (Joshua 17:8–10)

Moreover, the expression "and his flank shall rest on (*ad*) Sidon" is unclear, and many commentators have debated its meaning.[11] In the book of Judges, we learn that the tribal territory of Asher bordered on Sidon, which indicates that Zebulun's tribal territory could not have been in this same region:

> Asher did not dispossess the inhabitants of Acco or the inhabitants of Sidon, Ahlab, Achzib, Helbah, Aphik, and Rehob. So the Asherites dwelt in the midst of the

> Canaanites, the inhabitants of the land, for they did not dispossess them. (Judges 1:31–32)[12]

Continuing the discussion of geographical realities, it is hard to understand the use of the pluriform "seas" in Jacob's blessing to Zebulun. Moses also mentioned "seas" in his blessing: "For they draw from the riches of the seas." It is not clear whether this is intended literally or figuratively.[13]

Perhaps the key to bridging the gap between the literal meaning of the words and the facts on the ground can be found by contrasting the words of Jacob's blessing with those of Moses. Unlike the ships of Zebulun and the donkey of Issachar that appear in Jacob's blessing, Moses said: "Rejoice, O Zebulun, on your journeys and Issachar, in your tents." (Deuteronomy 33:18)

To understand Moses's intention here, begin by noting that all of Moses's blessings, beginning with the tribe of Joseph ("Blessed of the Lord be his land"), are economic in nature. The blessing given to Joseph and his tribal territory are about natural resources. He is blessed with delicacies and natural water sources. His tribal territory is sun-drenched, and its fruit and grain grow by the moon:

> And of Joseph he said: Blessed of the Lord be his land with the bounty of dew from heaven, and of the deep that couches below; with the bounteous yield of the sun, and the bounteous crop of the moons; with the best from the ancient mountains, and the bounty of hills immemorial; with the bounty of earth and its fullness, and the favor of the Presence in the bush. May these rest on the head of Joseph, on the crown of the elect of his brothers. Like a firstling bull in his majesty, he has horns like the horns of the wild-ox; with them he gores the peoples, the ends of the earth one and all. These

are the myriads of Ephraim, those are the thousands of Manasseh. (Deuteronomy 33:13–17)

Thus, in the blessings of both Jacob and Moses, Joseph represents the extreme blessings of bountiful and abundant nature.

Though it bordered that of Asher and Manasseh and appears right after Joseph in the verses, Zebulun's territory lacked the special properties that theirs did. Zebulun had to *go out* to earn a living. As 13th century French Exegete Rabbi Hezekiyah Ben Manoah, also known as Hizkuni explains: "'Rejoice O Zebulun'—Zebulun resented his allotment." Landlocked, without a natural maritime border, as demonstrated above and as corroborated by the map, Zebulun would have had to work that much harder. In his blessing, Jacob almost mocked Zebulun: "Zebulun shall dwell by the seashore."

But embedded in this mockery was a challenge and an opportunity. The natural adversity would drive him, out of necessity, to be daring and innovate. In order to make a living, Zebulun would need to blaze a trail to the sea. Without his own shoreline, he would need to work hard and be enterprising to reach the shorelines of the neighboring tribes of Manasseh and Asher. From these beaches—called "harbors" because they were not part of his ancestral lands, merely places to anchor his ships—Zebulun would need to load merchandise bound for the corridors of international trade in Sidon. The geographical and topographical constraints, the lack of natural resources, and absence of natural trade routes spurred Zebulun toward innovative breakthroughs—[14] breakthroughs whose rewards are meaningful like Moses promised ("the riches of the sea").

At first glance, the fact that Zebulun did not have natural access to the sea seems to limit him. In truth, however, it would actually grant him greater flexibility to engage in a variety of activities in numerous maritime locations, on the shorelines of a few tribes. This is why both blessings invoke the plural, "seas."

Since Zebulun needed to innovate and invest in infrastructure and transportation[15] in order to leave his comfort zone and succeed, he was blessed (and expected) to be happy with his portion: "Rejoice, O Zebulun, on your journeys." Joy would come on the heels of challenges and creative solutions, breakthroughs, and successes. Zebulun was a "rich man who is happy with his lot" because there is no joy like the joy of an entrepreneur who leaves doubt behind, forges a new path, overcomes obstacles, and succeeds.

Even after Zebulun broke through to the sea, he did not have a natural land route for trade, so he would need to partner with Issachar, whose territory lies on a major east–west trade route forking from the Via Maris. Issachar's "strong-boned donkey" would become the logistics division of the entrepreneurs of Zebulun.

Zebulun's challenge was international trade, and he was consequently in charge of imports and exports for the whole country. He was the entrepreneur among the tribes. He received a small tribal territory, without natural bounties, access to the sea, and proper trade routes. His landlocked territory lay between the natural trade route that passed through the lands of Issachar and the coastal territories of Manasseh and Asher. Zebulun had to cooperate internally, among Israelites, and also externally, with foreign actors like the Sidonians. Seafaring was risky. Manasseh and Asher, who bordered the sea, were far more conservative, perhaps because their territory was larger and provided for them sufficiently.[16] They enjoyed the coast and the comfortable climate and were in no rush to be enterprising and take on risk.

Zebulun, however, needed to take risks in order to support himself and to develop his economy joyfully and optimistically. He would need to set out on adventures in order to realize his ambitions and succeed economically. As *Mishlei* (33:14) states: "She is like a merchant fleet, bringing her food from afar."

Obviously, this challenge suited Zebulun's personality and temperament, which is expressed in Deborah's song: "Zebulun had no qualms about risking his life." It is also mentioned in later historical accounts—Zebulun provided far more soldiers to King David's army than the other tribes (Book of Chronicles 1 12:34)—and this is especially remarkable given Zebulun's small population and territory compared to other tribes. As Shadal, Ibn Ezra, and others explained, his willingness to enlist "to the aid of the Lord among the warriors" was not limited to war. Zebulun had the mindset of an entrepreneur; he was wired to take risks, leave his comfort zone, and think optimistically. At the very core of Zebulun's character was the attitude that it was possible to emerge victorious. He and his descendants were the people who would set out to sea and succeed: "He shall be a haven for ships."[17]

A LIGHTHOUSE

One of the key attributes of a successful venture capitalist is knowing when to surround the entrepreneurs we invest in with professional managers. Entrepreneurs and managers are different, with distinct personality traits and areas of expertise. Entrepreneurs break paradigms, imagine new solutions, and shape new landscapes. They tend to be undaunted by constraints—and are sometimes even blind to them. New companies, industries, and business empires are painted onto a new canvas after entrepreneurs envision and create them.

Managers run and scale businesses. They think more systematically and operate via efficient and repeatable processes and methods to launch and scale the company's products and solutions in the market. They ensure that you can safely, effectively, and efficiently distribute and drive these products into the hands of more customers. Generally, they are less daring and creative than entrepreneurs. But they are no less important.

This distinction between entrepreneurs and managers also helps explain how the tribe of Issachar functioned as the business managers of the adventure-seeking entrepreneurs of Zebulun. In my personal experience, which is corroborated by many studies, every entrepreneur needs a manager by his side who takes care of logistics, accounts, payments, expenses, delivery, and distribution. All of these things are critical in order to innovate, break into new markets, and make well-timed decisions without error or delays. The people of Issachar were the business managers for the tribe of Zebulun, and they also opened the east–west trade route. They dealt with finances, logistics, distribution, and administration.

The tribe of Issachar loaded merchandise on its shoulders and worked like donkeys for the wages that Zebulun pays. They are the managers and workers of the tribe of Zebulun. In the words of Moses: "Rejoice, O Zebulun, on your journeys, and Issachar, in your tent." The tribe of Issachar sat in tents because they were responsible for the logistics and management of Zebulun's business.

Among the somewhat opaque verses from The Book of Chronicles 1 on the topic of King David's coronation, it is stated: "Of the Issacharites, men who knew how to interpret the times, to determine how Israel should act; their chiefs were 200, and all their kinsmen followed them" (The Book of Chronicles 1 12:33). These verses state that all the tribes supplied tens of thousands of soldiers to David's army. As mentioned above, the tribe of Zebulun provided the most soldiers of all. Issachar, in perfect contrast, supplied only 200 personnel. This reflects that they were managers and not warriors, as the verse continues "and all their kinsmen followed them."

Expounding on the expression, "the times" (*itim*), the sages understand the "knowledge" of Issachar as referring to the calculation of months, intercalation of years, and the like.[18] Given our interpretation that the Issacharites were in the "tents" of administration, managing the accounts of the entrepreneurial Zebulunites, we can interpret this verse as saying that Issachar managed the accounts of David's military, as well. The Issacharites were the financial managers and accountants of the ministry of defense's budget and perhaps all governmental bureaus. Keeping track of cash flow and logistical operations and making sure all reports are filed in a timely manner requires outstanding time management skills: "men who knew how to interpret the times."[19]

Thanks to the cooperation between these two tribes, business with the Phoenicians, who wanted to reach the markets east of the Jordan, flourished. From the ninth through sixth centuries BCE, the seafaring Phoenicians, who lived to the north in modern-day Lebanon, spread out across the Mediterranean and controlled its trade. They settled and established many trade posts: first in Cyprus, then in the Aegean islands, Sicily, Malta, Sardinia, North Africa (where they established their largest colony, Carthage), and ultimately Iberia and the Maghreb.

It is therefore fitting that Zebulun precedes Issachar because the entrepreneur precedes management; they set up the business and create the opportunities. Much as Steve Jobs brought in Tim Cook, Mark Zuckerberg brought in Sheryl Sandberg, and Bill Gates brought in Steve Ballmer, the visionary entrepreneur sweeps us all into the future while great managers ensure that the trains run on time.

Perhaps the connection between Issachar and Zebulun also cloaks a deeper idea, beyond the ongoing practical activities of entrepreneurship and management. Since Zebulun did not have access to the sea, which necessitated settling by someone else's coastline, it is puzzling that Jacob did not link him to the tribe of Asher, whose tribal territory actually bordered the sea. In fact, it seems that by promoting intertribal cooperation in matters of commerce, Jacob also drove home a point.

Jacob was an economic migrant: someone who had moved away from the land of Israel for more than twenty years and built his family and fortune, only to leave again years later and travel to Egypt. He also saw his sons travel back and forth to Egypt to buy food and eventually settle. He therefore understood the value of building a strong chain of commerce that would connect land and sea and whose nerve center would be in the heart of the land of Israel.

Every society needs an economy of imports and exports. Jacob, therefore, goaded the risk-taking entrepreneurs of Zebulun to engage in it. But it was also important that their role in developing the economy did not cause prolonged absence from their homes,[20] land, values, and birthright.

At the end of the book of Joshua, the midrashic *Sefer HaYashar*, which was written in the Middle Ages by an unknown European author, describes: "And they buried the coffins of their tribal patriarchs...each in the tribal territory of his sons.... And the bones of Issachar and Zebulun were buried in Sidon, in the portion that fell to their sons." *Seder HaDorot*, the 18th century book of biographies written by Rabbi Yechiel Halpern of Minsk, cites the following from *Gelilot* Eretz Yisrael: "And the bones of Issachar and Zebulun are in Sidon, which is the great

Sidon on the coast of the Mediterranean, and beyond the city limits is the domed grave of Zebulun, and there is a synagogue there." Putting aside the historical reliability of these descriptions, they bring out the built-in tension of "here vs. there" that comes with forging significant foreign trade relationships.

Jacob did not want Zebulun to follow the path of the Phoenicians, establishing colonies throughout the Mediterranean that slowly developed from ports of call and trade posts into permanent settlements and full-fledged cities.[21] He wanted Zebulun to work with the Phoenicians, but he did not want him emigrating from the land of Israel. The challenges that Zebulun faced in his tribal territory, which was less fertile and had no port or access to the sea, both spurred him to be an entrepreneur and kept him close to home. This was the purpose of the vital link with Issachar—"the tent dwellers" who were extremely attached to their territory, its mountain ridges, and its lands in the heart of the country—instead of Asher, whose territory abutted the sea, and the Sidonians who "dwelt among the Canaanites."

According to their tradition, the Jews of Djerba, located off the coast of Tunisia, and Crete are descendants of the tribe of Zebulun, as cited by Professor Nahum Slouschz in *Ha-I Peli* (Dvir 1957). This would indicate that Jacob's fears were somewhat warranted. Slouschz cites dozens of customs of the Jewish community of Crete that give expression to the tradition that they are descendants of Zebulun. Regarding the Jews of Djerba, Slouschz writes: "According to the Torah scholars of Djerba, the island upon which they live is actually a tract of land from the land of Israel...."

One of Zebulun's sons was Sered. In his book *Mi Hayu Ha-Finikim*, N. R. Genor speculated that members of the Sered clan may have settled the island of Sardinia. Similarly, in The

Book of Chronicles, the lists of tribal lineages from the early Second Temple period do not include an up-to-date lineage for Zebulun. The Book of Chronicles includes nine chapters of genealogical lists. While Bible critics assert that The Book of Chronicles was written in the Persian period (fourth century BCE), tradition avers that it was written by Ezra and Nehemiah, the leaders of Jews who returned to the land of Israel in the early Second Temple period. The lists are both a census of those returning to the land and an identity marker for Jewish or Israeli lineage. Therefore, Zebulun's absence may mean that Zebulun did not return to the land of Israel after the first exile, following the destruction of the First Temple. Indeed, the Jews of Djerba have a tradition that Ezra the Scribe visited their island in an attempt to persuade them to return, but they refused.[22]

"HIS FLANK (YARKHATO) SHALL REST ON SIDON"

In its simplest sense, the Hebrew word *yerekh* denotes an extremity, side, flank, or wing. For example: "And for the rear [*yarkhetei*] of the Tabernacle, to the west, make six planks; and make two planks for the corners of the Tabernacle at the rear" (Exodus 26:22–23). Accordingly, the phrase "His flank [*yarkhato*] shall rest on Sidon" means that the border of his tribal territory—or more precisely, his business activities, which will be conducted via ship—will reach Sidon.

In a wider sense, the rear of the Tabernacle was not only the back part, but also the narrowest part, the part with the least planks, and therefore the most vulnerable. Or in nautical terms: "Jonah, meanwhile, had gone down into the hold (*yarkhetei*) of the vessel" (Jonah 1:5). This refers to the belly of the ship or part of the vessel where a single hole can sink it. Later in the story, it becomes clear that Jonah is the "hole" that threatens to capsize the entire ship.

"His flank shall rest on Sidon" does not refer only to opportunities but also to the challenge Jacob posed. Jacob wanted Zebulun to engage in international trade with the Sidonians for the greater welfare of the Israeli people, but his irregular use of the word "flank" connotes a warning, as well. In the associative world of Jacob and his sons, *yarkhato* evokes the word *yerekh* (thigh, extremity),[23] a part of the body that, like all instances of the root "YRKh," is vulnerable.[24] The man who fought with Jacob, on the night prior to his encounter with his brother Esau, could not emerge victorious, but he was able to injure Jacob in a sensitive place,[25] his *yerekh*, an Achilles heel of sorts.

In other words, trade with the Sidonians was an opportunity, but leaving home for extended, difficult journeys abroad could make Zebulun susceptible to influence from the cultures he encounters and their behavioral norms.[26] Zebulun is vulnerable, especially morally, to the harmful influence of the Sidonians. In *Zohar* (p. 242b), the phrase "And his flank shall reach Sidon" is expounded: "Rabbi Abba began, 'Gird your sword upon your thigh [*yerekh*], O hero, in your splendor and glory....'" (Psalms 44:4) The word *yerekh* is explained there as circumcision and as the Wayfarer's Prayer.

It seems that both of these are linked to Zebulun, who must preserve his identity during his travels. Therefore, Jacob's message to Zebulun was twofold. Firstly, just like the belly of a ship is narrow and sharp, so too, his exposure to Phoenician culture must be as narrow and limited as possible because he is vulnerable. Secondly, it must always be that "His flank shall rest on Sidon"—his back must face Sidon because his face will always be directed towards the land of Israel.

In his prophecy of doom about the Phoenician cities—Sidon and its successor, Tyre[27]—Isaiah warned against the corruption caused by a culture of wealth, commerce, and maritime activity.[28] Tyre had commercial ties, engaged with neighboring and distant kingdoms (as the prophet mentions: Tarshish, Kittim, Egypt, Canaan, and Sidon), and became wealthy. Isaiah described her as a "merry city in former times of yore"; "her feet carry her off to sojourn far away"; "crown-wearing Tyre"; and "whose merchants were nobles, whose traders the world honored." But resilience does not last forever. Isaiah[29] shows contempt for wealth, pride, and honor and predicted their downfall due to these attributes: "The Lord of Hosts planned it—to defile all glorious beauty, to shame all the honored of the world."[30] Modern day bible scholar Rabbi Yoel Bin-Nun, based on the words of Isaiah's "harlot's song" (Isaiah 23:15–16), adds that Tyre was the cultural capital of Canaan and its sexual cult of Baal and Asherah.[31]

In *The Rational Optimist*, Matt Ridley is sensitive to the tension between the Phoenicians' successful international trade and the ethical dangers that lurk in the shadow of wealth. In this context, he relates to the words of the prophets with a mocking tone:

> Travelling farther afield, the Phoenicians' innovations multiplied: better keels, sails, navigational knowledge, accounting systems, log-keeping. Trade, once more, was the flywheel of the innovation machine. To the south, steeped in their religious obsessions, the Israelite pastoralists looked on in puritan horror at the explosion of wealth thus created. Isaiah cheerily anticipates Yahweh's destruction of Tyre, the "market of the nations,," to humble her pride. Ezekiel vents his Schadenfreude

> when Tyre is attacked: "When thy wares went forth out of the seas, thou filledst many peoples; Thou didst enrich the kings of the earth with thy merchandise and thy riches.... Thou art become a terror; and thou shalt never be any more."[32]

As noted, Zebulun and Issachar worked together the entire time. Due to the ethical hazards of doing business with Tyrians and Sidonians, the Issacharites took responsibility for ensuring that all business activities would be conducted justly, in both appearance and reality. Their worldview would not change; they would pursue neither the haughtiness of Tyre nor the mocking spirit of Ridley.[33] Beyond his managerial position, Issachar was also a spiritual and moral anchor. Accordingly, Moses stated in his blessings: "They invite their kin to the mountain, where they offer sacrifices of righteousness. For they draw from the riches of the seas and the hidden hoards of the sand."

In what appears to be the straightforward meaning of the text, the key is that all peoples, even the other tribes of Israel, said that sacrifices of righteousness were offered in the mountains of Zebulun and Issachar in the Lower Galilee. They dealt fairly and justly. Their altars and their religious rites were righteous. All their wares, food and sacrifices came from trustworthy, reliable, well-considered sources, free of extortion and fraud.[34]

In contrast to the vile norms of the Phoenicians, Zebulun and Issachar "draw from the riches of the seas"—they gathered treasures and abundance from maritime trade. This phrase is a double entendre; the word "draw" (*yinaku*) invokes the Hebrew phrase for unblemished (*neki kapaim*).[35] "And the hidden hoards [*sefunei*] of the sand" means they did not hide any of their riches in the sand. Everything was kept out in the open, on the deck (*sipun*). Everything was transparent, clean, and just because the tribe of Issachar oversees the entrepreneurial business activities of the tribe of Zebulun. All of the merchandise, the treasures, and the international commerce were well documented by provenance and volume. Even those things that sailors generally "bury in the sand" to avoid detection were kept in the open, plain for all to see. These things teach us about "sacrifices of righteousness."

THE INSTITUTE OF STANDARDS

As we have seen, the blessings both assign a role and predict a destiny. Like the monarchy, which was granted to the tribe of Judah in the context of the blessings, Jacob and Moses entrusted Zebulun and Issachar with an important job. On one hand, the role is a financial one, which deals with enterprise and commerce. On the other hand, it is an ethical role, which ensures that imports to and exports from the land of Israel do not come under foreign influence.

Importers determine more than a financial agenda when deciding what to import. Conducting business with foreign elements is liable to entrench norms that diverge from the spirit of the Torah. It is therefore imperative to monitor and, perhaps, limit such interactions. Had the Phoenicians arrived on the shores of Eretz Yisrael to conduct business, their potential impact on Jewish society would have been far greater than when the Zebulunites controlled the sea routes and conducted business in the distant markets of Tyre and Sidon. When business was conducted within the land of Israel, foreign nations quickly established envoys, who brought both their merchandise and their culture.[36]

From a historical perspective, Jacob's and Moses's concern that trade routes would nourish negative spiritual influences was not unwarranted. Such fears materialized in several different time periods. Thus King Solomon married princesses of gentile nations near and far, and they inclined his heart toward sin.[37] Ahab married Jezebel, the daughter of Etbaal, king of Sidon, and she promoted the Baal cult in the land of Israel and persecuted the prophets of God.[38] There is also the episode recounted in the books of Ezra and Neḥemiah, wherein the Phoenicians sold raw materials for the construction of the Second Temple,[39] leading them to settle in Jerusalem and making it difficult for the Jews to observe Shabbat properly: "Tyrians who lived there brought fish and all sorts of wares and sold them on Shabbat to the Judahites in Jerusalem" (Neḥemiah 13:16).

The final example fits well with the aforementioned fact that no lineage of the tribe of Zebulun appears among the lists of pedigrees that returned to the land of Israel with Ezra and Nehemiah. We can speculate that no tribe returned to Zion from colonies they had established across the sea, be it Djerba, Crete, or Sardinia. Since Zebulun did not return and life does not occur in a vacuum, their role was taken over by the Phoenicians, who thought their commercial activities and hence their culture could penetrate Eretz Yisrael.

THE SAILOR'S KNOT[40]

By linking Issachar to Zebulun, Jacob and Moses attempted to construct the optimal synthesis of entrepreneurial spirit and careful management. They wanted to be certain that international trade would not be left to foreigners, both so that economic prosperity would serve Israelite business interests and that imported goods would fit with the nation's value system. They sent Zebulun the entrepreneur to carry out this task, but, there was the risk that the Zebulunites would be blinded by the wealth and opulence of the nations and forget where they came from, just as Ridley mockingly expressed.

Jacob and Moses wanted them to support themselves honorably and beyond the shadow of doubt. They wanted them to interact with the Sidonians without being influenced by their debased value system or their idolatry. This was not the puritanism described by Ridley but the upholding of a moral standard. Jacob and Moses shared a worldview that sanctifies enterprise and risk-taking but counterbalances—and even magnifies their value—through a deep connection to the work of porters and managers, who are anchored in the native values of ancient Israel.

In many ways, the Phoenicians are the perfect foil to the Israelites—and the message of the book of Genesis. Asceticism has been practiced by many religions from Hinduism to Christianity to certain Jewish sects. However, this is not the way of the Torah. The Jewish state also stands in opposition with the hedonistic Phoenicians and the sybaritic Sodom. It is the use, not the avoidance of wealth, that Jacob and the book of Genesis are interested in.

Abraham was wealthy. Isaac was wealthy. Jacob was wealthy. Joseph was an economic entrepreneur and minister. It is completely consistent that when Jacob blessed his children, he blessed them both with wealth from natural resources and from commerce. However, he admonished them not to use their wealth to bully others and descend into debauchery like the Phoenicians, and he warned them not to be selfish like Sodom.

The Torah thus seeks to model a successful society from both a material and spiritual perspective. That spirituality grounds the ethics that drive success in business. It promotes the transparency seen with Zebulun and in Abraham's encounters with the King of Sodom and the Hittites who sold him the burial plot. It stimulates the innovation that increases prosperity, as with Isaac's well-digging and Joseph's far-sighted storage of grain.

It does not always go according to plan. Sometimes significant innovation and economic activity and prosperity can lead to unfortunate outcomes such as Joseph's economic planning that enabled an Egyptian narrative to enslave the people of Israel or Jacob's economic and ethical tussles with his father in law Laban or even modern day internet innovations that enabled growth in binary options trading, correctly outlawed by the State of Israel in 2017. But that spiritual and ethical aspiration to build wealth and promote innovation is what creates the possibility of Israel being a light unto nations.

Acknowledgments

I am so grateful to the many people who have helped me in writing this book. First and foremost, my parents, Rabbi Barry and Debra Eisenberg, who raised me and my siblings, and who influence my children and grandchildren to be Zionists; feel responsibility for the Jewish people; and live a life of loyalty and devotion to the timeless Jewish tradition and law. "The glory of children is their parents." Likewise, my grandparents, with whom I was very close,—Charles (of blessed memory) and Els Bendheim (may she live and be well), and Isaiah Jacob "Sonny" and Sarah "Tootsie" Eisenberg (may their memories be a blessing)—were kind and generous people, guided by deep integrity. My in-laws, Martin and Miriam Knecht, have always been supportive, and my wife's grandparents, Avraham and Rachel Kurtzfeld (of blessed memory), a daily presence in our children's lives. They were spared from the flames of the Holocaust and have been privileged to raise five generations of offspring.

My *ḥavruta* (study partner) for this book is Rabbi Amit Misgav. When I sought an editor for the Hebrew version, I thought I would need to find two people, a Torah scholar and an economist, to weave together the different elements of the book. Amit is not only both an economist and a Torah scholar; he is also an original, creative, and eloquent person. He took an unripe text and transformed it into the book before you, and he became a *ḥavruta* and friend in addition to an editor. He challenged and improved every idea and every textual analysis, adding volume, depth, and an interesting, readable style. I am grateful to Rabbi Benny Lau for introducing us (albeit for a different purpose), thus begetting this fruitful collaboration. There are no words for me to thank Amit for his strenuous, sharp, and energetic work. We have already published the Hebrew version of the second and third volume on Exodus and Leviticus respectively. Two more to go. This book is his book, as well.

Adam Bellow taught me how an editor impactfully helps to craft a story. His experience and attention to detail come to the fore in the significantly better manuscript that is before you. His structural precision and insistence of getting rid of superfluous text that make the book harder to read significantly improved the English version of this book.

Rabbi Joseph Wermuth, (of blessed memory), was the devoted Ritual Director and Torah reader at the Jewish Center on the Upper West Side of Manhattan for half a century. He taught me and countless other young men to read and chant the Torah for their Bar Mitzvah. He taught me to read the Scroll of Esther as well. It was thanks to the love that he imbued in me that I learned to chant other parshiyot and continue to read the Torah in public for a long while.

My rabbis and mentors in various realms over the years have influenced me. I wish to name them, and I beg forgiveness of anyone I may have forgotten. Some of them are colleagues in economic activities, and some are from the realm of Torah. Rabbi Dr. Aharon Lichtenstein, whose aforementioned exemplary moral character influenced anyone who knew him (or even just saw him); Rabbi Yehuda Amital, who, as I wrote, challenged me to move to Israel and was the first person to open my eyes to viewing economics through the lens of Torah and mitzvot; Rabbi Michael Hecht, who taught me to love Torah and sent me to study at Yeshivat Har Etzion; Rabbi Ezra Bick, who taught me to read texts with care and precision; Rabbis Eliyahu Blumenzweig, Michael Rosenzweig, Yaakov Neuberger, Mordechai Friedman, Yitzchak Cohen, Moshe Yaged, and Chaim Gold; Rabbis Menachem Leibtag and Yaakov Medan, who influenced the way I read the verses of Scripture; my *ḥavrutot* through the years: Rabbi Ezra Wiener, Adi Lamm, Rabbi Menachem Penner, Rabbi Yaakov Blau, Michael Selesny (of blessed memory), Rabbi Simcha Krauss, Rabbi Binyamin Krauss, Rabbi Yonason Shippel, Micah Gimpel and Simcha Axelrod; and, of course, my father. He brought me to love the Torah from a young age and continues to serve as a role model for setting aside time to study Torah and with whom I have been fortunate to learn with for many years in a consistent, diligent study partnership. Gratitude is also due to my dear friend since our time together at Yeshivat Har Etzion, Aviad Friedman, who made direct and helpful comments on the Hebrew draft and has been a pillar of support for me and our family since we moved to Israel.

During my career, many people helped me and influenced my thinking. Dr. Shlomo Kalish of Jerusalem Global; Jon Medved and Neil Cohen, my partners in Israel Seed; Adv. Daniel Chinn; Bruce Dunlevie (the biggest mensch in our craft and a true mentor); and Bill Gurley (one of the smartest people I have worked with), some of my wise and understanding Benchmark partners, whose impact on my path has been tremendous. Arad Naveh, Elie Wurtman, my partners at Benchmark Israel. Eden Shochat, Yael Elad and Aaron Rosenson, my partners at Aleph, and people who devoted precious moments of their time for small tips at the beginning of my career: Henry McCance, Edward Cohen, Kevin Compton, Jack Nash (of blessed memory), Ludwig Jesselson (of blessed memory), and legendary "coach" Bill Campbell (of blessed memory).

I owe a debt of gratitude to all the entrepreneurs who shared their best ideas with me, agreed to work with me, challenged me, and gave me the opportunity to invest with them. I learned a great deal from all of them. I also want to thank the internet entrepreneurs from PictureVision, the first company I invested in—Yaacov Ben Yaacov and Elliot Jaffe—and the people of Shopping.com: Amir Ashkenazi, Dan Ciporin, and Nahum Sharfman (of blessed memory).

To the weekly WhatsApp group where I began distributing these essays while they were still (very) unripe: You know who you are. Thanks for the feedback. A special thank you as well to Rabbi Dr. Hillel Novetsky and family, who started and run the site Alhatorah.org, which I live on in order to write these books. Hillel also pushed me hard to put out the English version.

To the literary editor of the Hebrew edition, Rabbi Avichai Gamdani, who also edited *Ben Barukh*, my book on *Jerusalem Talmud Tractate Berakhot*. R. Avichai is a special and talented person who gave the book a beautiful form and flow. To Mara Sarnoff, my copyeditor for the English version of the book who upgraded my written English to 21st Century norms and syntax. To my publisher in Hebrew, Rotem Sela, who also published *The Vanishing Jew*, reviewed drafts of this book, and made helpful comments.

This English translation would not have been possible without the excellent work of my translator Rena Siev. I tried a few translators before finding someone who had both the textual understanding and translation skill to bring this together. Rabbi Elli Fischer served as editor and supervisor of the English translation. I am indebted to both of them as well as my cousins Aliza and JJ Sussman, who suggested that Elli would be a good choice for the project.

Our children and their spouses—Tamar, Yosef, Sonny, Chaim, Gabriella, Sarah, Yehuda, Moshe, Batsheva, and Nili—were the first audience for these ideas at our Shabbat meals at home. They encouraged me to spend my mornings writing at home, supported the publication of the book, and took interest in it. None of this is self-evident. You are my inspiration for this book and the pride and joy of my life.

This book is dedicated to my beloved wife, Yaffa. No one carries the banner of moral principles and their importance and application more than her. She even tries to improve my approach every day, commenting on such matters with a special sweetness.

What is mine and yours is really hers.

She heroically supported the many hours I invested in learning Torah, in my work, and in the numerous lectures I give. She provided ongoing encouragement of my efforts to publish this book, read multiple drafts, and made many good and helpful comments about its content and approach. Thank you from the bottom of my heart.

My dear wife and life partner, we have an agreement not to speak about or compliment one another in public. It must therefore suffice to quote the words of the wisest of all men:

Live joyfully with the wife that that you love all the days of the life of vanity, which He has given you under the sun, all the days of your vanity. For that is your portion in life and in your work that you labor under the sun. (Kohelet 9:9)

To this I will add the words of Proverbs (18:22):

He who finds a wife, finds good, and obtains favor of God.

I have found that which is exceedingly good.

I conclude with a prayer that we merit experiencing pride, *nachas,* in our descendants for many more years, in health and abundant love.

Michael
2021

Notes and Insights

1. It is really an even more extreme home-run business. According to the data, there has been $482 billion of venture capital funding in the last ten years. The combined value of the ten largest venture-backed companies is $213 billion. So ten venture-backed companies are valued at half the industry's deployed capital.
2. Space does not allow us to touch even the tip of the iceberg of this issue, which begins with the Torah verse, "do what is upright and good" (Deuteronomy 6:18); continues with various commandments that end with the coda "and you shall fear your God"; and has branched out through generations of Jewish thought and halakhah (including cases where one is technically or formally exempt from a payment but must still pay "in order to fulfill his duty in the eyes of heaven" (e.g. Babylonian Talmud Bava Kama 59b and many more)
3. https://www.wsj.com/articles/im-leaving-seattle-for-texas-so-my-employees-can-be-free-11593211124

PARASHAT BEREISHIT

1. *Lonely Man of Faith* (New York, 2009), pp. 15-16.
2. Background on the proposal: "The universal need for basic income. What can be done about poverty? Often, poverty is tackled through a symptomatic approach rather than by treating the underlying cause. For historian Rutger Bregman, the solution to poverty is simple: universal basic income. We should change the

context in which poor people live by giving everyone a monthly allowance to pay for basic needs. This idea is more than five hundred years old, first introduced by Thomas More in *Utopia* and, Bregman says, it's proven to be successful. In 1974, an experiment in Dauphin, Canada, showed how basic income could allow everyone to not only survive but thrive. According to Bregman, a basic income in the United States would cost $175 billion, just a quarter of the US's military budget. And universal basic income impacts the future of work itself—it's a complete rethink of what 'work' actually is. Ultimately, Bregman believes in a 'future where the value of your work is not determined by the size of your paycheck, but by the amount of happiness you spread and the amount of meaning you give'" (TED Talks Vancouver 2017). For additional information, see the Wikipedia entry on "Universal Basic Income."

3. https://www.wired.co.uk/article/finland-universal-basic-income-results-trial-cancelled. See also the argument as to why the UBI test in Finland "failed" (or did it?): https://www.nytimes.com/2018/05/02/opinion/universal-basic-income-finland.html
4. "We should have a society that measures progress not just by economic metrics like GDP, but by how many of us have a role we find meaningful. We should explore ideas like universal basic income to give everyone a cushion to try new things. We're going to change jobs many times, so we need affordable childcare to get to work and healthcare that aren't tied to one company. We're all going to make mistakes, so we need a society that focuses less on locking us up or stigmatizing us. And as technology keeps changing, we need to focus more on continuous education throughout our lives. And yes, giving everyone the freedom to pursue purpose isn't free. People like me should pay for it. Many of you will do well, and you should, too." (Mark Zuckerberg, Harvard Commencement Speech, 2017)
5. "Silicon Valley is so excited about the concept of universal basic income, or stipends paid to people regardless of whether they work. The message is: 'We don't need you. But we are nice, so we'll take care of you.'" Yuval Noah Harari https://www.nytimes.com/2018/11/09/business/yuval-noah-harari-silicon-valley.html

Unlike Harari, the Torah understands that man was created in God's image, meaning that man can create and invent. This godly ability that was breathed into him both confers great responsibility upon him and endows him with a life full of meaning, making him personally accountable for his continued existence.

6. The Mishnah (*Ketubot* 5:5) cites a similar debate:

> And these are tasks that a wife must perform for her husband: She mills [wheat], bakes, launders clothes, cooks, and nurses her child, makes her husband's bed, and spins wool. If she brought him one maidservant (into the marriage), [the wife] need not mill, bake, or launder clothes. If she brought him two maidservants, she need not cook or nurse her child. If she brought him three maidservants, she need not make his bed or spin wool. If she brought him four maidservants, she may sit in a chair like a queen. Rabbi Eliezer says: Even if she brought him a hundred maidservants, he could compel her to spin wool, since idleness leads to licentiousness. Rabban Shimon ben Gamliel says: Even one who vows that his wife must not do work must divorce her and pay her *ketubah*, since idleness leads to boredom.

Rabbi Ovadia of Bartenura explains: "'Boredom'—panic." The Targum translates the words *u-vetimhon levav*' (Deuteronomy 28:28) to mean "*u-vesha'amamut liba*." The dispute between Rabbi Eliezer and Rabban Shimon ben Gamliel regards a woman who is not idle, but rather amuses herself in a variety of ways. Such a woman is likely to become involved in licentious behavior, whereas boredom is a function of complete idleness and inactivity. The *halakha* follows the opinion of Rabbi Eliezer.

7. Malbim (ad loc.) comments:

> In any event, it is not possible that they would have continued to exist had not man been created. This is on account of two reasons: (a) The vast majority of plants do not grow on their own. They require man to plow the soil

and sow seeds. This is true with regard to trees as well: they, too, require man to plant them and cultivate the land; (b) Vegetation cannot grow without rain, and rain is a matter of divine Providence. Rainfall comes on account of man's merits and his prayer.

8. Some commentaries assume that the "Eid" is a flow of water from the ground and not a mist.
9. As the river said to Rabbi Pinḥas ben Yair: "You are going to perform the will of your Maker and I am going to perform the will of my Maker, to flow in my channel. With regard to you, it is uncertain whether or not you will perform His will successfully. I will certainly perform His will successfully" (BT *Ḥullin* 7a).
10. R. Aharon Lichtenstein, *By His Light* (Hoboken, 2003), pp. 8-9.
11. https://basicincome.org/news/2016/06/would-a-universal-basic-income-make-us-lonely/
12. Mishnah *Avot* 2:2 states:

    > Rabban Gamliel, the son of Rabbi Yehuda the Nasi said: Excellent is the study of the Torah together with a worldly occupation; for the exertion expended in both causes sin to be forgotten. Ultimately, all Torah study that is not accompanied with work is destined to cease and to cause sin.

    Rambam (*Mishneh Torah*, Laws of Torah Study 3:11) states similarly:

    > It is virtuous for a person to derive his livelihood from his own efforts. This attribute was exhibited by the pious of the early generations. In this manner, one will merit all types of honor and benefit in this world and in the world to come, as it is written: "You shall enjoy the fruit of your labors...."

13. Mishnah *Avot* 4:15 states: "Rabbi Yanai says: We do not have the ability to explain the tranquility of the wicked or even the suffering of the righteous."

PARASHAT NOAH

1. In this time period, when people lived upwards of 900 years and continued to have children, the rate of reproduction was extremely high. Halting population growth for a few hundred years would not have endangered the survival of humanity.
2. Some of the commentators, including Rashbam, suggest that Noah was born right after Adam passed away. According to their explanation, with Adam's passing, the curse of thorns and thistles was also abolished, enabling better agriculture and food supply.
3. Jerusalem Talmud, *Bava Metzi'a* 4:2. The Mishnah on which this passage comments states:

   > If the buyer acquired produce from the seller, but the buyer did not yet give the seller their value in money, he may not renege on the transaction, but if the buyer gave the seller money but did not yet pull produce from him, he can renege on the transaction, as the transaction is not yet complete. But with regard to the latter case, the Sages said: He Who exacted payment from the people of the generation of the flood, and from the generation of the division (i.e., that of the Tower of Babel), will in the future exact payment from whoever does not stand by his statement. Just as the people of those generations were not punished by an earthly court but were subjected to divine punishment, so too though no earthly court can compel the person who reneged to complete the transaction, punishment will be exacted at the hand of Heaven for any damage that he caused.

4. https://www.wsj.com/articles/SB10001424052702304840904577422090013997320

PARASHAT LEKH LEKHA

1. Each of the early commentators formulated his own list. Rambam writes:

> The ten trials of our father Abraham are all listed in the Torah. The first was his migration, when God told him, "Go forth from your native land...." The second was the famine that he encountered upon arriving in the land of Canaan. Abraham's destiny was "I will make of you a great nation," so this was a most difficult trial, wherein it states, "There was a famine in the land." The third was the lawlessness of the Egyptians who abducted Sarah to Pharaoh's home. The fourth was the war with the four kings. The fifth was his marriage to Hagar, after he had despaired of having a child with Sarah. The sixth was his circumcision, which he was commanded to perform in old age. The seventh was the lawlessness of the king of Gerar who also abducted Sarah. The eighth was the eviction of Hagar, after he had a child by her. The ninth was the distancing of his son Ishmael. God said to him: "Do not be distressed over the boy," which indicates that it was extremely difficult for Abraham. Nonetheless, he followed the command of God and evicted them from his home. The tenth was the binding of Isaac.

R. Ovadiah of Bertinoro enumerates:

> One, Ur of the Chaldeans, where Nimrod threw him into the fiery furnace. Two, "Go forth from your native land." Three, "There was a famine." Four, "And the woman was taken into Pharaoh's palace." Five, the war of the kings. Six, the covenant of the pieces, when Abraham learned that his children would be subjugated by the kingdoms of the world. Seven, circumcision. Eight, "So King Abimelech of Gerar sent and took Sarah." Nine, "Cast out that slave-woman and her son." Ten, the binding of Isaac.

R. Yonah of Gerondi enumerates them as follows:

> Our father Abraham was tested with ten trials and he passed them all. The first was at Ur of the Chaldeans, when Nimrod threw him into a fiery furnace, and he was

saved. The second was when he was commanded to leave his land, as it is written "Go forth from your native land and from your birthplace," and he followed through. The third was with regard to the "famine in the land." Even though God had promised, "And all the families of earth shall bless themselves through you," Abraham did not doubt God when He brought a famine. The fourth was Sarah's abduction by Pharaoh. The fifth was the war of the four kings. Abraham fought with an army of only 318 soldiers and trusted in God. A miracle occurred and Abraham was spared and was able to save his relative and restore all of the stolen property of Sodom and Gomorrah. Abraham endured the entire episode, which is a testimony to his righteousness. The sixth was that "Abraham was ninety-nine years old when he circumcised the flesh of his foreskin." He endangered himself in his old age, and he was saved. The seventh was Sarah's abduction by Abimelech. The eighth was the expulsion of Hagar and his son Ishmael from his home. Although "The matter distressed Abraham greatly, for it concerned his son," he nonetheless followed God's command. The ninth was the binding of his son Isaac, where it is written "For now I know that you fear God." Is it possible that God did not know this previously?! After all, God is omniscient! Rather, it is at the point in time when it became clear to the rest of humanity that God declared, "For now I know that you fear God." The tenth was the burial of Sarah. Abraham was told "Arise, walk about the land, through its length and its breadth, for I give it to you." Yet when his wife died, he could not find a burial plot until he purchased one, but Abraham did not doubt God.

2. Abram and Sarai were the original names of Abraham and Sarah before they were changed by God.
3. Following Rashi's interpretation.
4. For additional discussion of this point, see my book *The Vanishing Jew: A Wakeup Call from the Book of Esther,* pp. 84–88

5. Ibn Ezra (12:20) explains "they sent him" (*va-yishleḥu oto*) means not that they expelled him, but that they granted him permission to leave, as in "Abraham went along with them to see them off (*leshalḥam*) (18:16). R. Eliyahu Mizraḥi goes further, explaining that "they sent him" means that they escorted him with great honor.
6. For a general survey of the wickedness of Sodom, see this article by Yoḥanan Cohen: http://www.daat.ac.il/daat/kitveyet/maaliyot/hetey-2.htm
7. The Talmud (*Megilah* 10b) states:

   > R. Ashi said: Instances of "It happened" (*vayehi*) can go like this or like that. "It happened in the days of" (*vayehi biymei*) always refers to distress. There are five instances of "It happened in the days of": "It happened in the days of Ahasuerus" (Esther 1); "It happened in the days when the judges ruled" (Ruth 1); "It happened in the days of Amraphel" (Genesis 14); "It happened in the days of Ahaz" (Isaiah 7); and "It happened in the days of Jehoiakim" (Jeremiah 1). In all those incidents, grief ensued.

   In *The Vanishing Jew: A Wakeup Call from the Book of Esther (42),* I explain that the phrase "it happened in the days of" is not merely an expression of sorrow but specifically sorrow that derives from an unethical economic decision.

8. From this point in the story, Abraham embarks on only one more journey, many years later—the journey to Gerar (Genesis 20:1).
9. My friend Moshe Bar Siman Tov, who was Director-General of Israel's Health Ministry during the COVID-19 virus, said this about the spread of the virus. In commenting on the third volume of this series entitled *Roaring Tribe* on the Book of Leviticus, which appeared in Hebrew in March 2021, he made the same remark about the economic principles of this book series.
10. Warren Buffett, *The Snowball: Warren Buffett and the Business of Life* (New York, 2008).
11. As the Babylonian Talmud (*Beitzah* 16a) states:

    > All of a person's sustenance is set for him between Rosh Hashanah and Yom Kippur, except for the expenses of

> Shabbat and Festivals and the expenses of [sending] his sons to study Torah; [regarding these expenses], if he decreased [his expected expenses] his [earnings] are decreased, and if he surpassed [his expected expenses] his [earnings] are increased.

Rashi comments (ad loc.):

> "All of a person's sustenance"—everything a person will earn over the course of the year, from which his sustenance will come, is set for him; he will earn such-and-such [an amount] in this year.

Rashi's explanation presents an extreme view; namely, that everything is determined by God and there is no room for human effort. However, Rashi himself was a vintner, and *Shitah Mekubetzet* (ad loc.) cites more moderate interpretations, according to which a person's efforts contribute to his financial success.

12. David Tzvi Hoffmann addresses this question.
13. Radak advances a similar approach. Ramban rejects the possibility that the land could not feed two flocks of sheep, but he does not see the blessing as the root cause of their separation:

    > And the land where they sojourned—that is to say: the city in which they lived, which is Hebron, where Abraham and Isaac had lived. Because the land of Israel can support more than a thousand times [the number of sheep that Esau and Jacob had]. When Esau saw that he would not be able to stay in his city and his place, he ceded the entire land to his brother and left.

14. Rashi, in the name of the midrash, chooses sides in this ethical argument. According to his approach, the argument revolved around stealing the grazing lands of the Canaanites and Perizzites, who governed the land of Canaan at the time.
15. Rashi, quoting the midrash, explains: "He journeyed away from the Creator of the Universe. He declared: I am not interested in Abraham or his God." Professor Yehuda Elitzur explained that the

word "eastward" hints to the place where Abraham constructed his altar—"east of Bethel,," meaning that Lot distanced himself from Abraham and from service of God. Thus, the straightforward meaning of the text and the midrashic explanation coincide. See http://www.daat.ac.il/daat/tanach/tora/elitzur-4.htm.

16. After the destruction of Sodom, Lot fled to the mountains. Alone there with his two daughters, he became drunk and incestuous. This portrayal is very reminiscent of Noah in the aftermath of the flood. In the chapter, "The Frustrated Inventor," we explain that Noah felt guilty for inventing the plow that led to breakdown of society and the destruction of human civilization, and he therefore became drunk in his tent. In the article "An Ember Saved from Fire" below, we expound upon the leadership of the king of Sodom and how Lot realized his own leadership ambitions. The composite effect of these three things—Lot's leadership, Lot's similarity to Noah, and Noah as "the frustrated inventor"—suggests a portrait in which Lot peers out from his cave onto the region that has been scarred by fire and sulfur, deeply frustrated that his leadership brought this catastrophe upon the land, just as his ideology and belief system caused him to lose all of his wealth.

17. Legendary investor Ray Dalio presents a similar message in his groundbreaking article: https://www.linkedin.com/pulse/our-biggest-economic-social-political-issue-two-economies-ray-dalio/

PARASHAT VAYERA

1. 19th century Biblical commentator Meir Leibush, also known as Malbim, writes:

> A poor man who withholds what is due to the wretched—this indicates that at times it is not the rulers who dominate, but rather the poor men who dominate through their rebellion, and all people will rule over one another. The poor men who have nothing will extort the destitute who have become impoverished on account of the

rebellion. This is similar to a destructive rain. The clouds split open, and the rain bursts forth and washes everything away, to the point that there is no bread. Rather than producing bread, the rain will destroy everything, and no bread will come on account of the rainfall. The same is true regarding the poor people. They will wash everything away, just like mighty, roaring water.

2. Abarbanel, commentary to Bereishit 14:21
3. Perhaps the "fugitive" was a preselected messenger in case Lot was captured in war.
4. "The sword comes upon the world because of the delaying of justice and the perverting of justice; and because of those that teach Torah not according to the *halakhah*" (*Avot* 5:8).
5. In his book, *Abram to Abraham: A Literary Analysis of the Abraham Narrative*, Professor Yonatan Grossman considers the double entendre of the verse: "Now the Valley of Siddim was dotted with bitumen pits; and the kings of Sodom and Gomorrah, in their flight, fell there, while the rest escaped to the hill country" (14:10). He explains that the phrase "fell there" suggests that they fell in battle, meaning that the kings were killed. He notes that the verses "play a trick on the reader"; when the king of Sodom comes out to meet Abraham, it becomes evident that the other kings fell into ditches and were not killed in battle. Based on our analysis in this essay, it follows that four out of five kings died in battle, and only the king of Sodom survived. In fact, Rashi on 14:10 seems to suggest that the king of Sodom was the only king who survived. However, one can read Rashi as saying that the King of Sodom survived, but he has no opinion as to the fate of the other kings.
6. Rashbam on 14:21.
7. This is reminiscent of the struggle of YIMBY and NIMBY in San Francisco: https://www.reuters.com/article/us-usa-realestate-sanfrancisco/yimby-call-to-build-more-housing-divides-booming-san-francisco-idUSKCN1J11SS
8. In effect, the entire Chapter 23 of Jeremiah deals with the corruption of justice in Judea: "They are all murderers"; "Uphold the rights of the orphan; defend the cause of the widow"; etc.

9. For further discussion of this point see: https://www.tandfonline.com/doi/full/10.1080/15299732.2017.1295373; https://www.theguardian.com/society/2013/sep/17/breaking-the-cycle-of-abuse

10. A similar progression of denying rights to the weakest and ignoring the divine imperative, leading to an ever-deteriorating situation, is described in Mishnah *Avot* 5:8:

    > Seven kinds of punishment come to the world for seven types of transgression: When some give tithes and others do not give tithes, a famine from drought comes; some go hungry, and others are satisfied. When they have all decided not to give tithes, a famine from tumult and drought comes; [When they] do not set apart the dough-offering, an all-consuming famine comes.

11. See the commentary of R. David Tzvi Hoffmann to 18:20:

    > The outcry—It is not necessary to say that this outcry protested Sodom and its wickedness. As can be explained on the basis of other verses, it seems more correct to us that this is the image of the city of Sodom, from which the outcry to avenge the wrongs that have been committed there reaches the heart of the heavens.

12. "The two angels arrived in Sodom in the evening, as Lot was sitting in the gate of Sodom. When Lot saw them, he rose to greet them and, bowing low with his face to the ground, he said, 'Please, my lords, turn aside to your servant's house to spend the night, and bathe your feet; then you may be on your way early.' But they said, 'No, we will spend the night in the square.' But he urged them strongly, so they turned his way and entered his house. He prepared a feast for them and baked unleavened bread, and they ate. They had not yet lain down, when the townspeople, the men of Sodom, young and old—all the people to the last man – gathered about the house. And they shouted to Lot and said to him, 'Where are the men who came to you tonight? Bring them out to us, that we may know them.' ... Then the men said to Lot, 'Whom else have you here? Sons-in-law, your sons and daughters, or any-

one else that you have in the city—bring them out of the place. For we are about to destroy this place; because the outcry against them before the Lord has become so great that the Lord has sent us to destroy it.'" (19:1–13)

13. "It was written at the entrance to Cappadocia: *Anpak, anbag, antal*" (*Bava Batra* 58b). Rashbam explains: "They wrote this in order to teach the residents of the city that these three terms are the same measurement. The practical ramification is for business: If one stipulated to sell his fellow this measurement, whichever term he used he gives the same measurement."
14. This echoes the cry of Joseph: "Take everyone out from before me" (45:1).
15. The vast majority of commentators maintain that the demand "that we may know them" has a sexual connotation.
16. Isaiah (3:1–12):

> For lo! The Sovereign Lord of Hosts will remove from Jerusalem and from Judah all leaders and officials, every official who dispensed food, and every official of water. Soldier and warrior, magistrate and prophet, augur and elder; Captain of fifty, magnate and counselor, skilled artisan and expert enchanter; and He will make boys their rulers, and babes shall govern them. So the people shall oppress one another—each oppressing his fellow: The young shall bully the old; and the despised [shall bully] the honored. For should a man seize his brother, in whose father's house there is clothing: "Come, be a chief over us, and let this ruin be under your care." The other will thereupon protest, "I will not be a dresser of wounds, with no food or clothing in my own house. You shall not make me chief of a people!" Ah, Jerusalem has stumbled, and Judah has fallen, because by word and deed they insult the Lord, defying His majestic glance. Their partiality in judgment accuses them; they avow their sins like Sodom, they do not conceal them. Woe to them! For ill have they served themselves. Hail the just man, for he shall fare well; He shall eat the fruit of his works.

> Woe to the wicked man, for he shall fare ill; as his hands have dealt, so shall it be done to him. My people's rulers are babes, it is governed by women. O my people! Your leaders are misleaders; they have confused the course of your paths.

17. Jonah 3:4 it states:

    > Jonah started out and made his way into the city the distance of one day's walk, and proclaimed: "Forty days more, and Nineveh shall be overthrown [*nehepekhet*]!"

    The word "overthrown" (*nehepekhet*) is a double entendre. Either the city would be destroyed or the inhabitants would repent, have a change of heart, and improve their actions. Sodom was given many opportunities to repent and mend its ways, but it did not internalize the message. Ultimately, the destruction, in the form of fire and sulfur from the heavens, was inevitable.

18. In Deuteronomy (29:22), the Jewish people are warned that if they do not abide by their covenant with God, He will destroy the land of Israel as He destroyed Sodom: "All its soil devastated by sulfur and salt, beyond sowing and producing, no grass growing in it, just like the upheaval of Sodom and Gomorrah, Admah and Zeboiim, which the Lord overthrew in His fierce anger." It seems, contrary to what the daughters of Lot imply when they say, "there is not a man," that the city of Zoar was not included in the cities that God destroyed. It is possible to resolve this incongruity by saying that Zoar was destroyed in a different fashion. With the destruction of her allies, in the absence of appropriate social and governmental infrastructure, Zoar collapsed on its own.

PARASHAT SARAH

1. An instructive description of the nuances of Biblical language in negotiations can be found in Elhanan Samet's *Iyunim BeParashat HaShavu'a*, second series, pp. 86–89.
2. 57 Babylonian Talmud *Ketubot* 99b. This halachic principle avers that if real estate is sold at well above market value, the buyer has

no claim on the difference. According to some commentators, the reason is: "People are wont to forgive [what they overpaid] for land, because land is priceless."

3. Ramban connects Onkelos's explanation that the land was worth four hundred silver shekels with a statement of Babylonian Talmud (*Bava Metzia* 87a): "According to our Rabbis, Ephron set a very expensive priced, at his whim, yet Abraham generously accepted and did as he wanted—and more." Although the Talmud says, "a very expensive price,," the meaning seems to be that Ephron insisted on payment in the more valuable currency that merchants used, *over la-soḥer* ("at the going merchant's rate") instead of standard coinage. That is, Ramban understands that the price of the field was the regular price, but Ephron "spoke a lot, but did little" in the sense that he first offered the field to Abraham free of charge and ultimately demanded the full sum of the field in a specific expensive currency.

   The Talmud goes on to name three different types of coins—expensive and inexpensive—in order to establish the disparity between Ephron's public declaration—that the money would be paid in standard currency—and what he actually took. Note, however, that according to historical research, coins were only invented several centuries later.

4. Commentary of the JPS Pentateuch to Genesis 23:15
5. The Vilna Gaon, in *Kol Eliyahu*, connects the price of the cave of Machpelah and the fixed price of a field in the book of Leviticus. Accordingly, since the value of Ephron's field was 400 shekels, and given that one who consecrates an area that is one *beit kor* (a Talmudic measurement) can redeem it for fifty shekels, it follows that the area of the field was eight *batei kor*.
6. My father commented that perhaps there is a difference between the money that Abimelech gave to Abraham and the money that Abraham paid to Ephron, given that the money that Abimelech gave is described as "one thousand silver pieces" without mentioning "shekels" or *over la-soḥer*." Although there are those who understand the term differently, I maintain that *over la-soḥer* refers to a system whereby the money is placed in escrow, under

the auspices of an individual who will ensure that the money is indeed used for the stated purpose and that the land transaction is completed. Further, although Abimelech did not invoke the term "shekel," it is hard to imagine that the king would use coinage that was not *over la-soḥer*," certainly if the sum was paid out in coins (as opposed to the weight of the silver), given that the king was the one who minted the coins. Similarly, it is said of King Solomon: "Solomon had a vineyard in Baal-Hamon. He had to post guards in the vineyard: A man would give for its fruit one thousand pieces of silver" (Song of Songs 8:11). While this verse does not specifically note the currency used, it is obvious that it is referring to the crop's value.

7. The Babylonian Talmud (*Bava Metzi'a* 62a) records a Tannaitic dispute that is reminiscent of the Prisoner's Dilemma:

> Two were walking on a path and there was a jug of water in the possession of one of them. If both drink, both die. If one drinks, he will reach a settled area. Ben Petora expounded: Better that both drink and die, so no one watches his friend die. Along came Rabbi Akiva and taught: [The verse states,] "And your brother shall live with you"—your life precedes the life of your friend.

Since, in this case, the water (the decision) belongs to only one of them, there is no bilateral strategy of two players, and this is not perfectly comparable to the Prisoner's Dilemma. Nevertheless, the personal conflict in which each individual player finds himself in the Prisoner's Dilemma—to inform or to remain silent—is analogous to the question of whether to share the water (sharing the water is equivalent to the decision not to inform). Ben Petora demands complete solidarity with the dehydrated friend, even to the point of literally giving up one's life. His words, "so no one watches his friend die," redound in the words of Hagar as she wanders in the desert with Ishmael, with no water left: "For she said, I shall not watch the boy die" (Genesis 21:16). Ben Petora, that is, demands that people have solidarity at the level of the bonds between mother and son. R. Akiva's view could have been explained as a complete rejection of Ben Petora's view and a championing of free competition in which each person maximizes his personal gain. However, in light of the verse that R. Akiva quotes, "And your brother shall live with you" (Leviticus 25:36), which imposes responsibility for the life of a friend, and in light of R. Akiva's words, "Love your neighbor as yourself is a great principle of the Torah" (*Bereishit Rabbah* 24:7), it seems that his opinion should be explained another way.

R. Akiva advocates a mixed model, in which principles are not utopian, but are expressed in reality. R. Akiva was not willing to sacrifice more life on the altar of the moral principle of solidarity. From his perspective, the anti-practical demand, "they both die," runs counter to the general approach to life, which demands the integration of principles into the routine of life. Put differently, if principles improve the optimum, as we discussed in the main text with regard to the case of a mother and son Prisoner's Dilemma, we must adhere to them. In a situation where it seems that the moral world limits and brings the minimum (in the case of the two who were walking on the path to total loss), the world of principles must be reexamined.

8. Mishna, *Berakhot* 7:1: "Three who ate together are obligated to form a *zimmun* [i.e., to recite the blessing after the meal collectively]." In the Babylonian Talmud (45a), R. Yoḥanan and Rav debate whether two may form a *zimmun*. The Jerusalem Talmud (7:1) relates this law to a dispute about the number of judges required to constitute a rabbinical court. I expound on this equation and its significance in my book *Ben Barukh* (pp. 227-9).

9. Shechem, the son of Hamor, employed a similar line of reasoning when he persuaded the men of his city to undergo circumcision to facilitate his marriage to Dinah, the daughter of Jacob:

    > But only on this condition will the men agree with us to dwell among us and be as one kindred: that all our males become circumcised as they are circumcised. Their cattle and substance and all their beasts will be ours, if we only agree to their terms, so that they will settle among us. (34:22–23)

10. Numbers 13:22 states: "Now Hebron was founded seven years before Zoan of Egypt." The Talmud (*Sotah* 34b) comments that Zoan was built by Ham, the son of Noah. As Hebron was already a built-up city, Abraham's extended presence there as a nomad, living in a tent (13:8: "And Abram moved his tent, and came to dwell at the terebinths of Mamre, which are in Hebron; and he built an altar there to the Lord"; see also 18:1–10), projects this exact message. Abraham was "a resident alien."
11. Their custom was to bury in the ground for twelve months, during which the flesh would decay, leaving only bones. The bones were then collected and moved to a familial repository of bones.
12. See the definition of "otherish" givers: https://www.conversationagent.com/2017/09/successful-givers.html; and *Give and Take* by psychologist Adam Grant. See also http://knowledge.wharton.upenn.edu/article/givers-vs-takers-the-surprising-truth-about-who-gets-ahead/.
13. It is possible that the term *over la-soḥer* reflects the understanding that although Ephron was the one who personally received the cash in hand, he would use this money in Hebron in the future, so the money would somehow benefit everyone.
14. "We should use the transition to a better energy strategy as an opportunity to create a better economy and a better country all around." Van Jones, *The Green Collar Economy: How One Solution Can Fix Our Two Biggest Problems*

PARASHAT TOLDOT

1. "Abraham willed all that he owned to Isaac." (25:5)
2. Commentary to 26:1. Thank you to Rabbi Hillel Novetsky for referring me to this comment.
3. Abraham was born when Terah was seventy years old. Abraham left Haran when he was seventy-five years old, which means that Terah was 145 years old when Abraham left. Given that Terah lived to the age of 205, it follows that he lived another sixty years in Haran after Abraham left.
4. For example, Abraham arrived in Gerar in the context of his travels (20:1), whereas Isaac came to Gerar on his way down to Egypt

in a time of famine. Abimelech abducted Sarah (20:2) but did not abduct Rebecca. Abraham was not exiled from Gerar, and he admonished Abimelech for stealing the well from him, whereas Isaac was exiled from Gerar and did not rebuke Abimelech.

5. Meah Shearim is a neighborhood in Jerusalem primarily populated by ultra-Orthodox Jews, many of whom rejected the early Zionist pioneers. Baron Rothschild was a funder of the early Zionist cause. *Meah Shearim* is also the amount of wheat Isaac harvested in that year of bounty.
6. Perhaps Abraham's purchase of a field (and not just a burial cave) from Ephron signaled to Isaac that the time for settlement, and perhaps even agriculture, had begun. Thus, when Rebecca first laid eyes on Isaac, he was out in the field, engaged in an activity (*lasu'aḥ*) that can be interpreted as agricultural labor, specifically planting trees (see Rashbam to 24:63).
7. http://www.lifewater.ca/drill_manual/Section_2.htm; http://wtamu.edu/~cbaird/sq/2013/07/16/how-do-wells-get-their-water-from-underground-rivers/
8. https://harvesttotable.com/how_to_grow_lentil/
9. 18:8: "He took cream and milk and the calf that had been prepared and set these before them; and he waited on them under the tree as they ate."
10. My father suggested that against this backdrop, Rebecca's desire to send Jacob to her brother Laban is better understood. Laban was a shepherd and Jacob and his sons, who would be nomads in the future, needed to learn the profession.
11. Rashi cites a midrash that states that Esau would ask his father: "How do you tithe salt?" This is generally understood as a display of false piety by Esau towards his father, given that salt is not tithed, though crops are. In line with the analysis presented in this article, though, the example brought in the midrash is not incidental, as Esau's false piety related to the laws crops and produce. There is an additional layer to the midrash: Esau is deriding the lifework of his father Isaac.
12. Rashi comments on the verse "Give me some of that red stuff to gulp down" (25:30):

> Red lentils. On that day Abraham had died, so that he would not see his grandson Esau becoming depraved, for this would not be the good old age that God had promised him.... ...Jacob cooked lentils to provide the customary first meal for the mourner. Why [did he specifically cook] lentils? Because lentils resemble a wheel, and mourning is a wheel that revolves in the world and affects everyone sooner or later.

According to the analysis presented here, it is possible that Esau, whose personality was aligned with his grandfather Abraham and the campaigns that he conducted, relinquished the birthright on the day that Abraham died. In Esau's mind, with the death of Abraham, the era of Abraham ended forever, and Isaac's movement to settle the land took hold permanently. At this point in time, Esau felt that he had been ousted from the family ethos. It is possible that in a similar context, Esau elected to specifically marry Hittite women. Abraham saw himself as "a resident alien" among the Hittites and even bought the cave of Machpelah and a field from them. It is entirely possible that Esau, as a person who felt connected to Abraham and his nomadic journeys and saw Abraham as a role model, spent time alongside him when Abraham lived and operated among the Hittites and therefore married Hittite women. When Esau saw that Canaanite women displeased his father, though, it is written: "Esau realized that the Canaanite women displeased his father Isaac. So Esau went to Ishmael and took to wife, in addition to the wives he had, Mahalath the daughter of Ishmael son of Abraham, sister of Nebaioth." Esau, who was connected to his grandfather Abraham, turned to the family of Ishmael, who led a nomadic style in the desert, and therefore the verse goes to lengths to describe Ishmael as the "son of Abraham."

13. The verse notes: "Rebecca then took the best clothes of her older son Esau, which were there in the house, and she placed them on her younger son Jacob" (27:15). Considering that Jacob was no longer a child (he was over forty years old), it stands to reason that the Rebecca did not actually dress her younger son. It is

far more likely that "she placed them on her younger son Jacob" means that she put Esau's clothing over the clothing that Jacob was already wearing, creating the perfect outfit.

14. "Esau took his wives, his sons and daughters, and all the members of his household, his cattle and all his livestock, and all the property that he had acquired in the land of Canaan and went to another land because of his brother Jacob." (36:6)

PARASHAT VAYEZTEI

1. See Arrow, K. J. (1972) "Gifts and Exchanges" *Philosophy and Public Affairs,* pp. 343-362; Guiso, L., Sapienza, P., & Zingales, L. (2006) "Does culture affect economic outcomes?" *The Journal of Economic Perspectives,* 20(2), 23-48. See recent work by the OECD https://read.oecd-ilibrary.org/economics/trust-and-its-determinants_869ef2ec-en#page12
2. The Talmud asks how we know that a rotten date tree grows among barren trees, meaning that something negative joins other bad things or bad environments, and cites several sources for the existence of this phenomenon:

    > He said to him: This matter is written in the Torah, repeated in the Prophets, and triplicated in the Writings, taught in a Mishnah, and repeated in a *baraita*. It is written in the Torah, as it is written: "And so Esau went to Ishmael" (28:9). It is repeated in the Prophets, as it is written: "And there were gathered vain fellows to Yiftah, and they went out with him" (*Shoftim* 11:3). And it is triplicated in the Writings, as it is written: "All fowl will live with its kind, and men with those like him" (*Ben Sira* 13:17). It is taught in a Mishnah: "All that is attached to that which is ritually impure is ritually impure; all that is attached to that which is ritually pure is ritually pure" (*m. Kelim* 12:2). And it is repeated in a *baraita*: "Rabbi Eliezer says: Not for naught did the starling go to the raven, but because it is its kind." (*Bava Kama* 92b)

According to this Talmudic statement, even as he was attempting to respect Isaac's wishes, Esau searched for a wife in a dreadful environment. Moreover, he deserves criticism for this, as "All that is attached to that which is ritually impure, is ritually impure." Following the Talmud's critical stance, biblical commentators (Ramban and Malbim, for example) critique Esau for not fully heeding Isaac's directive and going to Haran to find a wife. This approach disregards the Torah's descriptions of Haran in general, and Laban's home in particular.

3. Ralbag, in the "practical benefits" (*to'alot*) section of his commentary, uses this to teach a critical life lesson:

> The fourth benefit relates to character traits, namely, that a person should rise up with all his might to help his relatives, and must not ignore them. As a case in point, as soon as Jacob saw the flocks of his mother's brother Laban, and Rachel, the daughter of Laban, his mother's brother, he roused himself to quickly give water to the sheep, and rolled the large stone, which all the shepherds would gather together to roll, by himself. We also see from here that Jacob possessed exceptional strength, which is one of the prerequisites for prophecy, as our Sages taught: Prophecy does not descend except on one who is wise, strong, wealthy, and of stature.

R. David Tzvi Hoffmann comments:

> Our forefather was well-known for his strength. He could roll the large stone, which the shepherds could not move without cooperation, by himself. Through this episode we incidentally learn about the incredible physical strength of our forefather. And yet, we do not find that Jacob used this strength to subdue those who were weaker than him, aside from one episode, in the dark of night, in a defensive battle. When Jacob learned that his sons used their strength to kill people on a different occasion, he was extremely distressed to the point that he cursed his sons,

even though their actions were motivated by righteous indignation in the aftermath of a despicable crime.

4. Shadal adds another dimension to this discussion, one reminiscent of a classic "tragedy of the commons":

   They placed a stone over the mouth of the well to ensure that each shepherd could only give his sheep water in the presence of all the other shepherds, so that nobody would waste water. In truth, the stone was not that large, and two or three shepherds could easily roll it off, but the shepherds watched one another, and did not let anyone violate the treaty.

5. Francis Fukuyama, *Trust: Human Nature and the Reconstitution of Social Order*.
6. People do not just behave in consonance with the economic background in which they grew up. They also adapt their behavior to different economic situations. A recession, or alternatively, a bull market, influence the behavior patterns of individuals and societies. Issues like interpersonal trust are heavily influenced by the circumstances that prevail in the economy and vary in accordance with the forces and circumstances that act on society. For example, studies show that people who grew up under economic duress have fewer children. For further discussion about the impact of changing economic situations see:

   https://www.nytimes.com/2010/08/08/magazine/08FOB-wwln-t.html;

   https://www.ncbi.nlm.nih.gov/pmc/articles/PMC5818567/;

   https://www.jstor.org/stable/24541683?seq=1#page_scan_tab_contents.

   As noted, economic background, economic change, and individual and social change are as just relevant to the analysis of biblical figures and the various societies that the Bible describes. For example, in the broader context of the various branches of Abraham's family, Nahor had eight children with his wife Milcah and another four by his concubine Reumah. It is unclear how many children Nahor's son Bethuel had, given that the Torah focuses exclusively on his daughter Rebecca before her marriage to Isaac and later on her brother Laban. We do not know whether there were any other siblings, though according to our analysis, Haran experienced an economic recession that led to a lower birthrate.

7. The essay, "The Birthright and the Blessing" (above, p. 46ff.) devotes a broad discussion to the disagreement between Ibn Ezra and Ramban regarding Isaac's financial status. Either way, Isaac, together with the other residents of the region, experienced a serious economic crisis, even if he ultimately preserved his wealth.
8. Robert Axelrod, *The Evolution of Cooperation* (New York, 1984). This book expounds on the research conducted by Axelrod and Dr. William Hamilton, a professor of evolutionary biology, that was published in 1981 in the journal *Science*.
9. Shiller and Akerlof, *Animal Spirits: How Human Psychology Drives the Economy and Why It Matters for Global Capitalism* (Princeton, 2009).
10. See also: *The New Famines* by Stephen Devereux, who describes the breakdown in trust in societies in rural Malawi where there is famine. Communal values and reciprocal arrangements also eroded as individualism took over due to famine and food scarcity.
11. For a psychological description of how children reflect and perpetuate the parental behaviors experienced in their childhood homes, see: https://parenthood.library.wisc.edu/Popenoe/Popenoe-Modeling.html

PARASHAT VAYISHLAḤ

1. In a related message, the Babylonian Talmud tells us the following:

   Rav Ḥisda says: A person should never impose excessive fear upon the members of his household, as the husband of the concubine of Gibeah imposed excessive fear upon her and this ultimately caused the downfall of many tens of thousands of Jews in the resultant war. Rav Yehuda says that Rav says: Anyone who imposes excessive fear upon the members of his household will ultimately come to commit three sins: Engaging in forbidden sexual intercourse, committing murder and desecrating the Sabbath... Rabbi Abbahu says: A person should never impose excessive fear upon the members of his household. When a great man imposed excessive fear upon his household, they fed him something that carried a great prohibition... And what was this? A limb from a living animal. (BT Gittin 6b–7a)

2. In a famous case still taught in law schools, the inventor of Listerine mouthwash crafted a one line agreement that entitled him, his heirs, and his executors a royalty from all sales of Listerine. This simple contract with no penalties remains unbroken until this day despite attempts by former pharmaceutical company Warner Lambert to challenge it in the 1950s. https://www.bloomberg.com/news/articles/2020-07-13/bad-breath-offers-a-rare-payoff-in-listerine-royalty-stake-sale
3. According to the sages, Jacob stayed in Succoth for eighteen months. They criticize Jacob for this decision (*Megilah* 17a, *Bereishit Rabbah* 78:16). See Netziv's commentary *Harḥev Davar* to Genesis 33:17 for further discussion of this point.
4. See also Jerusalem Talmud *Sheviit* 9:2.
5. See "Living on the Margins: Livelihood Strategies of Bedouin Herd-Owners in the Northern Negev, Israel." This article demonstrates that the gifts that Jacob sent were quite large relative to the size of a typical herd.
6. "Of the twenty years that I spent in your household, I served you fourteen years for your two daughters, and six years for your flocks; and you changed my wages time and again. Had not the God of my father, the God of Abraham and the Fear of Isaac, been with me, you would have sent me away empty-handed... And Jacob swore by the fear of his father Isaac" (31:41–53).
7. "Now he heard the things that Laban's sons were saying: 'Jacob has taken all that was our father's, and from that which was our father's he has built up all this wealth.' Jacob also saw that Laban's manner toward him was not as it had been in the past" (31:1–2).

8. "Jacob then got fresh shoots of poplar, and of almond and plane, and peeled white stripes in them, laying bare the white of the shoots. The rods that he had peeled he set up in front of the goats in the troughs, the water receptacles, that the goats came to drink from. Their mating occurred when they came to drink, and since the goats mated by the rods, the goats brought forth streaked, speckled, and spotted young. But Jacob dealt separately with the sheep; he made these animals face the streaked or wholly dark-colored animals in Laban's flock. And so he produced special flocks for himself, which he did not put with Laban's flocks. Moreover, when the sturdier animals were mating, Jacob would place the rods in the troughs, in full view of the animals, so that they mated by the rods; but with the feebler animals he would not place them there. Thus the feeble ones went to Laban and the sturdy to Jacob. So the man grew exceedingly prosperous, and came to own large flocks, maidservants and menservants, camels and asses" (30:37–43).

9. When Jacob escaped from Esau he swore:

> If God remains with me, if He protects me on this journey that I am making, and gives me bread to eat and clothing to wear, and if I return safe to my father's house—the Lord shall be my God. And this stone, which I have set up as a pillar, shall be God's abode; and of all that You give me, I will set aside a tithe for You. (28:20–22)

This vow provides another explanation for Jacob's extended delay in Succoth. Jacob had promised to tithe his profits in exile, but then he used this wealth to placate Esau. Perhaps Jacob felt that he had misappropriated assets that should have been designated for God, and he therefore lingered in Succoth to rebuild his wealth and offer a generous tithe to God. It is important to note that while the Sages determined that Jacob stayed in Succoth for eighteen months, this period of time is not explicitly stated in the narrative. In my humble opinion, Jacob stayed there longer in order to rebuild his wealth.

10. Archeological research indicates that coins were not yet invented in this time period.
11. Shadal (ad loc.) offers this explanation as well.
12. In the essay, "The Birthright and the Blessing" (above, p. 49ff.), we analyzed a similar economic move undertaken by Isaac, who exchanged the family's moveable assets for arable lands. That said, it is important to note the differences between these two land purchases. Isaac invested in agriculture at the height of an economic crisis caused by famine, and his success aroused the Philistines to be so jealous and resentful that they eventually banished Isaac from their land. Jacob's decision to settle in Shechem was not impacted by any external factors and was therefore perceived as an expression of trust.
13. This is akin to Baron Edmond de Rothschild's purchase of land for Jewish settlement in Eretz Yisrael. See also Mishnah *Bava Batra* 1:5: "How long must a man dwell in a town to count as one of the men of the town? Twelve months. If he has purchased a dwelling place, he immediately counts as one of the men of the town." One who purchases land from the locals, immediately becomes part of that city or country.
14. https://hbr.org/2010/09/the-five-powers-that-bring-upl.html
15. "If an injury has to be done to a man it should be so severe that his vengeance need not be feared." —Niccolò Machiavelli, *The Prince*
16. See R. Yaacov Medan's article, "Anyone who Says that Reuben Sinned," on this topic.

PARASHAT VAYESHEV

1. https://mastersofscale.com/bill-gates-how-to-accelerate-history/
2. https://www.cnbc.com/2020/02/24/bill-gates-was-difficult-boss-in-early-microsoft-days-but-employees-still-liked-him.html
3. R. Yaacov Medan likewise explains thus in his book on Bereishit, *Ki Karov Elekha* (pp.339–340).
4. "Tended" (*haya ro'eh*) is an expression that has two entirely different connotations: tended (*haya ro'eh*) can refer to an ongoing activity or an event that happened previously at an earlier point

in time. It is possible that both apply to this situation. Perhaps Joseph tended the sheep alongside his older brothers, and when he began to bring back negative reports about them to his father, they could no longer continue working with him, leaving Joseph out of the family business.

5. Similarly, the verse "Lot, who went with [*et*] Abram, also had flocks and herds and tents" (13:5) describes Abraham and Lot's return from Egypt, which is immediately followed by their separation.
6. A different Harvard study demonstrates that in family businesses, first-generation managers adopt the business leadership style of "conqueror," a manager who works hard to implement the business strategy of the firm that he established. The study found that in the second-generation, after the business has already been established, it is preferable for the firm to be managed by a multidimensional leader. It seems that Simeon and Levi, and the sons of Leah in general, were closer to the aggressive style of management of the environment of Haran, where they grew up, than a multi-dimensional style of leadership based on trust and open to change. For further discussion, see https://hbr.org/2014/12/family-businesses-need-one-person-to-conquer-and-another-to-rule.
7. *The Five Addresses* (pp. 15–35). In this speech, Rabbi Soloveitchik discussed his positive endorsement of Zionism in contrast to the opposition to Zionism expressed by his grandfather and his family.
8. The JPS Pentateuch (ad locum) notes that in Bereishit, all dreams are understood as prophecy.
9. Rabbi Samson Raphael Hirsch (commentary to 37:7–8) explains that binding sheaves is the final stage of wheat production that immediately precedes distribution.
10. In the sale of Joseph (37:26–28), the verses recount that the brothers utilized an Ishmaelite caravan that transported spices to Egypt. Essentially, the brothers used the precise distribution system that Joseph had dreamt of (and sermonized about) against him. This sheds new light on their statement: "We shall see what comes of his dreams!"

11. According to R. Soloveitchik, the transition to agriculture would enable them to survive in Egypt, and not in the land of Israel. R. Soloveitchik explains that Joseph knew that the exile was imminent on account of the divine promise in the Covenant Between the Parts, and he therefore wanted to prepare the family for exile.
12. More than a decade later, when Joseph was the ruler in Egypt and the brothers traveled to Egypt to buy food, the verses state: "He recalled the dreams that he had dreamt about them" (42:9). The use of the phrase "dreamt about them" (*ḥalam lahem*; lit. "dreamt for them") as opposed to "dreamt" (*ḥalam*) possibly indicates that Joseph hoped that his dreams would help his brothers—in the sense that they would devise new strategies to deal with their economic challenges. I thank Dr. Benny Gesundheit for this insightful comment.
13. R. Soloveitchik is apparently addressing the position espoused by many European rabbinical figures that secular and scientific studies—as well as Zionism—are new things that do not derive from traditional Judaism. In contrast to this worldview, R. Soloveitchik explains that changing times calls for changing measures.
14. It is interesting to note that Joseph is called on to interpret Pharoah's dream in Egypt, whereas here, he merely tells of his own dreams. Oftentimes, business changes require proficient storytelling in order to penetrate and succeed. As my friend and former Timberland CEO Jeffrey Swartz taught me, it is not enough to change the narrative, you must narrate the change. In this case, it seems that Joseph failed to narrate the change to his brothers and father.
15. Grote relates the story of Joseph and his brothers as the prototype of this psychological phenomenon: Jim Grote, "Conflicting Generations, A New Theory of Family Business Rivalry," *Family Business Review*, June 2003.
16. Most commentators ask the opposite question: since Jacob knew that the brothers hated Joseph, why did he send him? They do not question why Joseph agreed to go.
17. The verses use two words, *bar* and *okhel*," to refer to food, and it seems impossible to make a clear distinction as to when one is used and when the other is used. As Shadal wrote:

> "As food (*okhel*) to be stored in the cities" – this modifies the earlier statement of "let the grain (*bar*) be collected under Pharaoh's authority." Meaning, food will be accumulated in each and every city. The phrase "to be stored" (*ve-shamaru*) is connected to the phrase 'be collected' (*ve-yitzberu*). This is in line with the cantillation signs. Although there is a difference between *bar* and *okhel bar* is the grain that has been separated from the chaff, and *okhel* includes all foodstuffs, in this section they are used interchangeably. The distinction that I made in *Bikurei HaItim* is incorrect, since Joseph's brothers declared: "We will go down and procure food (*okhel*) for you" (43:4), even though they had already traveled to Egypt and seen that only grain (*bar*) was sold there; it seems that Joseph stored not only grain.

In contrast, Netziv explains: "'All the food'—even the food that does not yet exist, and it is called food (*okhel*) because it is usually consumed raw."

18. According to Netziv, Joseph divided the land of Egypt into five different districts (*hamesh*). According to other commentators, this word alludes to the system of taxation that Joseph established, whereby one-fifth of the population's produce was assessed to fund Pharaoh's empire.
19. For example:

> When a man gives money or goods to another for safekeeping, and they are stolen from the man's house—if the thief is caught, he shall pay double; if the thief is not caught, the owner of the house shall testify before God that he has not laid hands on the other's property. (Exodus 22:6–7)
>
> When a person sins and commits a trespass against the Lord by dealing deceitfully with his fellow in the matter of a deposit (*pikadon*) or a pledge, or through robbery, or by defrauding his fellow...." (Leviticus 5:21)

20. When I was fifteen years old, my study partner Ezra Wiener (today a rabbi in Teaneck, New Jersey) told me in the name of someone who I do not know personally by the name of Gershon Kramer, that Jacob's assessment of the absurdity of Joseph's dream is embedded within Jacob's response to the dream: "And when he told it to his father and brothers, his father berated him. 'What,' he said to him, 'is this dream you have dreamed? Are we to come, I and your mother and your brothers, and bow low to you to the ground?'" The Hebrew words "*Raḥel meitah*" (RḤL MTH; "Rachel is dead") are spelled out in the Hebrew words "*asher ḥalamta havo*" (AShR ḤLMT HBA; "you have dreamed, are we to come").
21. The Babylonian Talmud (Berakhot 55a) states:

    > Rabbi Berekhyah said: Even though part of a dream is fulfilled, all of it is not fulfilled. From where do we derive this? From the story of Joseph's dream, as it is written: 'And he said: Look, I have had another dream: And this time, the sun, the moon' and at that time his mother was no longer alive... R. Panda said that R. Naḥum said that R. Birim said in the name of one elder, and who is he? R. Bena'ah: There were twenty-four dream interpreters in Jerusalem. One time, I dreamed a dream and went to each of them to interpret it. What one interpreted for me the other did not interpret for me, and, nevertheless, all of the interpretations were realized in me, to fulfill that which is stated: All dreams follow the mouth [of the interpreter].

22. The fact that standard methods of storage are useful for a maximum of two years beyond the agricultural cycle is seen in the context of the Biblical command of the sabbatical year:

    > You shall observe My laws and faithfully keep My rules, that you may live upon the land in security; the land shall yield its fruit and you shall eat your fill, and you shall live upon it in security. And should you ask, 'What are we to eat in the seventh year, if we may neither sow nor gather in our crops?' I will ordain My blessing for you in the sixth year, so that it shall yield a crop sufficient for three years.

> When you sow in the eighth year, you will still be eating old grain of that crop; you will be eating the old until the ninth year, until its crops come in. (Leviticus 25:18-22)

23. Rashi (47:19) explains that the famine ended earlier than predicted on account of the blessing that Jacob bestowed upon Pharaoh. From his explanation, it seems that in the absence of this blessing, it is doubtful that Pharaoh and his magicians would have successfully avoided the ominous predictions, even with Joseph's ambitious plan.
24. Matt Ridley, *The Rational Optimist*, p. 158.
25. At times, this can play out differently with automation and mechanization, making farmworkers and others superfluous and causing them to migrate to cities in search of new opportunities.
26. Assuming that most of the populace lived in villages and farmsteads along the Nile, the urbanization of the populace was necessary to spur them to acquire new professions so that they would have relevant skill sets during the seven lean years. A large group of people cannot withstand seven years of idleness and purposelessness, even when food is not lacking. This insight is discussed at length in the chapter, "Mission (Im)Possible: Universal Basic Income" (above, p. 2ff).
27. Joseph was also in the city, as the narrative later notes: "They had just left the city and had not gone far, when Joseph said to his steward, 'Up, go after the men!'" (44:4).
28. Understanding the market potential of the city is reflected in an earlier story, as well. Hamor attempted to convince Jacob's sons to reside within their city: "Intermarry with us: give your daughters to us, and take our daughters for yourselves: You will dwell among us, and the land will be open before you; settle, move about, and acquire holdings in it" (34:9-10). See also *Shabbat* 32b, where Shmuel avers that Jacob improved the city of Shechem by establishing a market there.
29. Babylonian Talmud Sanhedrin 16a:

> Rabbi Shimon Ḥasida said: A lyre hung above David's bed, and once midnight arrived, a northern wind would blow on it and cause it to play of its own. David would

> immediately rise up and study Torah until the break of dawn. Once dawn broke, the sages of Israel would enter. They said to him: Our lord, the king, your people Israel needs sustenance. He said to them: Go and sustain one another. They responded to him: A handful [of food] does not satisfy a lion, and a cistern will not be filled merely from [the rain that falls directly into] its mouth. He said to them: Go and take up arms with the troops....

Like David's statement of "Go and sustain one another," Richard P. Moth notes, in his article, "Differential Growth Among Large US Cities" (in: Quirk and Zarley, *Papers in Quantitative Economics* [1968], pp. 311–335) that cities develop according to their human capital. According to his research, factories are built in population centers. This challenges the prevailing understanding that people migrate to where they can find jobs.

30. There are several historical accounts of famine in ancient Egypt, as noted in the JPS Pentateuch on 41:53–57.
31. This does not mean that manufacturing is not important. It actually has significant national security ramifications. It is just that commerce and finance enables faster and more diversified growth. See for example: https://foreignpolicy.com/2020/08/12/china-industry-manufacturing-cold-war/
32. In Aramaic, an ant is called a *kamtza* (which is reflected in the word *k'matzim*, the Hebrew word for "abundance" in this verse). An ant is indeed symbolic of the process of hoarding food during a time of abundance and saving it for a time of deprivation.
33. Shadal and R. Samson Raphael Hirsch address this point. Shadal notes: "For it could not be measured—this is hyperbole. It is similar to the Latin words 'innumerable' and 'immenso.'" R. Hirsch explains that there was a precise accounting, but it was so large that the precision seemed meaningless.
34. Beyond the straightforward hypothesis that Joseph anticipated that he would need to provide for his family if the famine were to impact the entire region, in the chapter, "A Warning Sign: Over-Centralization and Economic Decline" (below, p. 85ff), I discuss

how Joseph managed the years of crisis and distributed food to the populace, ultimately leading his family's migration to Egypt.

35. The commentators disagree as to whether *vayishbor* ("and he dispensed") means that the people paid or that he dispensed the surplus for free.
36. Manna is the "bread" that fell from heaven and fed the Israelites during their forty-year sojourn in the desert.
37. Similarly, Prime Minister Benjamin Netanyahu often uses different Israeli innovation to strengthen the diplomatic footing of the State of Israel.
38. See Dr. Parag Khanna's discussion of the inverse relationship between active global supply chains and the potential for polar, territorial war in *Connectography*, Prologue, p. XVII
39. Perhaps this partly explains why Joseph and his servants returned money to the brothers. At this stage of the famine, Joseph did not charge money for food. He wanted the people to be dependent on him, so he dispensed the food for free. This was true for the land of Canaan, as well. Jacob's sons and their father understood that someone who remits payment for something is far more independent than someone who receives it as a gift. They therefore wanted to pay, even though Joseph wanted to dispense it for free.
40. For a discussion of the implications of the Unites States' decision to pull out of the Asian trade agreement, see my friend Parag Khanna's article: https://www.politico.com/agenda/story/2017/02/trade-grows-without-us-000321.
41. See, for example: 46:31–34:

> Then Joseph said to his brothers and to his father's household, "I will go up and tell the news to Pharaoh, and say to him, 'My brothers and my father's household, who were in the land of Canaan, have come to me. The men are shepherds; they have always been breeders of livestock, and they have brought with them their flocks and herds and all that is theirs.' So when Pharaoh summons you and asks, 'What is your occupation?' you shall answer, 'Your servants have been breeders of livestock from the start until now, both we and our fathers' – so that you may stay

> in the region of Goshen. For all shepherds are abhorrent to Egyptians."

Later on, the verses state: "Thus Israel settled in the country of Egypt, in the region of Goshen; they acquired holdings in it, and were fertile and increased greatly" (47:27). R. Shlomo Ephraim Lunschitz, author of the seventeenth century commentary *Kli Yakar*, states that this verse is actually an admonition of the Jewish people:

> This entire verse discusses the sin of the Israelites. God had decreed upon them "know well that your offspring shall be strangers" and here they seek to become permanent residents...The verse accuses them of settling in order to gain a homestead in a land not theirs...They became so embedded there that they did not wish to leave Egypt, until God had to take them out with a strong hand....

42. See the groundbreaking article by the International Monetary Fund on this topic: https://www.imf.org/external/pubs/ft/fandd/basics/trade.htm
43. Joseph was buried in Shechem, a city governed by his descendants (the tribe of Ephraim). In the chapter, "Land Reserve" (above, p. 71ff), I discuss the connection between Joseph's economic doctrine and the plot of land that Jacob bought in Shechem.

PARASHAT VAYIGASH

1. Abarbanel, commentary to *Parashat Vayigash*, seventh question.
2. The Babylonian Talmud (*Ḥullin* 60b) presents an even sharper formulation of the purpose of this episode:

> R. Shimon ben Lakish says: There are many verses that are seemingly fit to be burned as books of the heretics, and yet they are part of the corpus of Torah.... "And he removed the population town by town" (47:21). What is the practical difference? So that they would not call his brothers exiles.

Rashi (ad loc.) softens the Talmud's formulation: "The reader may assume that these texts should be burned, because they should not have been written, given that they do not seem to have any relevance to the Torah, and it is disgraceful to incorporate it with that which is holy."

3. Ralbag ad Locum. The sixth and seventh purpose.
4. For a more extensive analysis of these approaches, see http://alhatorah.org/Yosef's_Economic_Policies/2. My thanks to the Novetsky family for this important reference.
5. Other commentators—including Prof. Uriel Simon, Dr. Tamir Granot, and R. David Sabato—also adopt this approach. For additional discussion, see http://alhatorah.org/Yosef's_Economic_Policies/2 footnote 24. In *Ki Karov Elekha,* R. Medan agrees that the economic plan possibly caused resentment against the Israelites and may have caused their enslavement since some people turned the Joseph saving Egypt into an economic conspiracy. In his opinion, however, this was not a direct result of Joseph's economic policies.
6. For additional examples, see "The Questionable Legacy of Alan Greenspan" by Thomas Palley and *Greenspan's Bubbles* by William Fleckenstein.
7. Nassim Nicholas Taleb, in response to the great financial crisis of 2008: http://www.washingtonpost.com/wp-dyn/content/article/2009/03/12/AR2009031202181.html

   He continues:

   > People have the problem of denial. This is one of the things I learned in Lebanon. Everybody who left Beirut when the war started, including my parents, said, "Oh, its temporary." It lasted 17 years! People tend to underestimate the gravity of these situations. That's how they work.

8. While it is true that Ḥizkuni, Radak, R. Abraham ben HaRambam, and other commentators explain that Joseph sustained his family lavishly, this does not seem to be the straightforward meaning of the text, nor would it be prudent on the part of a leader. As explained above, my interpretation corroborates Ralbag, who

notes: "He only wanted to give his father's household according to their needs. For this reason, the verse notes (47:12) that he sustained them according to the [number of] little ones." This is also the opinion of Ramban and Rabbenu Baḥya, among others.

9. Rashi, following the approach of the sages, explains that the famine ended when Jacob came to Egypt and blessed Pharaoh. The famine therefore only lasted for a total of two years. According to the straightforward meaning of the text, however, the famine continued on. The two years described in the verses cited at the beginning of this chapter, where Joseph covered the cost of food by collecting all of the money and animals that belonged to Egypt's citizens, refer to the first two years that Jacob and his family lived in Egypt. This would actually make this the third and the fourth years of the famine. Ḥizkuni explains it this way:

    > "In the second year"—according to the straightforward meaning, this refers to [the second year] from Jacob's arrival, which was the fourth year of the famine. The produce that remained from the years of abundance, and the money that they had, lasted for three years; in the fourth year they gave their cattle [in lieu of payment]; in the fifth year, they gave their land; in the sixth year, they gave their bodies; and in the seventh year, he gave them seeds, and they planted and harvested the field's produce in the eighth year, when the famine ended.

    The Tosefta (Sotah 10:8) outlines a historical progression that combines these two understandings of the verses. According to the Tosefta, the famine stopped when Jacob came down to Egypt, but it started again after he died.

10. It is unclear if the famine continued to ravage "all of the lands" and the Torah only focuses on Egypt and Canaan, or if the famine continued and intensified only in Canaan and Egypt so that Jacob's family would relocate to Egypt.

11. The king is commanded: "Moreover, he shall not keep many horses or send people back to Egypt to add to his horses"

(Deuteronomy 17:16). A verse in Song of Songs (1:9) states "I have likened you, my darling, to a mare in Pharaoh's chariots."

12. For a fascinating discussion of the use of silver as a means of payment, see Tzilla Eshel's article: https://thetorah.com/how-silver-was-used-for-payment/
13. Dave Birch wrote (http://digitaldebateblogs.typepad.com/digital_money/2009/02/payments-without-banks.html):

> Between 1966 and 1976 there were three major "all out" bank strikes in Ireland that shut the retail banks for (in total) a year. There is a super case study, written a few years ago, on this called "Money in an Economy Without Banks" by Antoin Murphy of Trinity. I've sometimes referred to it when challenging people to think harder about how the payment system works, but of course it's taken on a new lease of life in current circumstances and in the context of the "utility vs. casino" strategy discussions.

14. R. Ḥofni Gaon comments on verse 21: "And when Joseph instructed them, 'bring your cattle,' he had their best interests in mind. He eased their burden of taking care of feeding [the animals], as pastureland was disappearing."
15. "Silver Hoards"—"In Israel, over the past one hundred years of archaeological excavations, more than thirty silver hoards have been found, containing varied numbers of silver pieces of different sizes. When the first hoards were discovered (for example at Gezer, published by Macalister in 1912), the excavators assumed that they had found a silversmith's shop and that this was raw material for melting into jewelry or other luxury items. As more and more such hoards were found however, it became clear that they were used as silver 'currency.' https://thetorah.com/how-silver-was-used-for-payment/. I am grateful to Rabbi Dov Kidron for this reference.
16. See 2 *Shmuel* 12:1–6:

> The Lord sent Nathan to David. He came to him and said, "There were two men in the same city, one rich and one poor. The rich man had very large flocks and herds, but

> the poor man had only one little ewe lamb that he had bought. He tended it and it grew up together with him and his children: it used to share his morsel of bread, drink from his cup, and nestle in his bosom; it was like a daughter to him. One day, a traveler came to the rich man, but he was loath to take anything from his own flocks or herds to prepare a meal for the guest who had come to him; so he took the poor man's lamb and prepared it for the man who had come to him." David flew into a rage against the man, and said to Nathan, "As the Lord lives, the man who did this deserves to die! He shall pay for the lamb four times over, because he did such a thing and showed no pity."

17. In the Torah's system of charity, even the gifts that are given to the poor, such as the gleanings (*leket*), the forgotten sheaves (*shikheḥah*), and the corner of the field (*pe'ah*), require the poor to make an effort. Similarly, it is better to support the business endeavors of a destitute person than to give him a handout. See the chapter, "Mission (Im)Possible" (above, p. 2ff) for further elaboration.
18. See Quinn, C. E., Halfacre, A.C., "Place Matters: An Investigation of Farmers' Attachment to Their Land." *Human Ecology, 2014.*
19. https://www.theguardian.com/us-news/2017/dec/06/why-are-americas-farmers-killing-themselves-in-record-numbers.
20. It is possible that the general public was not made fully aware of the scope and expected duration of the famine, so they would not become despondent from the very beginning or out of concern that they would take to the streets and undermine the stability of the regime.
21. Ridley, *The Rational Optimist*, p. 33 states:

> The decline in agricultural employment caused consternation among early economists. François Quesnay and his fellow 'physiocrats' argued in eighteenth century France that manufacturing produced no gain in wealth and that switching from agriculture to industry would decrease a country's wealth: only farming was true

wealth creation. Two centuries later the decline in industrial employment in the late twentieth century caused a similar consternation among economists, who saw services as a frivolous distraction from the important business of manufacturing. They were just as wrong. There is no such thing as unproductive employment, so long as people are prepared to buy the service you are offering. Today, 1 percent works in agriculture and 24 percent in industry, leaving 75 percent to offer movies, restaurant meals, insurance broking and aromatherapy.

22. In recent decades, billionaire Steve Forbes has been pressuring the United States government to institute a flat income tax rate of 17 percent: https://www.forbes.com/sites/steveforbes/2014/03/07/the-tax-code-make-it-flat/#745d31c27e0e.
23. Judaism, in general, and the Torah in particular, allows transgressions to save lives except in the areas of idolatry, incest, and homicide.
24. Australia is a case in point: https://www.abc.net.au/news/2017-07-12/australia-religion-census-2016-mapped/8660798.
25. There is a high correlation between low socioeconomic status and religiosity and religious extremism: https://www.citylab.com/equity/2013/04/americas-most-and-least-religious-metro-areas/5180/.
26. Pharaoh was an experienced king. Given that he did not know if Joseph's plan would work, he acted cautiously and transferred responsibility exclusively to Joseph: "And when all the land of Egypt felt the hunger, the people cried out to Pharaoh for bread; and Pharaoh said to all the Egyptians, 'Go to Joseph; whatever he tells you, you shall do'" (41:55).
27. Ridley, *The Rational Optimist*, p. 106:

> Since people have generally done more dying than procreating when in cities, big cities have always depended on rural immigrants to sustain their numbers. Just as agriculture appeared in six or seven parts of the world simultaneously, suggesting an evolutionary determinism, so the same is true, a few thousand years later, of cit-

ies. Large urban settlements, with communal buildings, monuments and shared infrastructure, start popping up after seven thousand years ago in several fertile river valleys. The oldest cities were in southern Mesopotamia, in what is now Iraq. Their emergence signified that production was becoming more specialized, consumption more diversified.

28. The people of Sodom underwent a similar process when they went from being enslaved to being exploiters of others, as described in the chapter "An Ember Saved from Fire" (p. 30ff). It is possible that this point is reflected in the Torah's comparison of Egypt and Sodom: "like the garden of the Lord, like the land of Egypt." In order to confront this mindset of vengefulness and vindictiveness, the Torah admonishes: "You shall not oppress a stranger, for you know the feelings of the stranger, having yourselves been strangers in the land of Egypt" (Exodus 23:9).
29. In June 2003, the Israeli government coalition led by Prime Minister Ariel Sharon, which included the Shinui Party and Benjamin Netanyahu as Finance Minister, dramatically cut state welfare payments. From Netanyahu's perspective, this move was designed to increase economic growth and save the country from an economic crisis: "The stipend cuts must continue. If we stop, the entire country will stop," he said. Many people critiqued Netanyahu, maintaining that this process, which seriously hurt the weakest segments of society, was implemented far acutely. A decade later, the National Insurance Institute published a study indicating that these cuts caused many handicapped people to become impoverished. Different political parties demanded—and with time succeeded—in restoring the payouts. See: https://www.calcalist.co.il/local/articles/0,7340,L-3673988,00.html; https://www.davar1.co.il/60353/

PARASHAT VAYEḤI

1. Obviously, there are exceptions such as King David who was the youngest in his family.

2. Numbers 2:3–9:

> Camped on the front, or east side: the standard of the division of Judah, troop by troop. Chieftain of the Judites: Nahshon son of Amminadab. His troop, as enrolled: 74,600. Camping next to it: The tribe of Issachar. Chieftain of the Issacharites: Nethanel son of Zuar. His troop, as enrolled: 54,400. The tribe of Zebulun. Chieftain of the Zebulunites: Eliab son of Helon. His troop, as enrolled: 57,400. The total enrolled in the division of Judah: 186,400, for all troops. These shall march first.

3. Malbim understood the relationship between Zebulun and Issachar as an archetype and explained that all of the blessings joined two tribes together:

> "And of Zebulun he said"—Following the blessing of Manasseh and Ephraim comes the blessing of Zebulun and Issachar. a) Because their territories were side by side; b) Because all of the blessings link two tribes together: Reuben with Judah in the blessing of life, Levi and Judah with regard to publicizing the divine and working to ensure that Israel follows the Torah, Judah and Benjamin through the place of the Temple and monarchy, Ephraim and Manasseh share the same blessing, and so too [the blessing given to] Zebulun and Issachar like a single blessing.

4. The tribe of Issachar produced two-hundred heads of Sanhedrin. All of their brothers would conduct themselves in accordance with the halakhic principles that they determined, and they would answer them with regard to each *halakhah*, according to the *halakhah* given to Moses at Sinai. How did Issachar obtain all this? From Zebulun who went about his business affairs and provide for Issachar who was involved in learning Torah. As it is written: "Zebulun shall dwell by the seashore." And when Moses prepared to bless the tribes, he put the blessing of Zebulun ahead of the blessing of Issachar: "Rejoice, O Zebulun, on your journeys and Issachar, in your tents." Zebulun rejoices when embarking

on his journeys because Issachar is in his tents. And some say [that the verse should be interpreted to read]: "There is a reward (*yesh sakhar* [which spells out the name of Issachar]) in the tents of Zebulun. (*Bereishit Rabbah* 72:5)

5. Rambam (Laws of Torah Study 3:10) vociferously disapproved of such arrangements:

> Anyone who resolves that he will study Torah and not work, and that he will be supported by charity—has desecrated the name of God, disgraced the Torah, dimmed the light of Judaism, caused himself harm, and took his own life in the next world, for it is forbidden to derive benefit from words of Torah in this world. The Sages said that anyone who derives benefit from words of Torah, has taken his own life from the world. They further instructed: "Do not make them [matters of Torah] a crown for self-promotion, nor a spade with which to dig." They further instructed: "Love work and hate authority. Torah that is not accompanied by work will ultimately be null"; this person will end up robbing others.

It is worth noting that Rambam may have learned this from experience, as his brother, who worked as a merchant and supported him, drowned at sea. As Rambam wrote to R. Yefet HaDayan:

> The greatest misfortune that has befallen me recently, worse than anything else that has ever happened to me... is the demise of the saint, may his memory be blessed, who drowned in the Indian Sea, carrying much money belonging to me and to others...He conducted business in the market and made profits, while I sat securely. (Letter 11, pp. 229-230, in the Shilat edition of Rambam's letters)

It was only in the aftermath of this tragedy that Rambam began to practice medicine, eventually becoming the physician of the royal court.

6. Some explain that the city of Haifa derives its name from the phrase "sea shore" (*ḥof yam*), even though the city of Haifa was not part of the Zebulun's tribal territory.
7. According to many scholars, the Phoenicians only ascended the stage of history after Jacob's time. In this chapter, we will address the Phoenicians in various contexts, including how they interacted with Israel in general and with Zebulun and his seafaring activities specifically. For example, the origin of the name "Phoenicians" is unclear, although it seems to have derived from Greek. In Greek, the words *phoenices* or *phoenicia* refer to the purplish color (Tyrian purple) that the Phoenicians expertly produced from the *Bolinus brandaris* and *Stramonita haemostoma* and traded. This corresponds to a Talmudic passage (Megilah 6a):

> Zebulun said before the Holy One, blessed be He: Master of the Universe! To my brothers, the tribes whose territory is adjacent to mine, You gave fields and vineyards, whereas to me You gave mountains and hills; to my brothers You gave lands, whereas to me You gave seas and rivers. God said back to him: Nevertheless, all will need you due to the *ḥilazon*, as it is stated: "They invite their kin to the mountain...and the hidden hoards of the sand" (Deuteronomy 33:19). R. Yosef teaches...this refers to the *ḥilazon*.

   Jacob's blessing was future oriented; he related to Sidon, the port city of the future.

8. As its name indicates, it primarily followed the Mediterranean coast from Egypt, across the Sinai (the shorter "Way of the Land of the Philistines" of Exodus 13:17) and north into the land of Israel. It then turned inland at Megiddo and continued through the Jezreel Valley, eventually skirting the Sea of Galilee and continuing across "Jacob's Ford" (Gesher B'not Ya'akov) to the Golan Heights. In the story of the sale of Joseph, the brothers, sitting in Dothan in the central ridge, saw a caravan of Ishmaelites traveling along this road. Megiddo was a strategic highland that controlled the Via Maris where it turned inland; it was therefore the

site of many battles throughout history and lends its name to the mythic final battle, "Armageddon." It is also worth noting that Israel's Route 6 closely tracks the route of the Via Maris and is part of Shimon Peres' vision of a "New Middle East," in which this road will once again link Egypt, Turkey, Lebanon, Syria, Iraq, and Iran through Israel.

9. Some commentators understand "and [he] became a toiling serf" to mean that he would serve an occupying nation that seizes control of the important trade routes. That is, Jacob's words, "He bent his shoulder to the burden and became a toiling serf," have a double meaning. The parallelism of the two parts of the verse might indicate Issachar's passivity as well as the sort of manual labor he would perform. Alternatively, the two parts can be distinguished: Issachar would indeed work in the transport industry, but in the future, the important trade route in Issachar's territory will attract empires and kingdoms to attempt to gain control of the region.

10. Yehoshua 19:10–16:

> The third lot emerged for the Zebulunites, by their clans. The boundary of their portion: Starting at Sarid, their boundary ascended westward to Maralah, touching Dabbesheth and touching the wadi alongside Jokneam. And it also ran from Sarid along the eastern side, where the sun rises, past the territory of Chisloth-tabor and on to Daberath and ascended to Japhia. From there it ran [back] to the east, toward the sunrise, to Gath-hepher, to Eth-kazin, and on to Rimmon, where it curved to Neah. Then it turned—that is, the boundary on the north—to Hannathon. Its extreme limits were the Valley of Iphtah-el, Kattath, Nahalal, Shimron, Idalah, and Bethlehem: twelve towns, with their villages. That was the portion of the Zebulunites by their clans—those towns, with their villages.

11. Rashi, R. Abraham ben HaRambam, Ibn Ezra, R. Joseph Bekhor Shor, and others explained the word "on" (*ad*) to mean "adjacent,," i.e., that the border of Zebulun reached Sidon. This explanation

fits neither the map nor the verses in Yehoshua. Netziv explains *ad* to mean "reliant on," meaning that his livelihood came from Sidon. Shadal explains that this word means "extremity" and does not necessarily refer to an actual border.

12. The Babylonian Talmud (Bava Batra 122a) notes that when the land was divided by lottery, the tribe of Zebulun received the area of Acco. Nevertheless, *Tosafot* (ad loc., s.v. "*Zebulun oleh*") comments: "This is not a reference to Acco itself, which was in Asher's territory, as it is written: 'Asher did not dispossess the inhabitants of Acco.' Rather, it means to say a region adjacent to Acco."
13. Some explain that the tribal territory of Zebulun was located between two seas, namely the Sea of the Galilee and the Mediterranean Sea, although it is worth noting that the tribal territory of Zebulun comes nowhere near the shores of the Sea of the Galilee.
14. See: https://hbr.org/2013/02/why-innovators-love-constraint.
15. Famous architect Frank Gehry commented that creative thinking is inspired by constraints and limitations. For a more complete discussion of this issue, see: https://www.forbes.com/sites/groupthink/2013/07/12/creativity-how-constraints-drive-genius/#477e740b3d89
16. Deuteronomy 33:24–26:

    > And of Asher he said: Most blessed of sons be Asher; may he be the favorite of his brothers; may he dip his foot in oil. May your door bolts be iron and copper, and your security last all your days. O Jeshurun, there is none like God, riding through the heavens to help you....

17. The verses in *Tehillim* (107:21–23) state:

    > Let them praise the Lord for His steadfast love, His wondrous deeds for mankind. Let them offer thanksgiving sacrifices and tell His deeds in joyful song. Others go down to the sea in ships, ply their trade in the mighty waters. (*Tehilim* 107:21–23)

    The Talmud (*Berakhot* 54b) expounds on this:

> R. Yehuda said that Rav said: Four must offer thanks: Seafarers, those who cross the desert, one who was ill and recovered, and one who released from prison. From where do we derive seafarers? "Others go down to the sea in ships, ply their trade in the mighty waters; they see the works of the Lord." And it says: 'For He commands and raises the stormy wind which lifts up the waves thereof. They mount up to the heaven, they go down again to the depths', And it says: "They reel to and fro, and stagger like a drunken man." And it says: "Then they cry unto the Lord in their trouble, and He brings them out of their distress." And it says: "He makes the storm calm." And it says: "Then are they glad because they become quiet." And it says: "They are grateful to God for His loving-kindness and His wonders for mankind" .... What blessing does he recite? R. Yehuda said: Blessed is He Who bestows loving-kindness.

18. Radak explains:

> "Of the Issacharites, men who knew how to interpret the signs of the times, to determine how Israel should act." Our Rabbis, of blessed memory, explained that they knew how to intercalate the years and how to establish the months, and that is [the meaning of what] is stated: "to determine how Israel should act." That is [also the meaning of the phrase] "knew how to interpret the signs of the times," meaning, the seasons of the world, as they knew how to calculate astronomical seasons and [the movement of the] constellations. This matter is mentioned here because the king needed to consult with them regarding these matters, because intercalation and setting [of the calendar] was determined by the king, as is known with regard to King Hezekiah (Babylonian Talmud *Sanhedrin* 12a). And Rabbenu Yonah (see Radak's *Sefer Hashorashim*, s.v. *ayin-vav-taf*) explains [that this is a reference to] legal matters, like the verse "the sages learned in procedure (*itim*)" (Esther 1:13), as it says "all

who were versed in law and precedent" (*ibid.*), and the verse "the heart of a wise man knows procedure (*et*) and law (*mishpat*)" (Ecclesiastes 8:5); and the king needed to consult with them about legal matters. But the phrase "to determine how Israel should act" does not fit this explanation, because it should have said "to determine how the king should act." However, according to the explanation advanced by our Rabbis, of blessed memory, "to determine how Israel should act" fits well—[they need to know] how and when to observe the holidays.

19. Ralbag explains:

> "Know how to interpret the times to determine how Israel should act"–It seems that they were wise and intelligent and people of good counsel. At all times they knew how to offer wise counsel as to what Israel should do at that time, given what would happen in the future, so they had a certain amount of prescience, and they all agreed to coronate David.

20. Each tribe had its own flag with an emblem that expressed its unique character, its primary occupation, or a foundational event in the history of the tribe's namesake. The mainstream view is that the flag of Zebulun featured a ship (*Bamidbar Rabbah* 2:7). Yet there is another opinion found in a different midrash:

> "The Israelites shall camp each with his standard, under the banners." This teaches that each and every tribe had an insignia of the tribal patriarch, and all of the flags had an emblem of the tribal patriarch. What were the emblems and insignias of the tribes? The emblem of Reuben...The emblem of Simeon...The emblem of Issachar had a donkey drawn on it, on account of what is said: "Issachar is a strong-boned donkey." Zebulun had a sort of house drawn on it, as it is said: "He will make his permanent home with me (*yizbeleni*)" (Genesis 30:20), and the Targum [of *yizbeleni*] is "home" [*mador*]. (*Midrash Agaddah al haTorah* [S. Baber ed., Vienna, 1894], Numbers 2:2)

According to this view, perhaps the Zebulunites maintained commercial relationships with the seafaring Phoenicians, and therefore dwelt near harbors but did not actually own ships. Either way, according to this midrash, the flag of Zebulun symbolized the return home.

21. From the ninth century through sixth centuries BCE, the Phoenicians spread out across the Mediterranean Sea and controlled its trade. They settled and established many trade posts, first in Cyprus, then on Aegean islands, followed by Sicily, Malta, Sardinia, and North Africa (where the Phoenicians established their most famous and strongest colony, Carthage), and ultimately Iberia and the Maghreb.

    At first, these colonies were no more than docking stations that provided port services to Phoenician ships and were a good starting point for searching for raw materials. With time though, specifically on account of extensive trade interests, most of these locations developed into central permanent settlements. (Wikipedia)

22. https://archive.org/details/in.ernet.dli.2015.88411/page/n271 (Page 258)
23. Rashi, in his commentary to Psalms 48, compares "the far-reaches (*yerekh*) of Zaphon" with the "northern flank of the altar."
24. Genesis 32:25–33:

    > Jacob was left alone. And a man wrestled with him until the break of dawn. When he saw that he had not prevailed against him, he wrenched Jacob's hip [*yerekho*] at its socket, so that the socket of his hip [*yerekh*] was strained as he wrestled with him. Then he said, "Let me go, for dawn is breaking." But he answered, "I will not let you go, unless you bless me." Said the other, "What is your name?" He replied, "Jacob." Said he, "Your name shall no longer be Jacob, but Israel, for you have striven with beings divine and human, and have prevailed." Jacob asked, "Pray tell me your name." But he said, "You must not ask my name!" And he took leave of him there. So Jacob named the place

> Peniel, meaning, "I have seen a divine being face to face, yet my life has been preserved." The sun rose upon him as he passed Penuel, limping on his hip. That is why the children of Israel to this day do not eat the thigh muscle that is on the socket of the hip [*yerekh*], since Jacob's hip [*yerekh*] socket was wrenched at the thigh muscle.

25. The sciatic nerve is responsible for moving the hamstrings and almost all the muscles of the calf and foot. It is also responsible for sensation of the skin on the back of the thigh and most of the calf and the foot.
26. Rashi similarly explains Jacob's words "I stayed with Laban" (32:5): "In numerology, 'stayed' (*garti*) is equivalent to 613, meaning, 'I stayed with the evil Laban, and I kept 613 *mitzvot*, and I did not learn from his evil ways.'" Shai Agnon devoted his novella *The Crooked Shall Be Made Straight* to a journey undertaken by the story's protagonist to make ends meet, which leads to the complete loss of his identity.
27. Shadal comments in our parashah that Tyre and Sidon represent the same phenomenon and society, but that Tyre was built after Jacob's time.
28. Isaiah 23:1-14:

    > The Tyre Pronouncement: Howl, you ships of Tarshish! For havoc has been wrought, not a house is left; as they came from the land of Kittim, this was revealed to them. Moan, you coastland dwellers, you traders of Sidon, once thronged by seafarers, Over many waters your revenue came: From the trade of nations, from the grain of Shihor, the harvest of the Nile. Be ashamed, O Sidon! For the sea—this stronghold of the sea – declares, "I am as one who has never labored, never given birth, never raised youths or reared maidens!" When the Egyptians heard it, they quailed as when they heard about Tyre. Pass on to Tarshish—Howl, you coastland dwellers! Was such your merry city in former times, of yore? Did her feet carry her off to sojourn far away? Who was it that planned this for crown-wearing Tyre, whose merchants were nobles,

> whose traders the world honored? The Lord of Hosts planned it—to defile all glorious beauty, to shame all the honored of the world. Traverse your land like the Nile, fair Tarshish; this is a harbor no more. The Lord poised His arm o'er the sea and made kingdoms quake; it was He decreed destruction for Phoenicia's strongholds. Behold the land of Chaldea—This is the people that has ceased to be. Assyria, which founded it for ships, which raised its watchtowers, erected its ramparts, has turned it into a ruin. Howl, O ships of Tarshish, for your stronghold is destroyed!

29. The prophet Ezekiel offers a similar description (Ezekiel 27:1–9, 16):

> The word of the Lord came to me: Now you, O mortal, intone a dirge over Tyre. Say to Tyre: O you who dwell at the gateway of the sea, who trade with the peoples on many coastlands: Thus said the Lord God: O Tyre, you boasted, I am perfect in beauty. Your frontiers were on the high seas, your builders perfected your beauty. From cypress trees of Senir they fashioned your planks; they took a cedar from Lebanon to make a mast for you. From oak trees of Bashan they made your oars; of boxwood from the isles of Kittim, inlaid with ivory, they made your decks. Embroidered linen from Egypt was the cloth that served you for sails; of blue and purple from the coasts of Elishah were your awnings. The inhabitants of Sidon and Arvad were your rowers; your skilled men, O Tyre, were within you, they were your pilots. Gebal's elders and craftsmen were within you, making your repairs. All the ships of the sea, with their crews, were in your harbor to traffic in your wares...... The merchants among the peoples hissed at you; you have become a horror, and have ceased to be forever.

30. This is based on: https://www.929.org.il/page/357/post/9405.

31. https://www.929.org.il/page/357/post/9406.
32. *The Rational Optimist* p. 112. For further discussion about the power of international maritime trade and the alliances it generated, see ibid., pp. 111–115. Ridley also notes that the Phoenicians developed their naval strength in the time period of the Judges, the same period in which the Philistines to the south increased their military strength and invented iron chariots.
33. Despite my disagreement with Ridley here, his books "The Rational Optimist" and "How Innovation Works" are must-reads in our home and have inspired me.
34. These righteous sacrifices stand in direct contrast to the city of Tyre, which will continue to do business corruptly even after her return to her former greatness, as described by Yeshayahu (Yeshayahu 23:1518):

    > In that day, Tyre shall remain forgotten for seventy years, equaling the lifetime of one king. After a lapse of seventy years, it shall go with Tyre as with the harlot's song: Take a lyre, go about the town, harlot long forgotten; sweetly play, make much music, to bring you back to mind. For after a lapse of seventy years, the Lord will take note of Tyre, and she shall resume her "fee-taking" and "play the harlot" with all the kingdoms of the world, on the face of the earth. But her profits and "hire" shall be consecrated to the Lord. They shall not be treasured or stored; rather shall her profits go to those who abide before the Lord, that they may eat their fill and clothe themselves elegantly.

    Therefore, against the backdrop of the biblical command, "You shall not bring a harlot's hire or the exchange for a dog to the House of your God for any vow for both of them are an abomination of your God" (Deuteronomy 23:18), Malbim explains the aforementioned verse in Yeshayahu:

    > "But her profits shall be"—this means to say that both her merchandise in her country—from the produce and from the metals that they would sell to other countries—

and the "hire"—the money and the silver and the gold that they would receive as payment for the merchandise—all of it would be consecrated for God, that they would send gifts to the house of God from both of these things. In the Second Temple period they lived in peace with the Jews, but, "They shall not be treasured" (which modifies the phrase "her profits"); their profits would not be brought into the Temple treasury. Sacrifices would not be offered from the animals, fine flour, or wine that they sent. "They shall not be stored" (this phrase modifies the phrase "and her hire"). The gold and silver that they sent to Jerusalem would not be used to fashion anything substantial in God's sanctuary, but would rather be dispensed to those who sat before God, meaning that the priests who worked in the Temple would divide it amongst themselves, and [the verse] clarifies that her profits will be used "that they may eat their fill"; the meat and the fine flour that they sent would be food for the priests, and the priests will take "her hire,," which refers to money, "and clothe themselves elegantly,," to purchase fine and expensive clothing for themselves.

35. "He who is unblemished and has a pure heart, who has not taken a false oath by My life or sworn deceitfully" (Psalms 24:4).
36. Rashi, too, explains that the ethical mission of Zebulun and Issachar is connected to the cultural–religious interaction that is an inherent part of business relationships, though his approach is far more optimistic, perhaps even utopian:

    "They invite their kin to the mountain"—Zebulun's business dealings will bring idol-worshipping merchants to his land, as he stands on the frontier. They say, since we have troubled ourselves to come this far, let us continue to Jerusalem and observe the religion and rituals of this nation. And they will see all of Israel worshipping the one God and eating one food, because among idol worshippers, the service of one god is unlike the service of another, and the food of one is unlike the food of another. And they will convert there, as it is written: "where they offer sacrifices of righteousness."

37. "In his old age, his wives turned away Solomon's heart after other gods, and he was not as wholeheartedly devoted to the Lord his God as his father David had been" (*1* Kings 11:4)
38. Elijah the prophet chose Mount Carmel as the location where he would deal with the threat posed by the prophets of Baal, who were the proteges of Jezebel, princess of Sidon. Mount Carmel rises high above the Mediterranean Sea, and it is possible that Elijah sought to give expression to the problematic nature of international relationships with countries across the sea. In this context, it should be mentioned that the book *Galuy U-Mutzpan* (p. 27) notes that, at a certain point in time, Mount Carmel marked the southern border of the Phoenician empire, and there was a temple that honored Baal there.
39. "They paid the hewers and craftsmen with money, and the Sidonians and Tyrians with food, drink, and oil to bring cedarwood from Lebanon by sea to Joppa, in accord with the authorization granted them by King Cyrus of Persia" (Ezra 3:7).
40. "These are the knots for which a person is liable: Camel-drivers' knots and sailors' knots. And just as one is guilty for tying them, so one is guilty for untying them" (Mishnah *Shabbat* 15:1).